LE LOT

Titles in the Travelscapes series

The Pyrenees · *Roger Higham*
Le Lot · *Helen Martin*
Poland · *Tim Sharman*

LE LOT

Helen Martin

COLUMBUS BOOKS
LONDON

First published in Great Britain in 1988 by
Columbus Books Limited
19-23 Ludgate Hill
London EC4M 7PD

Line drawing by Vera Brice

British Library Cataloguing in Publication Data

Martin, Helen
Le Lot —— (Travelscapes)
1. Lot (France) —— Description and travel
—— Visitors' guides
I. Title
914.4′7304838   DC611.L832

ISBN 0-86287-325-8

Designed by Vera Brice
Maps by Vera Brice and Leslie Robinson
Set in Linotron Ehrhardt by Facet Film Composing Limited
Leigh-on-Sea, Essex
Printed and bound by Richard Clay Ltd, Bungay, Suffolk

For Archie and May

CONTENTS

ILLUSTRATIONS

MAPS

The following symbols are used in the maps:

- ☦ Church or monastery
- ♖ Castle
- ∴ Ancient monument
- △ Mountain peak
- \\|/ Viewpoint
- ♈ Waterfall
- ✱ Windmill
- ∩ Cave
- π Dolmen

Preface

In the mid-fifties, when I was about eight years old, my father had what was for those days quite a novel idea: come the summer holidays, he packed my mother, brother and myself into the car, threw a tent into the boot behind us and set off to drive around Europe, setting a pattern for years to come. Some of those early trips were to Spain, a Spain with still unspoiled and as yet undeveloped Costas. There is only one real route to Spain from England – you drive through France, pick up the N20 at Châteauroux and follow it to the border.

For about a hundred kilometres of its distance, the N20 runs through the *département* of the Lot in south-west France and it was here, speeding down the road as fast as we were able (for in those days, and to a lesser extent, in these, it was a treacherous route of S-bends and steep climbs), that we first made acquaintance with the area. It would tantalize us: a river winding round the cliffs far beneath us, here, the turrets of a castle peeping over the horizon, there.

As with all nostalgic memories, it was hot, and never more so than when we trailed slowly up the hilly road caught behind a team of oxen, the heady scent of thyme and fennel pouring through the windows, and the wonderful exhilaration, on reaching the top, at being able to see for miles and miles across the countryside. Picnics, when we stopped, were a child's delight for the fields were brilliant and alive with butterflies, grasshoppers with primary coloured wings, and great green lizards.

Our detours and stop-overs became longer and took us further and further away from the road – trips to Padirac, trips to

Rocamadour and Pech-Merle and even trips to Lascaux, for in those days the Dordogne, too, was largely undiscovered. Eight years later the seduction was complete and it seemed that wherever else we went, separately or together, we would still need our annual 'fix' of the Lot.

What gradually became apparent was that there were no real guide books to the area apart from one long out-of-print book and Freda White's very excellent *Three Rivers of France* which became our well-thumbed Bible. Ms White's book, though, did have omissions, unsurprising in one covering such a wide area.

In more recent years, as books on south-west France proliferate, it has annoyed and irritated me to see the Lot gradually lose its identity as its many attractions get pulled into books about the Dordogne, as if the two *départements* were one and the same. The truth is very different. Where the Dordogne belongs to the Aquitaine grouping of western France, the Lot today belongs to the Midi-Pyrénées, reflecting its Quercy roots which delve firmly southwards towards Toulouse and the Languedoc. Where the Dordogne and its valley are neat, clean and green, wooded and pretty, the Lot is high, dry, arid and wild, a poor land of high limestone plateaux, known as *causses*, a land of sheep and dovecots.

This loss of identity stems partly from the popularity of the Dordogne with the British, with even Michelin pandering to this British influx and confusion by calling its English language version of the Green Guide to the area *Dordogne (Périgord-Limousin)*, unlike its French edition which is called, more correctly, *Périgord (Quercy-Limousin)*. Further confusion arises from the fact that the River Dordogne flows through the Lot *département*.

The Dordogne is a lovely *département*, rich in tourist sights and with a long historical pedigree, and clearly its proximity to the Lot must mean that there are similarities. But the treasures of the Lot – the cliff-hanging villages of St Cirq-Lapopie and Rocamadour (second tourist site of France after Mont St Michel), the romantic fortified bridge of Valentré at Cahors, the magnificent and famous caves of Padirac, the awe-inspiring cave art of Cougnac and Pech-Merle – all these have no place in a book purporting to be about the Dordogne – *département* or river.

My own book is arranged in two parts, the first part comprising what I call the introductory chapters, where I cover subjects such as history, architecture and gastronomy in detailed but non-geographical terms. The second part of the book is arranged geographically, and in this section I look at the main towns individually and then at the area that surrounds them.

I have arranged it thus for several reasons, but largely because I do not believe that many guide books are read at one sitting. People tend to dip into the bits which interest them, or the area they happen to be visiting. Following this arrangement, people with no interest in, say, prehistoric art can skip that chapter entirely. Second, it avoids repetition. The chapter on churches, for example, talks of the origins of the Romanesque tympanums which adorn many a church in the area. To repeat the salient points about tympanums each time we come across one is tedious for the reader, yet to mention them only once in context with, say, Cahors cathedral, would mean that visitors who never got beyond Souillac would be left in the dark unless they read the entire book. Third, I wanted the book to be fairly comprehensive, with enough background information to allow the reader to depend on it entirely, unless he/she wanted very detailed and specialized knowledge.

Lot – *Terre de Merveilles* is how the tourist literature describes it. This book is a plea for the Lot in its own right and, I hope, a not uncritical look at some of those marvels.

Acknowledgements

Many people have helped in the writing of this book, the majority of whom will not be able to read it in English, which is why I reiterate my thanks in French below.

Apart from those people, I should also like to thank M. de Chalain of the Comité Départmental de Tourisme du Lot; Lia and Renier Verwys; Gill Gibbins, my editor at Columbus Books for her support; my family for lots of help and enthusiasm; Jean-Louis Nespoulous for the photographs; and last, but most especially, Maryvonne Grellier for endless help with difficult translations, not to mention difficult transactions.

J'aimerais remercier tous mes amis du Lot, sans qui je n'aurais probablement jamais pu compléter ce livre. Leur gentillesse et leur chaleureuse hospitalité ont beaucoup contribué au développement de mon intérêt et de ma passion pour la région.

Je voudrais en particulier remercier M. et Mme Maury; la famille Czajkowski; la famille Rossignol; les Guitard; Geneviève Xiberas; sans oublier, bien sûr, Reine Oberti et son amie Huguette, qui depuis notre tendre adolescence m'ont aidé à découvrir les nuits folles du Lot!

Finalement il me faut remercier spécialement Alice et Georges Lacam de l'Hostellerie de la Bouriane, qui ont toujours fait preuve à mon égard d'une hospitalité à toute heure sans égal.

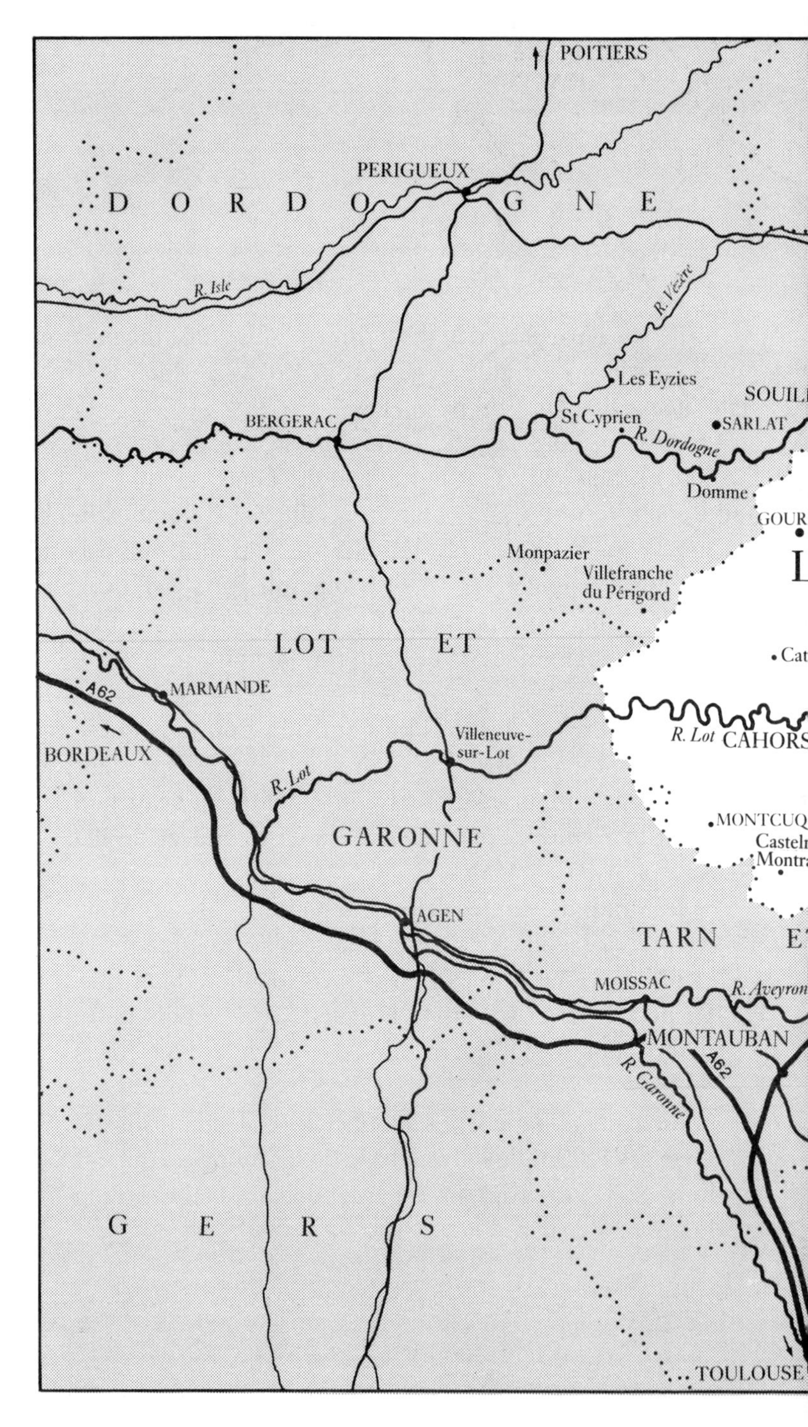
POITIERS
PERIGUEUX
D O R D O G N E
R. Isle
R. Vézère
Les Eyzies
SOUIL
BERGERAC
St Cyprien
SARLAT
R. Dordogne
Domme
GOUR
L
Monpazier
Villefranche
du Périgord
LOT ET
Cat
MARMANDE
A62
BORDEAUX
Villeneuve-
sur-Lot
R. Lot
R. Lot
CAHORS
GARONNE
MONTCUQ
Castelr
Montr
AGEN
TARN E
MOISSAC
R. Aveyron
MONTAUBAN
A62
R. Garonne
G E R S
TOULOUSE

CLERMONT-
FERRAND
TULLE
R R È Z E
Mauriac
C A N T A L
R. Maronne
ST FLOUR
Beaulieu
R. Cère
Martel
AURILLAC
Bretenoux
St Céré
Sousceyrac
Latroniquière
nadour
R. Truyère
O T
abastide-
urat
FIGEAC
Entraygues
R. Célé
Conques
Cabrerets
R. Lot
Capdenac-
Gare
R. Lot
A V E Y R O N
Limogne-
en-Quercy
R. Aveyron
Villefranche-
de-Rouergne
RODEZ
MONTPELLIER
Caylus
Najac
ARONNE
Cordes
Gaillac
ALBI
T A R N
R. Tarn

PART ONE

1

The Land

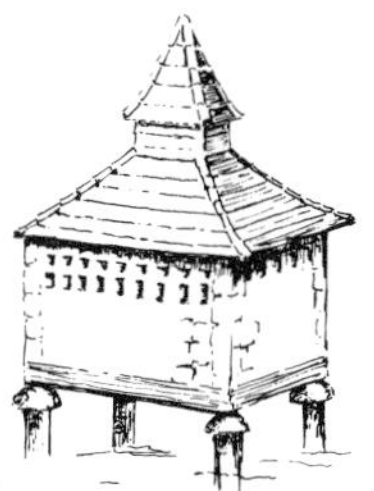

The *Gouffre* of St Sauveur is round and very deep, and of a colour so startling it seems almost sinister, an icy azure blue, or a deep jade green, depending on the season, which seems to reflect something of the woods which surround it and the sky above, but most of all something of the unfathomable depths to which it descends.

To find it you must drive past the vineyards of Bonnecoste, heading south, and take a tiny track to the left. Half-way – and a long way – down you wonder at the wisdom of bringing the car, but at the bottom there is plenty of room after all.

Looking up you see that you are in a well, surrounded on all sides by steep woods. The track has vanished. It is eerily quiet. Quiet, that is, except for the birds, of whose presence you suddenly become super-aware. Around you the cries of alarm go up. A blackbird screams a warning. A jay cackles. A kingfisher streaks past. There is a tendency to walk on tiptoe and speak in hushed voices, because you feel an intruder, because there is an echoing claustrophobia about the place, and because the water, when you suddenly come across its circular pool, is so arrestingly beautiful.

Not far away, and conveniently linked to the path of the Grande Randonnée 6, is the *gouffre* resurgence of Cabouy, where an equally blue-green pool flows out into the mini-canyon of the Ouysse, a deep, clear stream near its source here, overlain with mystery and legend, which link it to the village of Thémines about 30 kilometres away.

The story goes that the miller of Thémines was approached one winter's night by a smartly dressed man with a sparkling eye – the Devil. A very agitated Devil. He had been all day in the Ségala searching for souls, but lacked one to complete his collection, and he was prepared to offer the miller very favourable terms indeed for his. On enquiry the wary miller found that these terms included a long and healthy life and another mill on the same stream, so that he could easily work the two together. The miller of Thémines was a shrewd man. He thought about this proposition carefully and finally he gave his decision. It was a deal, he said, but on one condition: that he would not be required to hand over his soul until the morning. As soon as the first rays of sunlight hit the mill, the Devil could have his soul, but if perchance the day dawned dull and cloudy, the miller should have his long and healthy life and his second mill in exchange for nothing. Eagerly the Devil agreed, confident in the knowledge that influencing the weather was well within his possibilities. Both went happily to sleep and dawn found the two of them sitting on a big rock near the mill, waiting for the sunrise. The sky was clear and cloudless as the Devil had planned it should be, but as the sun rose not one ray fell on the mill. All day they sat there, but as dusk approached it became obvious to the Devil what the miller had known all along – that the mill was in too deep a hollow for the sun to penetrate in winter.

Swearing and angry, the Devil was forced to pay his dues, but in the matter of the mill he had his revenge. The mill at Cabouy – which no-one had ever noticed before – was indeed on the same river, but it was a long way from Thémines, where the Ouysse disappeared underground: one man could not possibly run both mills. Still, the miller sold the mill at Cabouy and became very rich on the proceeds, and true to the Devil's word he lived a long and healthy life.

Follow the Ouysse to its confluence with the Alzou and then climb upstream on the GR6 and you come to another beauty spot, the Moulin du Saut, a place of waterfalls and rocks and the sound of rushing water beside a ruined mill. Above you towers the limestone in rocky ledges and overhangs – a riot of butterflies and flowers in summer – and in spite of its weird and wonderful shapes, always a friendly rock because of the warmth of its colours. Look carefully as you walk for there are fossils, tiny shells and sea creatures, and because this is your first geography lesson. For the Lot is a land of *gouffres* – chasms – and wells, potholes and springs, resurgences (the emergence of an underground stream), rivers, caves, and canyons, and to know and love the Lot you have to know and love limestone.

About two hundred million years ago, south-west France lay under the sea and the rocky coastline of that sea was the foothills of the Massif Central. The tides ebbed and flowed, back and forth, day after day, year after year, century after century, grinding down the shells and the bones of sea animals and wearing away the hills, until the sea bed became nearly covered with a deep layer of lime thousands of feet thick: the Aquitaine Basin.

Meanwhile, slowly, slowly, the earth was rising out of the sea. Next came an era of great volcanic activity, the thrust of which not only threw up completely new mountain ranges like the nearby Pyrenees, but also altered the older hills of the Auvergne and the Cévennes significantly. Much higher now, these older hills, together with the neighbouring ranges of the Limousin and the Rouergue, squeezed the soft limestone until it cracked into huge faults.

Today, things are very roughly the same. There is the hard rock of the Massif Central to the east, forming a sort of westward-facing backbone to France. Northwards lies the Limousin and southwards the Cévennes and the Lozère, and in between these ridges is the limestone, lying in great plateaux and stretching far to the west before flattening out some distance from the sea. And because the land slopes south-westwards, the main rivers of the Lot, the Lot itself and the Dordogne, rise in the hard, high hills of the Limousin and the Lozère and flow through the limestone faults to the sea.

And it is the rivers and the limestone which must concern any visitor to the Lot, for it is the high, arid, stony expanses of the *causses* and the swift-flowing rivers carving their way through the limestone which give the Lot so much of its character.

The important thing to remember about limestone is that it is a relatively soft and extremely porous rock and water can therefore cut through it with some degree of ease and speed, causing the kind of scenery you can see on the road down to the old fortified mill at Cougnaguet near Rocamadour, for example, and also on the famous GR6; the sort of scenery where you half expect to be leaped on from a great height by a Red Indian.

When the rain falls on the *causses*, it does not, as in most other places, form rivers and streams; it simply seeps straight through the rock. Here it works away on the soft limestone in exactly the same way as it does outside, only now it is carving out an underground world of caves and caverns. The water, drip-dripping through the calcite in the limestone, produces the concretions and formations known as stalactites and stalagmites, which grow at the staggeringly slow rate of about one centimetre every hundred years.

If rivers and streams do not usually form on the surface, they quite frequently form underground, emerging at the foot of cliffs in resurgent springs. Sometimes the watercourse merely disappears underground to reappear later on.

Gouffres, great openings in the ground as at St Sauveur or Padirac, are formed by the hollowed-out roof of a cave falling in. The roof of the Grand Dôme at Padirac, some 90-odd metres high, lies quite near the surface of the Gramat *causse*, for example, and it is almost inevitable that one day this, too, will collapse to form another chasm. Thus you can see that the surface of the *causses*, and indeed their underneath, are both constantly changing as new wells, potholes and caverns are formed.

A large percentage of the Lot's 5,226 square kilometres is made up of this limestone *causse*-land, about 350 metres high and suitable for nothing much besides the grazing of a special breed of sheep with great black rings round their eyes like sunglasses. The sheep have good wool, but they are bred largely for their meat and *gigot de causse*, a barely cooked lamb cutlet, is considered a great local speciality. In the summer the sheep are shorn nearly to the skin, for then the sun seems almost to bounce off the rock and it can get very hot.

The wildest, biggest *causse* is that of Gramat, a desolate, beautiful plateau with little growing on it beyond scrub oak, maple and juniper, but heavily scented with thyme and fennel and slashed by the dramatic canyons of the Ouysse and, more especially, the Alzou. Further north is the *causse* of Martel, whilst that of the low-lying Cajarc is squashed in between the banks of the Lot and the Célé canyon, to the south. The *causse* of Limogne, in the extreme south-east of the *département*, is altogether different, having an almost Mediterranean look and feel to it and smelling heavily of lavender.

Hugging the foothills of the Auvergne are the atypical areas of the Châtaignerie, a chestnut-growing area in bygone days, and the poor land of the Ségala, coming from *seigle*, meaning 'rye', the only crop which would grow. Separating the *causses* from this mountainous stretch is the fertile, fruit-growing plain of the Limargue, with the ravine-ridden area of the Braunhie (pronounced as though spelt 'Brogne' in French) surrounding Gramat. To the east lies the verdant Bouriane, a land of pines and chestnuts, and south-west the aptly named Quercy Blanc, a wonderful sun-bleached sight in summer with its fields of giant sunflowers, heads turned in one direction as they soak up the heat.

Now we know how the land was formed, what and where *is* the Lot? Before the Lot existed as a *département*, the area was called Quercy, a land whose roots stretched down towards Toulouse and the Languedoc. Quercy belonged to the old province of Guyenne, a disparate province which linked the Atlantic shores of Bordeaux with the easterly reaches of the Rouergue.

The Lot itself, created in 1790, comprises most of Haut-Quercy, centred on Cahors; whilst Bas-Quercy, now largely Tarn-et-Garonne, was centred on Montauban. Cahors, capital of the Lot, lies about 570 kilometres south-west of Paris, about 200 kilometres east and slightly south of Bordeaux, and 110 kilometres north of Toulouse, the city to which the Lot looks and is economically attached.

The very thing which makes the Lot an attractive proposition for tourists – the high, poor *causse*-land, the small tumble-down farms and houses, the quiet peaceful villages locked into a centuries-old tradition – are the same things which are killing it as a viable economic *département*. It contributes hardly anything at all to the national economy. A hundred years ago the population of the Lot was around the 300,000 mark, but it has fallen to half that now. Villages that were once busy, bustling affairs, full of life, schools and shops, living a truly communal life of shared labour (and even shared stills) and adopting for the most part a barter system, are now little more than ghost villages, full of old people and foreigners' holiday homes. Homes that are lovingly restored, no doubt, but shut up for the best part of the year.

The exodus from the land, which was greatly abetted by the building at the turn of the century of that traveller's boon, the Paris-Toulouse railway line (which enables you to travel from London to Cahors in a day) was also encouraged by the Napoleonic laws of inheritance, which mean that any land has to be equally divided between all children, including the stepchildren, of the person concerned.

Subsistence farming such as was, and to some extent still is, practised in the Lot, meant large families to supply labour, so the land was divided into ever diminishing parcels, until there was simply not enough to go round. Even today, very few farms comprise more than twenty hectares, with the farmer almost always owning the land and referring to himself proudly as a *propriétaire*.

Nowadays, when many of the children move away and only one stays behind to look after the land, there is a move to encourage farmers to practise monoculture and to amalgamate the farms into bigger entities. Old habits die hard, though, and certainly the farm with which I am most familiar seems fairly steeped in the old polyculture.

Guy and Edith Rossignol farm their land themselves with the help of their daughter Catherine and occasional reciprocal help from neighbours at busy times of the farming calendar. Their main cash crop is tobacco, which is tended and cared for like a child from the planting of the tiny shoots through to the harvesting. Apart from the tobacco there is maize, largely grown for the cattle, and there are vines to tend, from which they make their own wine. They have quite a large dairy herd, a few sheep, some pigs and several goats, from whose milk Mme Rossignol makes cheese. This she sells along with the hens' eggs and the odd rabbit. Meanwhile she grows all her own vegetables and fruit.

If ever you thought life was bliss in the country, you only have to watch Cathy and her mother, bent double in temperatures of around 30°C, walking up and down the rows of tobacco plants, sometimes sown on steep gradients, weeding or fertilizing by hand, while Guy hares round the adjoining field in the tractor, trying to get the hay cut before the forecast thunderstorms. Someone will return to the farm in the early evening to milk the cows, but everyone will still be in the fields long after ten, gathering in the hay.

Yes, no doubt it is all grossly inefficient and even selfish, and yes, in spite of all the hard work, it is easy to romanticize about a life so different from one's own; but it is difficult not to be attracted by the homogeneity of life in the Lot. One can readily understand the conservatism of the *propriétaire*, used to being self-sufficient, in a life temporarily cushioned today by massive EEC grants.

And to the mere observer, freed from the worry of farming anywhere at all, there is another thing. In the Lot you can still find real meadows – meadows full of grasses and poppies, marguerites, mallow and vetch, wild sweet peas and campions, pimpernels and orchids, edged around with wild strawberries. There are still hedges and real forests and a life rich in tradition; a life still, for all the changes, well in touch with its roots.

Still in touch with its roots, yes, but changes are coming as French materialism creeps into the younger homes. The danger is either that these changes will come and destroy those roots, or that the land will be turned into a vast desert of holiday homes inhabited by Belgian, Dutch and British families, together with a few elderly French people, attracted to a lifestyle they find themselves creating because it no longer exists as a viable proposition for the majority of native inhabitants.

So far the Lot has been careful with its new hope for prosperity, the tourist industry. A careful control is kept on building; the Lot was the first *département* to offer architectural assistance to incoming foreigners with a booklet designed to show what materials and paint colours would be most acceptable. *Stations vertes*, or 'green zones', have been created around existing towns as rural holiday centres. Footpaths have been opened up and holiday chalet areas, where they exist, have been well camouflaged. Farmers are subsidized to renovate old farm buildings and houses into *gîte* accommodation, and the Syndicats d'Initiative all promote the more wholesome qualities of the area. With a lot of luck the Lot could retain its charm and find a modest prosperity because of the tourist industry rather than in spite of it.

But the Lot has a lot of luck. In spring the *causses* are ablaze with flowers, a veritable rock garden of pinks, rock-roses, convolvulus, thyme, saxifrage, flax and many wild versions of species one recognizes from gardens back home. The hedges are a tangle of honeysuckle, pink and yellow, although it is the yellow which smells sweetest. And there are the orchids. Come in May and June and the roadside verges and fields are thick with the magenta spikes of the common pyramid version, with shades ranging from the deep purple-pink through to pure white. There are straggly lizard ones with long curling tails, marsh orchids by the streams in shady places and, hiding away in private spots, rarely more than three together, are the exquisite bee orchids.

And through the flowers fly the butterflies, *Causses Bleus*, or Chalk Blues, fritillaries, Tortoiseshells, Swallowtails – white, red, blue, black, yellow; in summer the whole land seems a-flutter, with low-flying, slow-flying great black beetles, too.

A rustle in the roadside may mean a snake – an adder or the harmless grass snake – but more usually it is the big green lizard of Quercy, a mini-dinosaur which lies hidden in trees for hours until the wink of a small, black eye or the flick of a tongue gives it away. Courting lizards you cannot miss, for their engorged throats turn a bright royal blue.

Then there are the birds – buzzard, lark and kestrel on the *causse*; red-legged partridge, woodcock, cuckoo, warbler, golden oriol and even the red, black and white hoopoe for lucky people in the Céou valley on the right day. There is the ubiquitous jay, and along the rivers you find wagtails and kingfishers. At night the land hums to the odd sound of nightjars, and owls fly low over the fields. Pipistrelle bats squeak above you. In the woods you may see genets. And in the woods you find something else, too, just very occasionally, when you have given up all hope and don't really believe the stories any more. One day you may look up from gathering mushrooms, as Mme Guitard did recently, and come face to face with one. Later the same day we saw it, too, grazing in a clearing with its family of three adults and nine babies; coarse grey-brown hair, long snout and tusks – a wild boar.

2

Prehistory

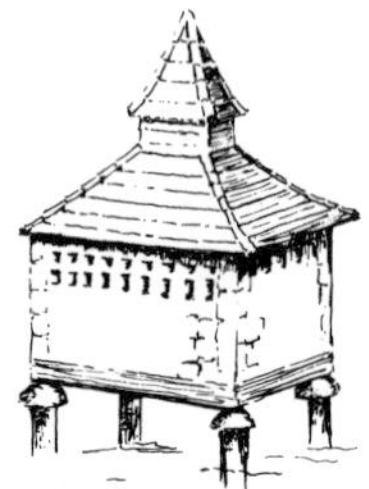

Painted caves

'It's like a tin of pâté,' the man said, 'It keeps quite fresh as long as the tin is closed, but once you open it . . .' So there I was, half-way up a rain-lashed hill in Montignac, thunder crashing over the distant *causse* as tins of foie gras tracked across my mind's eye.

But this was no chef speaking. Gaël de Guichen was a chemical engineer at Lascaux, that veritable temple of palaeolithic art, in the days just after it was closed to the public for good, and the pâté tin was an analogy of conditions which prevailed in the cave until its opening in 1940 broke the seal, so to speak.

Partly on M. de Guichen's recommendation, a facsimile has been built at Le Thot, though curiously it is experiencing difficulties not dissimilar to those at the real cave. That day, though, we waded through formaldehyde to the real thing. 'These old eyes have seen the marvel,' wrote Philip Hope-Wallace in *The Guardian*, after a similar experience, 'marvels I am not equipped to speak of.'

Whilst the Dordogne is the undisputed centre of cave art, and it would be churlish and foolish to pass so close without acknowledgement, the Lot is not without its own glories, and some would say that since the closing of Lascaux, Pech-Merle, on the Célé at Cabrerets, is now the finest of the painted caves still open to the public in France.

Abbé Breuil, one of several French priests to develop an interest in prehistory, called it 'a Sistine chapel of the *causse* plateau, one of the most beautiful monuments of the pictorial art of the palaeolithic age'. A Syndicat d'Initiative leaflet I came across said '... seven halls over a distance of one mile open the way to discover the exuberance and fabulous riches of subterranean sceneries'. Certainly it is one of the largest caves in the area.

If pressed, I should have to say that the painted caves are the show-piece of the region. The Lot is rich in so many things: churches, châteaux, gastronomy, stunning scenery and domestic architecture, but nothing quite epitomises the timelessness of the place as well as the caves.

To stand outside Cougnac on a hot day, sun filtering through the trees, sinister memories of Chabrol's *Le Boucher* stepping across your mind, then to enter the cool darkness and confront the red ibex or the fingerprints, fingerprints of Aurignacian man, is an experience which makes you grope for words.

> Me voici, imbécile, ignorant,
> Homme nouveau devant les choses inconnus.

Historically speaking the caves are, in any case, of enormous importance, and this geographical corner of south-west France and northern Spain is acknowledged to be amongst the most important in the world where cave art is concerned. If you have time for nothing else, therefore, visit the caves. Never put off till tomorrow . . . for tomorrow, sadly, they may be closed. Lascaux has gone. Already numbers at Altamira and Niaux are limited.

The problem is that the caves are often well below ground level, their original entrances sealed, and they have, therefore, been unaffected by the elements and any changes of temperature up until the time of discovery. Sometimes, as at Lascaux, the pictures have been painted on a thin calcitic film which served first as a base and then, as the action continued, as a varnish. Once human beings are introduced into a cave of this nature, their perspiration (40 grams of water per hour!) and the quantities of carbonic acid gas in their breath combine to dissolve the calcium carbonate surface and water then washes the paintings away.

In other caves the problem is the introduction of micro-organisms which encourage the growth of algae on the pictures, and thus it is that caves which have lain undisturbed and fresh for thousands of years can be suddenly destroyed by 'modern' man in the space of thirty.

But who were the artists and why is south-west France the cradle of so much palaeolithic art? The answer to the latter question is probably partly to do with the preponderance of limestone caves in the area, hollowed out by the action of water collecting in volcanic faults. Rivers, too, carved into the rock creating rock shelters or *abris* which still exist long after the river itself has shrunk to a small stream or vanished altogether. These U-shaped glacial valleys, straight out of a geography lesson with their steep-sided cliffs, are a feature of the Lot. You can see several around Rocamadour in the Alzou Gorge. Jagged limestone ledges, sometimes 60 to 90 metres high, descend to a narrow valley floor of lush pasture-land. Sometimes a small stream streaks across the greenery, its route traced by tall poplar trees, but often they are dry.

As for the artists, they were *Homo sapiens*, who appear to have occupied Europe during the last ice age. This was Stone Age man, although the ones who could paint are thought to have belonged to the more sophisticated Upper Palaeolithic period, when flints could be fashioned as sharp as a knife, and bone and horn instruments such as needles began to be used. With improved flints and harpoons came leisure time, evidenced by the shell bracelets and decorated tools of this period.

The climate was still quite cold and the glaciers, though they had begun to melt, were still very much in evidence. The people kept warm with fires and animal furs. The landscape was similar to part of the modern Russian steppe; wide open plains, over which roamed vast herds of animals – mammoths, horses and deer, as well as bears and hairy rhinoceroses.

It was these large animals – the bison, the mammoth, the deer and the horse, important sources of food – that the artists chose to represent most frequently, as opposed to birds and fish which seemed to figure largely in their diet if rarely in their art.

But whilst the drawings of the animals are sometimes quite startlingly fresh and alive, with a quite staggering, if arbitrary, attention to detail, those of man himself are far less well defined, risible almost: faceless pin men, sometimes masked – with a bird's head, as if taking part in a primitive dance ritual.

Prehistorians specializing in cave art (almost entirely a French-dominated science in its early years) have suggested that the purpose of the painting was magic, sympathetic magic, a process of vivid representation of an animal in the hope that this detailed concentration would act as a spell, a sort of painted prayer, enabling them to kill and eat, or, as with the paintings of pregnant animals, encourage the animals to breed. And not only paintings; some of the animals were carefully engraved into the rock, still others were sculptured.

There are, of course, societies today who still believe in sympathetic magic, but there are other facts too which would seem to bear the theory out. Not all the caves are painted and it is rare to find evidence of daily living in the decorated caves. They are sometimes quite inaccessible, which would seem to imply that they were not painted for pleasure in leisure hours for all to see but that it was the very act of creation which was the important thing. For this reason, superimposition of the drawings, which frequently occurs, may have been unimportant.

Of course we can all theorize and there are some who question the accepted theories of evolution. Maybe our dating system is all wrong, maybe we have overlooked clues of enormous importance and drawn the wrong conclusions, but the theory of sympathetic magic seems to me to be the right one and the one what will stand the passage of time. Dating is notoriously difficult, and even the advent of radio-carbon dating did not entirely eradicate doubt. Abbé Breuil fiercely disputed the radio-carbon dating of Lascaux.

The Upper Palaeolithic period is divided into four main traditions: the Aurignacian (35-18,000 BC), which overlapped with the Gravettian or Perigordian (35-30,000 BC), then the Solutrean (17-15,000 BC) and the Magdalenian (15-10,000 BC). Looking at the dates gives one an idea of how slowly man is thought to have developed during this time.

Cave art is thought to belong to the whole of the Upper Palaeolithic period, developing from mere sketches to the sophisticated techniques of clearer outlines and the clever use of colour, composed from the natural soil colours of yellow and red ochre and the mineral colours obtained from iron oxides – blues and greens are never seen.

'Naturalism' is the word preferred by Geoffrey Grigson to describe the paintings. They are indeed naturalistic and evocative and sometimes, as with the dappled horses at Pech-Merle, powerful and alive. Sometimes the curve of the rock is used to represent the back or muzzle of the animal; whatever suggested itself to the artist. Many, too, are painted in a curious 'twisted perspective' as Abbé Breuil called it; sideways on that is, but showing two horns or four sideways-turned hooves.

Naturally man was living much closer to nature 40,000 years ago, and the paintings and engravings reflect this, sometimes seeming not so much magical creations as a celebration of life itself.

On the practical side, wear good stout shoes. The floors of the caverns can be uneven, wet and slippery; and whilst temperatures may be even, that is not to say warm. If there are any limestone formations in the cave it will, moreover, be wet. Some caves are very *aménagées*, with electric light effects, but I think the best way to see the paintings is by the light of a torch played over the contours, giving one the glimmer of an idea of the difficulties faced by an artist working, very literally, in the dark. Some, like Pech-Merle, are vast, with handrails; others are quite cramped and you are forced to duck. One, I remember, had us all giggling helplessly as it blasted out a quadraphonic version of the slave song from *Nabucco*, while we struggled painfully on bent knees, in single file, down a small subterranean passage somewhere near the centre of the earth.

Padirac and the unpainted caves

After the painted caves, the unpainted ones seem almost ordinary and lacking in mystery. That being said, Padirac is generally considered to be one of the important sites of France, let alone the Lot, and of all the European countries France has the largest number of caves open and equipped for tourists. Those in Quercy and Périgord form a large and unique grouping.

The caves most often visited today tend to be those originally explored by that great pioneer of cave exploration, Edouard A. Martel. Padirac, discovered in 1889, numbers itself amongst these, and there would seem to be no doubt that the public at large find it a more attractive proposition than visiting, say, Cougnac. The number of visitors has increased steadily since 1920 until, by 1979, 395,000 people a year were visiting the cave, although the tiny hamlet of Padirac has not benefited from this influx; its population has steadily fallen.

Martel described his nine explorations in *Le Gouffre et la Rivière Souterraine de Padirac*, published in 1925. It was during these expeditions, which took place between the years of 1889 and 1900 with none of today's sophisticated equipment, that he realized the commercial potential of the place and set about acquiring the land and forming a society to protect the *gouffre*. In 1920, William Paul Beamish, a relative of Martel, was appointed a director of the Society and it was he who, in 1937, invited Guy de Lavaur to make further explorations. These were halted in 1962 by the discovery of a syphon, which prohibited further progress a mere 9,600 metres from the mouth of the cave.

This means that no one is quite sure where the underground river, which is such a feature of Padirac, exits although experiments with dye would seem to indicate that there is a link with the Fontaines de St Georges at Le Lombard near Montvalent. The river, therefore, remains nameless, though some writers refer to it as the Plane and others, tongue in cheek or merely gullible, as the Styx.

The other important feature of Padirac is the *gouffre* itself, whose impressive dimensions make it an awe-inspiring sight. The well is 75 metres deep, 110 metres round and just over 31 metres in diameter. An enormous gaping wound in the ground, it may be descended either by lifts or stairs, though I recommend the latter. Unlike the lifts, the stairs are open to the dark, dank rock. Plants cling rather precariously and with a certain desperation to the crevices and all eyes turn nervously upwards at the ever-retreating patch of circular sky. Blue sky seems to emphasize the darkness and depth. Grey skies confirm the needling thought that you are journeying into hell. Everything drips. Spare a thought for the cleaners who make this journey nightly and for the guides, too, whose light tolerance is dramatically reduced by spending so much time underground.

Reaching the bottom, finally, you enter the cave proper and make your own way through the darkness to the *barques*, which will ferry you deeper into the cave. Once aboard these traditional craft, which are really punts, you sit three abreast, those on the outside slightly too close, it seems, to the level of the water – loud screams as the boatman deliberately rocks the boat. Have plenty of loose change in your pocket; the boatmen, the liftmen and just about everyone else will expect a tip. After the boat trip the rest of the 800-metre trip is done on foot before you return to the *barques* to be punted back to base. The walk is not really strenuous but it does involve a great deal of slippery stair-climbing and is probably unsuitable, therefore, for the elderly or disabled, or indeed anyone who does not see too well in the dark.

The stalactites and stalagmites, the colour of the rock mirrored in the limpid water, itself a bright emerald green in places, the galleries, the lakes and the waterfalls are all amazingly beautiful, but it is the sheer size of the place which remains as a lasting impression. The roof of the Salle du Grand Dôme is a staggering 91 metres high. Only a very few European caves can match this.

The *gouffre* was long a place of refuge for the locals in times of trouble and war. There are legends, needless to say. St Martin figures prominently – he seems to be a *causse* hero – but my own favourite is the one of St Peter wandering the *causse* at dead of night looking for souls to take to heaven. The *caussetiers* seem to have been a bad lot, and he was empty-handed when his mule suddenly froze in terror. Peering through the blackness *'noir comme de la poix'*, St Peter perceived the Devil and all his retinue. The Devil had fared better. His bag was nearly full. The two men bargained for the souls, eventually agreeing that each would set the other a *saute* or obstacle. The one to jump over both obstacles would win the souls. The Devil went first, tapping his foot firmly on the ground, and the great well of Padirac gaped and opened up, *'bien large et bien profond'* as St Peter noted with some anxiety. Coaxed by his master's gentle voice, the mule inched forward to the edge of the chasm. 'Jump, in the name of the Father,' cried St Peter, and the mule sailed into the air, just gaining the other side without an inch to spare. Several stones were dislodged, and they say you can still see the hoof-prints. Meanwhile, at St Peter's invocation, the Devil had recoiled so violently that he split Le Corcudier in two; witness the two hills. St Peter eventually found him at the Source de Miers, to which the former had fixed a cross. This time the mule jumped easily across the water. Not so the Devil who, try as he might, could not get beyond the foot of the cross. After several attempts he admitted defeat and handed over his bag of *caussetiers*.

'You didn't tell me who was looking after the gates of heaven in your place,' said the Devil. 'Our Lord,' replied St Peter and at His name all the little demons in Lucifer's train vanished clean away. No one knows where they went, or which route they took. No one but the *causse* shepherds, that is. It does not surprise them that explorers in the underground caverns of Padirac have experienced all sorts of strange things. They know that if you follow the tunnels far enough you will arrive at the bottom of the world, for this is the road to hell. As for the people of the *causse*, they are said to be much more well-behaved these days.

If you are keen, try some of the numerous other caves; Bellevue at Marcilhac-sur-Célé, Presque, l'Hospitalet, Roland and Lacave, where a train pulls you into the mountainside amid much nervous giggling and shrieking as the speed gathers and the lights go out. For me, though, one stalactite starts to look very much like another after a while, and the grandeur of Padirac is in any case unsurpassed.

Megaliths

According to a 1977 inventory by Jean Clottes *(Inventaire des Mégaliths du Lot)*, there are more than 500 megalithic structures in the Lot; 572, to be exact, of which 540 are dolmens (table stones supported by three or more upright slabs) and only 10 are menhirs or standing stones.

The famous dolmen, the one in all the guide books, is Pierre Martine on the Gramat *causse*, but my own favourite, Rigou, lies on the Reilhaguet road, just off the N20.

On light June evenings I have walked up there; up the steep hill from bosky Mas de Cauze and eastwards towards Reilhaguet. Once you have crossed the road, quiet now because it is supper-time, you are on the *causse*, and the landscape changes dramatically from pastoral to plateau land, from no views to endless vistas, from damp to dry, from cattle to sheep, from orchids to sweet-smelling honeysuckle, which hovers on the air and hangs in thick streamers along the ragged hedgerows and the tumble-down dry-stone walls. Grasshoppers chirp noisily and spring up from under your feet, flashing red and blue. On the way back you may see glow-worms.

You clamber up the grassy bank, breathing in the thyme and juniper and there it is, part-hidden behind a bush; not a big dolmen, but definitely a dolmen for all that. Sometimes the field on whose edge it stands is ploughed; sometimes it is a wild meadow of swaying grasses and flowers. Eastwards lies Reilhaguet, presenting its gentle side, as if the land had been sculptured especially to fit around the houses, the red roofs, the little church. Beyond that, Calès straggles serenely across the ridge, and beyond again the hills of the Cantal rise purple and blue. Westwards lies Gourdon, although the twin towers of the church are just hidden.

There is a wonderfully exhilarating feeling one always gets on the *causse*; the feeling of being able to see for ever, of wanting to dance, Zorba-like, on the roof of the world for the sheer joy of being alive. I know of no other place quite like it, for it is in no way akin to the feeling of height one gets on a mountain. The sun is red now and sinking. In long-ago days it probably set between the two stones of the chamber but, sadly, not today.

Maybe our forebears danced on this plateau on midsummer's eve. What is certain is that they buried their dead here. Ritual burial began to be practised in Europe as long as 50,000 years ago and, whilst it is difficult to ascertain the exact purpose of the standing stones, there is no doubt that the dolmens were quite frequently, if not always, used as places of burial.

The weight of the table stones is often phenomenal. That of Pierre Martine near Livernon, for example, is calculated at 19.6 tonnes. To move a stone of that weight on the flat would take 40 men. Many dolmens, however, were sited on inclines, which required sophisticated mathematical and engineering skills as well as many more pairs of hands.

The dolmens of the Lot are considered an important

homogeneous group, although it is difficult to slot them into their proper place in history. They are characterized by their simplicity and the fact that many of them open to the east. That being said, it is thought that the megalithic rite spread progressively from the Atlantic to south of Larzac and on into Languedoc, whose dolmens have a certain affinity with those in southern Spain and the Mediterranean islands. A snag to this hypothesis, which prehistorians as yet seem unable to explain adequately, is that the Quercy dolmens appear to be contemporary with, if not more recent than, those of the Grands Causses to the south-east.

It is thought that the dolmen religion, whatever it was, lasted only about a thousand years in this area, from around 2,100 BC to 1,700 BC, the first ones being built by the Groupe du Cros and the majority by the Artenacians.

Menhirs remain something of an enigma, though the idea that they were some sort of astronomical instrument does not seem quite so outlandish now as it used to. Prehistory is a strange science. We seek desperately for links across the great divide and come up with things which further estrange us. Francis Hitching in *Earth Magic* notes that the word 'man' or 'men', meaning 'stone' in a megalithic sense, is common to countries as diverse as England and India.

As in Britain, the country people of the Lot attached great importance to the standing stones and there is a rich tradition of folklore surrounding them. Often they would be festooned with flowers to keep the peasants from fever; sometimes sick beasts would be paraded around them in the hope of a cure. Others, such as Croix Blanche at Lachapelle-Auzac, have little stone crosses built beside the pagan structures, as if the communities were hedging their bets. At Le Suquet there is a derelict house whose window is virtually obscured by a menhir, though whether it was built there in order to benefit from the magnetic field which some dowsers say they can feel tingling in their fingertips on touching a standing stone, I do not know.

Certainly the Church became upset in the eighteenth and

nineteenth centuries by the superstition surrounding the stones and had many of them destroyed. Henri de Briqueville, bishop of Cahors in the early eighteenth century, was one of the biggest culprits.

There are endless examples of *peyre, peyro* and *peyrière* (from *pierre* meaning 'stone') figuring in place-names where a standing stone is known to have existed. Certain villages are named after the description of the stone; thus we find Peyre Longue, Pierre Basse, Pierre Grosse or Pech de la Peyre, and numerous others. St Martin crops up here again, too, his name being quite frequently associated with megaliths; hence, of course, Pierre Martine, which in some parts of the eastern Lot has become almost a generic term meaning dolmen. Likewise Pierre Levée, in the different forms of *pierre lavado, peyro lebado*, has become a generic term among the Caussenards.

The main groupings are to be found around Assier on the Gramat *causse* and on the *causse* of Limogne.

The Lot is fairly littered with prehistoric remains. Some say that even the hunters' game routes date from neolithic times or earlier, as man penetrated the Ségala and his colonization began. It is a good idea, therefore, if the subject interests you, to visit the museums at Cahors and Pech-Merle, though it has to be said that the opening hours of the former are somewhat erratic.

If it's prehistory you want, it's all here in the Lot.

3

History

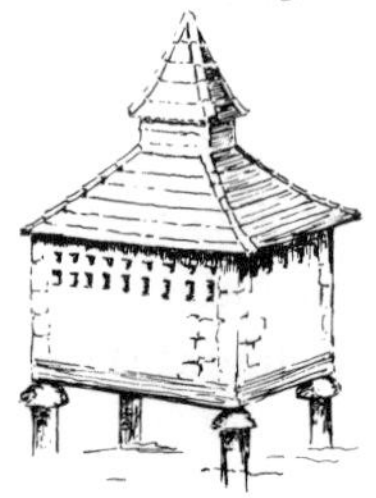

When the Roman army defeated the great Gaul leader Vercingetorix, Julius Caesar could have been forgiven for thinking that his trials in the conquest of France were over. He reckoned, however, without the Cadourques, the Celtish tribe who dwelt in the Lot, and who, with their leader Lucterius, holed themselves up in the oppidum of Uxellodonum and waited for the onslaught. It came and they survived it. Indeed it took Julius Caesar himself, in 51 BC, to defeat them, and that was by cunning rather than military might, for Caesar diverted the stream that fed the stronghold, thus delivering a psychological blow to the besieged Gauls. They surrendered, demoralized, thinking their gods had deserted them.

It is an infuriating fact that historians are quite unable to agree on where exactly Uxellodonum was, although most of the claimants are Lotois. Could it be the Gaulish town near Luzech? Could it be Capdenac-le-Haut, or the Puy d'Issolud above Martel, or the isolated excavated oppidum of Murcens (Ville des Murs) by the River Vers on the Gramat *causse*? No one knows, a lack of information which probably reflects the dearth of archaeological excavation in the Lot generally.

Uxellodonum was the last stand of the Gauls; with that, Rome had won. And it was not a bad thing. Cahors flourished into a wealthy city, trading in its rich, black wine and linen. Duravel and Varaire blossomed too. As many as ten roads criss-crossed the province, traces of which can be seen around the Catus region. They once linked Bourges and Bordeaux, the two provincial capitals of Aquitania.

The Romans stayed in the area for around four centuries, shaping a way of life which was to endure long after they had gone – education, the law, even the feudal system had Roman overtones. The Celtic tongue gave way to the *langue d'oc*, language of the troubadours and of most of the *causse* peasants today, as you will hear on market day. Today it is called 'patois' in a slightly disparaging way, partly because the very local variations make for confusion, but the Occitan nationalist movement has played a part in awakening people to their roots and there are now big university faculties at Montpellier and Toulouse devoted to the language and the culture it spawned.

That it is Latin-based you cannot doubt, with similarities to Spanish and to Catalan. An old farmers' proverb goes:

> Diù nos garda de la secada de Pentacòsta
> E de la plujado de Sant Joan
>
> (Dieu nous garde de la sécheresse pour Pentecôte
> Et des averses de la Saint Jean)

Even French, the *langue d'oïl* ('oïl' meaning 'yes' in the north just as 'oc' meant 'yes' in the south), is spoken here in an unforgettable, and to some incomprehensible, sing-song accent, with generally silent letters pronounced. There is, too, that ubiquitous reminder of Roman times in the number of place-names that end in 'ac', meaning 'belonging to'.

The Romans did not give the country Christianity, of course, but they tolerated it. Indications are that it arrived in the third century AD, though there are numerous legends which suggest an earlier date. And then it all collapsed. The Dark Ages arrived and wave upon wave of invaders plundered their way across the land. There were Vandals, Sarrazins from Arabia, Swabians and

Visigoths as well as the Franks, who gave their name to the country, and the Alemans or Allemands. Invader fought invader. The Franks were brought in to expel the century-old Visigoth rule; the Arabs were stopped at Poitiers by the famous Charles Martel in 732. Last of all there were the Vikings, who ventured deep inland up the long, long rivers. What a sight they must have been, moving up the Lot in their fearsome boats before they, too, were finally defeated.

Of the history of the Franks and the somewhat bloody Merovingian rule there is ample evidence, not least in the charming works of Gregory of Tours, Gallo-Roman bishop of that town from 573 until his death in 594. Cahors is mentioned frequently, indicating that it was still an important town. We learn particularly of its bishops, whom Gregory documents with an attention to detail that is quite riveting. 'Maurilio, Bishop of Cahors, suffered badly from gout. He added terrible tortures of his own to the pain which this affliction caused him, for he would occasionally apply a red-hot poker to his shins and feet in order to increase his suffering. There were many candidates for his bishopric, but he himself favoured Ursicinus ... In his later years Maurilio used to pray that Ursicinus would be elected. Then he died. He was a man of great charity and extremely well-versed in the Holy Scriptures, to the point that he could recite from memory the list of genealogies set out in the Old Testament, which very few know by heart. He was just in his decisions and ... he protected the poor of his diocese from the hand of unfair judges...'

Ursicinus was elected, later excommunicated and finally canonized – there is a church in Cahors dedicated to him.

Modern French history really begins, though, with the election of Hugh Capet on 5 July 987 to be King of France, thus giving birth to a dynasty which endured for 800 years, and which was often to find itself at odds with the claims of the English kings.

Hugh Capet's power did not extend to Quercy, however, which was then in the feudal grip of the powerful families of the area, and in the grip too of religious revival. In October 1096, the powerful count of Toulouse, Raymond IV, set off on the First Crusade, taking with him a mighty army of Midi barons, which included Géraud de Gourdon and knights of the houses of Thémines, Cardaillac, St Cirq-Lapopie, Pestillac, Luzech, Castelnau-Bretenoux, Castelnau-Montratier and Cabrerets, who in turn led their vassals. In order to recognize each other in the throng they devised signs. Cardaillac wore a silver lion, Thémines chose two goats – coats of arms had been born. They made their way across the Alps and headed for the Holy Land, or Outremer as the Templars called it, where they distinguished themselves in two sieges, those of Antioch and Jerusalem.

After the taking of Jerusalem a secret enclave was held to decide who should be King. It seems that it was Raymond, or Raimon, who received most of the votes, but for some reason he refused the title and it was offered to the hero of the hour, Godefroy de Bouillon. There is evidence to show that Godefroy had fully expected to be elected and had even sold all his fiefs and goods in expectation of spending the rest of his life in the Holy Land, so it would be interesting to know why Raymond turned the title down.

The Crusaders – those of them that remained – returned home, and in 1108 Raymond's son Bertrand set out on the same trail, never to return. Bertrand chose the sea route and took with him Géraud III, bishop of Cahors, who was to return so delighted by what he had seen that he insisted on cupolas for the Cahors cathedral. Enthusiasm for the Crusades now began to die out in Quercy, but there were lasting effects – windmills put in an appearance, along with peaches, apricots and plums and all the exotic fruits of the Middle East.

But we must not forget the Templars. A papal bull of 1139 had rendered them totally independent of all authority, secular or ecclesiastical, save that of the Pope himself. This was heady stuff and the bearded white knights grew very powerful indeed as, shielded from all criticism, they protected pilgrims on their travels and collected donations from people who did not wish to go on Crusades themselves. In Cahors they established themselves as an important force right through until the thirteenth century (the Templars were dissolved in 1307), but they also had *commanderies* dotted all over the *causses*, most notably at Le Bastit and other spots on the pilgrimage route to Rocamadour and Compostela.

In 1152 Eleanor of Aquitaine, recently divorced from Louis VII, married the man who was soon to become Henry II of England. Henry was a Plantagenet king, count of Anjou, lord of Maine, Touraine and Normandy. Eleanor brought with her as her dowry Guyenne, Périgord, Limousin, Poitou, Angoumois, Saintonge, Gascony, the viscounty of Toulouse and the suzerainty of the Auvergne. Within two years of their marriage they owned more of 'France' than any French king, upsetting an equilibrium which was never really re-established until 1453. In its early stages it was a dispute between the count of Toulouse and his fiefs all over the Lot and the Duke of Aquitaine, to whom the viscounts of Turenne and with them the Gourdonnais owed allegiance. Later on, when the duke begame Henry II of England, things became even more serious. Land changed sides hither and yon, treaties were made and broken, other wars intervened, local lords changed sides, but through it all, Guyenne, the province to which Quercy belonged, was to be tossed back and forth between the two countries for the next three centuries.

It is important to see Quercy at the beginning of the twelfth century in its role as part of the nether reaches of the Languedoc, an independent principality to which Quercy was bound by the counts of Toulouse, who owned much of both regions. To this extent the antics of the French and English kings were irrelevant, since northern France was, in those days, as isolated from the Languedoc as it could possibly be – isolated by language, by culture and by political outlook. But it was the culture that was the important thing. For in the Languedoc flourished a culture of such sophistication that it was unmatched anywhere in Christendom. Education, poetry and philosophy walked hand in hand with religious tolerance. This last was probably made easy by the fact that the Roman Church, although undoubtedly a powerful force, was so corrupt as to be despised by many people of the Languedoc. Around the countryside roamed the troubadours, singing their songs of chivalry and love:

> She's gracious, she is gay
> She charms with courtesy
> Her face all love to see
> The lovely girl I sing...

sang Uc de St Cirq in Provence, Italy and Spain as well as in his native Lot, much against the wishes of his father, who had wanted him to be a priest.

The corruption of the Church paved the way for the next major war to hit the area – the Albigensian Crusade – for it gave impetus to the Cathar or Albigensian heresy which spread like wildfire through the area and was easily tolerated in the liberal attitudes which prevailed.

The Cathar heresy was a form of Gnostic Christianity which had its roots in Persia and the East. It was a dualist movement which subscribed to direct mystical contact with God, thus eliminating the need for priests or bishops, and reincarnation. The teachers, of both sexes (and Catharism was way ahead of the Church today in that it gave women spiritual equality), were called *perfectis* or *parfaits*, literally 'good men'.

In the years leading up to the Crusade, the Church tried persuasion as a means of turning the heretics back to the true path, but these gentle self-denying vegetarians, who lived in poverty and practised meditation and birth control, were not easily convinced, and enjoyed the friendship and tolerance of those around them. Even the nobility, such as the counts of Toulouse, looked on them fondly, if pragmatically at times. Unlike the established Church, the Cathars did not demand high taxes; the emphasis was on spiritualism with low material demands.

The rite the Cathars practised was that of the *consolamentum*, usually administered on death beds to *crédants* by *parfaits* to reduce the risk of sinning again before death. The standards of austerity set by the simple-living *parfaits* were too great for the majority to take on.

Because the heresy was particularly prevalent around the town of Albi (Tarn), although it ran rife through most of Languedoc, the Cathars were also known as the Albigensians. Believing as they did that all things that truly existed were spiritual, their heresy, in the eyes of the Church, lay in their dualism, which denied Jesus as the Son of God, denied transubstantiation and denied, too, the Crucifixion, on the grounds that creation and the Cross were both essentially evil. God, they thought, would not give His son to the world through pain and agony. Jesus, indeed, could not even be God's son, unless he existed in spirit only, and clearly a spirit could not be crucified.

Officially the Crusade began on 14 January 1208, when papal legate Pierre de Castelnau, having excommunicated the count of Toulouse, Raymond VI, for being too tolerant towards the Cathars, was assassinated. This was the excuse the Church had been waiting for, for their alarm at the spread of the heresy had been growing for some years. They felt vulnerable and threatened. Northern France felt jealous. The seeds were sown. Pope Innocent III ordered the domestic Crusade to begin and put Simon de Montfort, a courageous and cruel fanatic and father of the English Earl of Leicester, at the head of military operations, aided by Dominic Guzman, father of the Dominican order.

Civil war had begun, and Quercy was more divided than most, with Bas-Quercy in the south suffering the trials of the Languedoc, very often at the hands of Haut-Quercymen who had joined the Crusade further north. Simon de Montfort was given a warm welcome in the essentially Catholic town of Cahors when he passed through in 1211. But not all the Lot was so glad to see him. The entire town of Montcuq fled when they heard he was on his way. Figeac, likewise, was wary. And with good reason, for these Crusaders, who fought with a cross on their chests for a mere forty days in return for remission of sins and a place in heaven, were slaughtering with gay abandon. In Béziers (Hérault) thousands were killed with no regard to what faith they practised. In the anonymous 'Song of the Albigensian Crusade', thought to have been written by the daughter of Bertrand de Cardaillac-St Cirq, we read of terrible deeds.

But in spite of his victories Simon de Montfort could not command any great loyalty, and many of the Lot lords, among them Bertrand de Gourdon, Bernard of Castelnau-Bretenoux and Guillaume de Cardaillac; deserted him to become direct vassals of the French king, who had not personally joined the Crusade. The lord of Castelnau-Montratier changed sides completely and became one of Raymond VI's most faithful followers. Even Cahors was moved to shut the gates in the face of the papal legate, but then hurriedly sent two people off to the Pope to apologize personally. The Languedoc was closing ranks.

Raymond VI had played a clever game of cat and mouse throughout, insisting on joining the Crusade as it headed towards his arch-enemy, the neighbouring family of Trencavel at Carcassonne. Thus his own land fell under the protection of the Church, who had to cease their attacks on Quercy as a result. His attitude infuriated de Montfort, for how could he attack heretics in the Trencavel lands when they had to be tolerated in Toulouse? Trumped-up charges were laid at Raymond's door. He was accused of being a heretic himself and of murdering Pierre de Castelnau. He was excommunicated again. As he refused a peace offer to help the Church suppress Catharism in his own lands, Toulouse found itself at war with the Crusade and, through a series of complicated developments, so did Aragon. But Peter of Aragon, who had come to the aid of Toulouse, was killed at Muret, and a stalemate ensued.

It had become a war of land – de Montfort's claim to Toulouse. The Pope died and de Montfort, too, in 1218, as he besieged Toulouse yet again. The Trencavels and Count Raymond had recovered most of their lands. Amaury de Montfort, Simon's heir but not of the same mettle as his father, gave up and returned to

Paris, ceding all his Languedoc claims to the new French king, Louis VIII.

The new Pope, Honorius III, was furious. The heresy would continue to flourish, he thought, and so, recognizing Louis VIII as Amaury's heir, he set about excommunicating Raymond VII of Toulouse, who had succeeded his father in 1222. Another Crusade was launched against the Languedoc, but this was led by a king allied to a pope. Raymond VII knew when he was beaten. Peace was made at Paris in 1229, at which he surrendered his lands and castles, undertook to prosecute heretics and promised to crusade in the Holy Land for five years. As deals go it could have been worse. Raymond was allowed to keep nearly all his land west of the Rhône, but the Languedoc countryside was devastated, the Cathars seemed as strong as ever and only the Cahors bankers were smiling.

The Inquisition which followed did finally make some inroads into the heresy. In the Lot, the Inquisitors went to those towns where it had flourished most strongly – Gourdon, Montcuq and Castelnau-Montratier. Sentences grew more severe as time went on, and Bernard of Castelnau, lord of St Cirq-Lapopie, was condemned not to a Crusade in the Holy Land, but to life imprisonment in a harsh Dominican prison, his lands and property confiscated. This was generally the sentence for someone whom the Inquisitors felt had made an insincere repentance or who might lapse into heresy again. Those who refused outright to repent, usually the *perfecti*, were burned alive.

The Inquisition, too, was recorded in the troubadours' song:

> And when at Toulouse as bishop he was named
> the fire he stoked across the whole land flamed.
> No water on earth could have quenched it then,
> small folk or great, in all 10,000 men
> lost their lives, lost bodies and spirits too.
> My faith! By his deed, his words, you'd think it true
> and by his way of acting, that he had come
> as Antichrist, not as messenger from Rome…

There were no clear winners; except, perhaps, for the French Crown. The Church was positively harmed, and E. Le Roy Ladurie, in his best seller *Montaillou* records plenty of Cathar activity in that gloomy little village and its surroundings, high in the Pyrenees, as the thirteenth century drew to a close.

It was the new Mendicant Orders who did much to kill Catharism, by challenging it head on. As Bernard Hamilton wrote in a pamphlet for the Historical Association, '...the friars taught that it was possible for all men to imitate Christ in this life and thereby fulfilled a spiritual need which Catharism had never fully met.'

The official dates of the Hundred Years War are 1337-1453, but, as we have seen, trouble between the English and the French, or more correctly between the Plantagenets and the Capetians, dated back much further than 1337.

As long ago as 1159, Henry II had presented himself at the gates of Cahors in pursuit of his claim to the viscounty of Toulouse, of which Quercy, and thus the Lot, was part. The gates were opened and Henry continued on to Toulouse, where they were not quite so accommodating. When he returned to Cahors, he found that the town had had second thoughts, this time staying loyal to Toulouse. But Henry forced his way in and an English garrison was established under the orders of Thomas à Becket, who was to remain in the town as governor for three years.

In 1173 prudence reigned and the count of Toulouse, whilst acknowledging his fidelity to the French Crown, declared himself a vassal of Henry II and his son Richard, and thus was Quercy returned to Toulouse, whilst paying the English an annual revenue of 1,000 silver marks.

A quick pen sketch of the actual years of the war show that, in spite of the Treaty of Paris in 1259 between St Louis and Henry III, Edward III of England seventy years later was still repeatedly laying claim to his uncle's French throne. Losing patience, Philippe VI confiscated Guyenne. This signalled the beginning, and Edward arrived in France to fight for the claim, and for

Guyenne, in 1338. The line of battle stretched across Haut Quercy, now the Lot. Those *bastides* already built were hurriedly fortified. Others were newly constructed.

In 1355, Edward's son, the Black Prince, landed at Bordeaux and the next year scored a coup at the Battle of Poitiers, by not only defeating the French but capturing the French king, John the Good, as well. The warring continued in all directions. France was hopelessly divided – a north-south divide at first glance, but in reality much more complicated. There were wars within wars. The so-called English (the Black Prince could barely speak the language, after all) sought the allegiance of the south, but feudal law meant that the south really owed allegiance to the king in the north of the country. The result was that loyalties remained intensely local and pragmatic.

And so it continued, on through Henry V and Agincourt. It took a woman to bring it all to an end. Joan of Arc marched forth to help Charles VII, and with the help of the fortune of Jacques Coeur a fight to the death began, ending in the battle of Castillon at Libourne in 1453. The English claim was in tatters.

That is the official chain of events. But how did Quercy fare in all this? The answer is, not very well. When Philippe VI arrived in the south on a massive public relations trip in anticipation of the war, Cahors, for one, gave him a rapturous welcome. But the following year, when the king levied a subsidy on Quercy to support 200 soldiers, the people of Cahors massacred the unfortunate men sent to collect it. And although Hugues de Cardaillac fortified all his châteaux against the English, as did the Thémines family at Gourdon, many of the local *seigneurs* – Philippe de Jean of Les Junies, Bertrand de Pestillac, the Stéphani of Gigouzac and others – supported the English.

In 1360, following a rampant outbreak of the Black Death, which further added to Quercy's trials, the Treaty of Bretigny was signed. Although Paris was happy enough with this Treaty, the people of the Midi were less so, for Aquitaine, of which Guyenne and thus Quercy were part, was handed over lock, stock, and barrrel to the English, as was the promised ransom of 3,000,000 écus for King John the Good.

To ensure payment of this sum the English had asked for hostages, amongst them two inhabitants of Cahors. John Chandos arrived to take possession of his new lands on behalf of Edward III, but the local barons felt furiously betrayed and some took to armed resistance. It was the levy to pay for the Black Prince's expedition to Spain in a victorious fight against Du Guesclin that was the last straw. Everyone without exception wanted to be French again. King Charles the Wise of France (Charles V) saw his chance, did a deal with the count of Armagnac and called the prince before parliament. He took prisoner the man sent to fetch him.

Once again war was inevitable, but now the towns which had refused to pay the levy at any cost, which had wanted to return to France and French rule, had second thoughts, fearing English anger. Geoffrey de Vayrol, archbishop of Toulouse, was sent among the Quercynois to woo them back to France, and maybe it was because he came from Cahors that most of Haut-Quercy was persuaded. Montcuq was not, and neither, further south, was Montauban.

Back and forth, back and forth; of all the regions it was perhaps Quercy which suffered most. By the time the decisive French victory at Castillon came, she was in pieces. Maybe that was why one of the first actions of the French king was to write a letter to the consuls at Cahors, telling them that he was now in control and that he knew how happy this news would make them. 'Nous avons mis et réduit en notre obéissance tout notre pays et duché de Guyenne; nous vous écrivons ces choses parce que nous savons que vous en serez bien joyeux.'

Quercy, one of the richest parts of the old province of Guyenne, lay in ruins. Many of the noble families had completely disappeared. The countryside was depopulated. The remaining peasants were racked by famine and plague. I doubt they cared very much any more.

Things were certainly not quiet between the ending of the Hundred Years War and the start of the Wars of Religion. For one thing, the people still fell victim to roving bands of brigands who came to be known as the Grandes Compagnies, soldiers left over from the war who pillaged, robbed, blackmailed and preyed on the population at large. There were feudal revolts, the beginning of the Croquants revolts, or Tardavisés as they were called, in Quercy. And who could blame them, the peasants were starving. There were the Italian wars and, in the run-up to 1562, when the religious wars started, there was the usual quota of deaths and even a small massacre at Cahors, in which 35 Calvinists were killed.

Nevertheless this could be considered a respite and Quercy, ever resilient, flowered briefly, although it never recaptured its thirteenth-century wealth. The builders were hard at work in the towns and countryside, most notably at Montal and Assier, a Protestant stronghold. The University at Cahors prospered and flourished, leading to a bonanza for the Cahors printers. The Lot poets and writers wrote furiously; not only Marot, but Hugues Salel of Cazals who translated the *Iliad*, the satirist Guillaume Dubuis, the moralist Charron, friend of Montaigne, and of course de Magny.

It was all too brief. Before long, war overtook the region again. Again it might have been contained had it not been for the warring families of Guise and Bourbon adopting the troubles as an excuse to fight. Once again Quercy found itself in the front line, for there were many stolidly Protestant towns in the region, most notably Montauban, but some of the Lot barons were Protestant, too: Antoine de Gourdon, viscount of Cénevières, the Hébrard of St Sulpice, Jacques de Crussol of Assier, the Cardaillac and others, many of them owing allegiance to the viscount of Turenne who had become a Huguenot too.

The reason people refer to the Wars of Religion in the plural is that there were nine of them, and since the majority of the Lot remained Catholic, it was the Protestant army led by Duras which tended to do most of the damage there. With Assier in the centre of the Lot, it was hardly surprising that most places suffered. Gourdon, Le Vigan, Catus, Carennac, Souillac, Martel – hardly anywhere escaped, and untold damage was done to the churches.

Then, on 24 August 1572, at the marriage of Henry of Navarre, a Gascon Huguenot, to the Catholic Marguerite de Valois, which should have cemented some sort of peace, came the massacre of St Bartholomew, when all the Protestants in Paris for the wedding found themselves under attack.

It was Catherine de Medici's dearest wish to see a France united under the absolute monarchy of her children, with herself pulling many of the strings. It was with some annoyance, therefore, that she had watched one of her weakest children, King Charles IX, fall under the increasing influence of the Protestant Admiral de Coligny. Nor did she approve Coligny's plan to launch an attack on Spain. In this she had an ally, arch-Catholic Duke Henry of Guise, who held Coligny responsible for his father's death.

A plan was hatched to put an end to Coligny's interference for good, and the date chosen was 22 August 1572, when Paris would be full of high-ranking Huguenots for the marriage of Henry of Navarre. Although the plan failed, it did allow Catherine to convince her son the king that unless the Huguenots were dealt with straight away there would be reprisals and that the traitors amongst them would threaten his crown. So, in the early hours of 24 August, the massacre of St Bartholomew's Day began. Jacques de Crussol escaped – by recanting – but Coligny fell, and among the dead also was Beaudine of Assier.

Horrified at this treasonable action, the Protestants went on the war-path for the fourth time. This time it was the Catholics of St Céré who were murdered in their beds. Towns were falling – Gramat, Cabrerets, Montfaucon, Cardaillac, Latronquière and Cajarc, where the locals decided to embrace the new cult. From these centres the Calvinists could conduct a kind of guerrilla warfare, making brief and murderous sorties out into the countryside.

In spite of peace-making efforts, the fifth, sixth and seventh wars all erupted, and in a curious twist to the tale Catholic Cahors found itself 'owned', as part of a dowry arrangement, by Henry of Navarre. The Cadurciens refused to recognize the authority of the Protestant chief, soon to be heir presumptive. Henry resolved to take the town by force, but it was only after three days of fierce fighting that Cahors fell.

The Treaty of Fleix led to the departure of the Protestant army on 8 February 1581, and as the Huguenots left by the Pont Neuf, the Catholic fugitives and three companies of the Royal Army arrived by the Pont Vieux. In an act of revenge Henry razed the château of St Cirq-Lapopie to the ground because it had had to be returned; the Cadurciens, in their turn, set fire to the château of Vayrols, where the *seigneur* of Cabrerets had received Henry of Navarre.

The Holy League had been formed in 1576 by Duke Henry of Guise, a body as hostile to the king as it was to the Protestants. Cahors was a League city. Figeac, on the other hand, was anything but. Still the Lot was torn in two, and the fighting continued. A three-year truce was signed at Castelnau in 1593 and on 25 July of the same year, Henry of Navarre, now king, renounced his Protestantism in the interests of the country.

The general treaty for all France was published at Cahors and the League began to fall apart; reluctantly, though, for the townsfolk did not like the idea of recognizing Henry as king. Finally, on 1 May 1594, a huge bonfire was lit alongside the Pont Valentré – the Cadurciens had returned to the fold.

By now you know better than to imagine that things started to improve. Skirmishes continued, another outbreak of plague left 2,000 people dying in Cahors while famished wolves took care of the country people. The peasant revolts were now in full flood; the peasants fed up with the back-breaking taxation which left them so hungry.

1598 saw the Edict of Nantes, which granted freedom of worship to the Protestants. Toulouse was not pleased but was rebuked by Henry. 'I want Catholics to live in peace in my kingdom.' But they were incapable of it. One hundred years later the Treaty would be revoked, with Alain de Solminihac, later bishop of Cahors and son of an old League family, preaching the 'true' religion with such force that many Calvinists returned to Catholicism. The revocation of the Nantes Treaty led to many Lot families leaving the country for good, but some did stay, and Protestants were still practising in Latronquière in 1720.

History, of course, did not stand still after the Wars of Religion, but the influence had changed completely now. The French kings were firmly established in the north and their influence extended further and further south. Quercy was no longer a powerful adjunct of the Languedoc; the English kings had gone away. After long and bloody years of fighting, Quercy was on her knees and no one wanted her very much any more. In 1790 the *département* of the Lot was created, splitting the once proud region of Quercy in two and separating the Lot from her southern roots.

During the Revolution Quercy followed the Commune, the leftist municipal body representing Paris; not surprisingly, for the agricultural poor of the country had long suffered under the yoke of feudalism, which was finally swept away in 1789. Modern history is a barren time for the Lot, although the period of the Empire brought some wealth and notoriety to the area. Napoleon's own son was brought into the world by a Gramat doctor, Antoine Dubois, and three sons of the Lot distinguished themselves on the battlefield – Générals Ambert, Dufour and Maréchal Bessières. Murat, of course, was king of Naples. Later on, in the nineteenth century, one name dwarfs all the others. Gambetta was founder of the Third Republic, Minister of the Interior and, later, President of the Chamber of Deputies. He was honoured with a state funeral on his death. It was Gambetta who uttered the famous comment which came to be adopted as official policy: 'Clericalism – there is the enemy.' Perhaps he spared a thought for the Lot as he said it.

In considering the history of the area, it is impossible not to mention the Resistance movement of the Second World War, for if there is sometimes criticism of France's national role, this is surely not true of the south-west.

The wild *causse* land was made for guerrilla action, of course, and no one could hope to know the countryside as well as the inhabitants themselves, familiar with every farm track, every isolated barn and every secluded valley. Once it was realized that the Germans had infiltrated the Resistance in the Lyon area, the emphasis on activities in the south-west increased. The contribution made by many people in the Lot was encapsulated in a warm letter of thanks from Maurice Buckmaster to the Resistance workers of St Céré. Colonel Buckmaster was head of the French section of the Special Operations Executive, responsible, among other things, for recruiting the agents who would work in France:

> ...we who have had the honour of being associated with your work, which has so largely contributed to the liberation of your beautiful country, wish to express our admiration, our respect and our profound gratitude. Long Live France, Long Live the Allies

he wrote on 17 December 1944. And indeed he had reason to be grateful to the St Céré resistance, who had worked tirelessly within their own group and with the Allies and the agents. Three Resistance leaders at St Céré, Georges Bru, Louis Lavaysse and Raoul Dufour, had, between them, virtually sewn up the town. No one could enter or leave without their knowledge; they even persuaded the *gendarmes* to look the other way when parachute drops were expected. Many Jews sought refuge in St Céré.

But it was not just St Céré. All over the Lot there were groups of Resistance leaders playing out their parts in a fight against a common enemy. Many are the reminders of this unhappy time – streets named after town inhabitants quite frequently carry a rider in italics, '*Shot by the Germans on...*'. Even the most casual visitor to the area cannot fail to notice the ugly Resistance monument which towers above the windmill near Lamothe-Cassel on the N20. On the *causse* at Loubressac you will see a little plaque which marks the spot where British and American agents were dropped. Once, on an annual visit to Rocamadour, I came across a group of Americans and Canadians revisiting the area for the first time since the war and re-establishing links with the many families who had helped and hidden them during their escape across the Pyrenees to Spain and beyond.

Much has been written of the political manoeuvring which sometimes threatened to destroy the effectiveness of these little groups. And it is true that many in the Resistance were motivated by Socialist and Communist principles. This is hardly surprising. The Lot, long an economically depressed area, has traditionally voted left-of-centre.

> Ohé Partisans
> Ouvriers et paysans
> C'est l'alarme
>
> Ce soir l'ennemi
> Connaîtra le prix du sang
> Et les larmes...
>
> Ici, nous, vois-tu,
> Nous on marche et nous on tue
> Nous on crève.

This was a popular song with the Resistance, reflecting those ideals. Many were the groups, many the opinions, many the quarrels; and many, often for pragmatic reasons as much as political ones, ended up merging with the Communist FTPF (Franc-tireur partisan français). This included the trade unionist leader Jean-Jacques Chapou, well respected by most and something of a legendary figure in the annals of the Resistance. Intended as a regional commander in spite of his move from the Mouvements unis de Résistance to the FTP, he fell in an ambush in the Creuse. There is a bust of him in Cahors.

George Hiller and Cyril Watkins (alias Maxime and Michel) were just two of the British agents who dropped from the sky one dark night in January 1944 above Loubressac and who had nothing but praise for the men of the Vény groups they worked with. They talked of their warm friendship, their gaiety and their great courage, their heroism, their kindness and their generosity. And indeed, if the description had not some element of truth about it, these British men could not have survived the experience. Hiller wrote, too, of the help they received from anonymous villagers and neighbours, who knew of their presence but resisted any temptation to denounce them, in spite of the dangers they faced.

The job of Hiller and his radio operator was to infiltrate the area and do as much as they could to disrupt the railways and the telecommunications, and at the same time to help coordinate and unify the various Resistance groups, some of whom called themselves Les Groupes Vény, after Colonel Vincent.

Together Vény and the Britons organized parachute drops, each with its code name, many in receipt of BBC coded messages, something George Hiller had reason to be thankful for. On 22 July 1944, whilst Hiller was travelling in a car with André Malraux and others, they rounded a bend at Couzou, straight into an SS patrol. The Germans opened fire, capturing Malraux, whom they took to be a Canadian officer. Hiller managed to escape, severely injured in the thigh. The wound looked nasty, but transfer to an ordinary hospital was unthinkable for safety reasons, so he stayed put at the field hospital set up in a house at Magnagues by Marie Verlhac, wife of one of the Resistance leaders. 'Ici fut soigné George Hiller CMG DSO Major britannique auprès des groupes Vény, blessé par les SS en juillet 1944' reads the plaque on the house.

An urgent message was sent to London warning of Malraux's capture and asking for medical supplies – anti-tetanus and anti-gangrene serums – to be dropped as soon as possible, for they had had to operate on Hiller. Security reasons prevented the message being transmitted until the morning of 24 July, but that night, at seven and nine o'clock, the BBC broadcast the message they had been listening for: *'Le précipice se trouve au coin,'* which was the code for the Vayrac drop. Within twenty-four hours Hiller was on the mend, none the worse for his operation, which was performed without an anaesthetic, but with the aid of three-quarters of a bottle of *eau-de-vie de prune* instead.

It was dangerous work for the Resistance, and it increased in volume after the Normandy landings, when they were instructed to do everything in their power to slow down the German advance northwards. Now the Resistance could take openly to arms and the guerrilla action was stepped up. In theory they were protected by the Allies' pronouncement that they were to be regarded as prisoners of war. In practice they were treated as outlaws, liable to be shot on the spot – or worse.

The German SS division, 'Das Reich', moving slowly northwards from Montauban, became infamous for the terrible reprisals they perpetrated on the civilian population of the area, which reached its climax in the terrible slaughter of 650 inhabitants of Oradour (Hte Vienne); but already there had been indications of what was to come.

It was at Frayssinet-le-Gélat on 21 May 1944, a tiny community of fewer than 400 people today, that a taste of Nazi barbarism was to be experienced. It was towards evening that two Nazi columns passed through the village and stopped. Shortly after 6.30 p.m., and joined now by a third column, the Germans began a search of the village followed by an order that all village men should assemble in the square. Arms in the air, knives and lighters confiscated (and in this country region all men carry knives), identities checked, resisters beaten, the men stood until suddenly a shot rang out from a house that the 'boches' had been trying to enter. A soldier fell. At this, all pretence at order left the Nazis. They ransacked the village, piling up property onto lorries. The house from where the shot had come was set alight. Women, children and old folk ran to join the men in the square. Guarded there by machine guns, a makeshift gallows was made on an electricity post and Mme Agathe Pailhès, an old woman of eighty, was the first to be hanged that evening, followed later on by her two nieces. Some time afterwards she would be cut down, dragged round the village and thrown onto the flames of the burning house.

The children were herded into the church and the rest of the population told that, as a woman had shot a soldier, they would all be dead in ten minutes if they did not own up. No one spoke, no one, that is, except the poor simpleton Yvonne Vidilles. Wrongfully denounced by a collaborator, Mlle Vidilles was dragged off by her hair and beaten.

Next the crowd were asked to denounce the Maquis, but once again no one spoke so the men were selected for retribution, twenty at first but reduced to ten. Five by five they were lined up and shot, with all the village forced to crowd round and watch. Once again resisters were beaten; one who tried to flee was killed, his skull crushed, his eyes pulled out. The women and children were then allowed to go home, forced to file past the bodies of their men but not allowed either to touch or even lean over towards them. The surviving men were herded to the cemetery to dig a ditch. Under pain of death it had to be dug, in an obscure corner, without speaking, without crying, and in under two hours. The bodies were searched and valuables removed by the Nazis, then the men were herded back to the church where they spent the night. Many women and children fled to the woods and just as well, since the pillaging continued all night. Altogether fifteen people were killed.

Three villagers escaped the worst of the Nazi horrors, indeed entertained the officers throughout the night. But when the Germans moved on next day leaving orders to extinguish the fire, wash away all trace of blood and avoid the cemetery, they faced their neighbours. It's hard to imagine the feelings of everyone involved. A few hundred souls who lived together, day in, day out, in an isolated country area where the land was still farmed with oxen, where everyone knew each other intimately. The Maquis were called in, maybe they were there the whole time, and Maquis justice was done. Cruel solutions for cruel times.

There were twelve people taken at Domme and Cénac, who were marched to a spot near the Abbaye Léobard and gunned down at the side of the road and M. Vernezoul, innocently working his fields at Payrignac when the Germans passed; shot dead for existing. There were 22 hostages taken from Gourdon at the end of June and massacred at Boissières. One man escaped. He came from Lorraine and, understanding the German command to fire, dropped to the ground seconds before the bullets flew. And there was Antoinette Buffières, who endured endless questioning and torture before being finished off in a wood at Prouilhac. She did not betray her Maquis friends. Her name is commemorated in a street at the side of the Hostellerie de la Bouriane in Gourdon. Sixteen hundred people crowded into the square in front of St Pierre at Gourdon on the day of the funeral for the hostages. Shops were shut, children were told to leave their lessons, everyone but the officials of Vichy turned out. It was a sad gesture of defiance from the little town.

But there were good moments too, as Hiller and Watney described. There was the time they sat convivially round the table at the Verlhacs' home in Les-Quatre-Routes, the whole family busily making the explosives which were to destroy the Ratier factory at Figeac, which made propellers for the Fokker Wulf 196 aircraft, pride of the Luftwaffe. There were the gendarmes of St Céré who forgot to patrol on the day parachute drops were expected; the camaraderie forged out of dangerous times; and there was the big drop of 14 July 1944, when 60 American planes appeared above the *causse* at Padirac and dropped no fewer than 617 containers, coloured red, white and blue and full of arms and ammunition for which Hiller and the Vény groups had been pleading.

Now the end was in sight, and a thousand men stood around the designated spot waiting for the planes. At the sound of their arrival the *causse* was suddenly alive with people – all the peasants and their families had come out to help.

4

Food and Drink

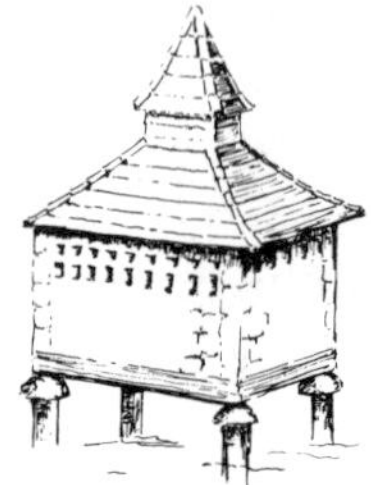

You arrange to meet at half-past five in the morning. Bleary-eyed, you rise and throw open the shutters to the day. The sky is white-blue and a thin summer mist like half-whipped egg white swirls over the valley beneath you, smothering the familiar landmarks. Only the *pigeonniers* can pierce it. It looks like a gigantic plate of *îles flottantes*. As the mist lifts you see smoke rise from the cottage chimney. Across the fields you can hear the children shouting and then the slow rumble of the car. You pile in on top of the chatter and drive to the farm.

Everyone is up already, so we leave the children and plunge down the meadows behind the farm buildings towards the woods. Our feet are wet. The grass is soaked with dew. Through the woods we go, heads down. 'Attention vipères!' says Reine, but we do not see any snakes.

We are mushrooming, and our eyes are skinned for the little yellow *girolles* with wavy up-turned caps, and big bold ceps. The floor of the wood is soft with the mould of centuries. It rained yesterday and our feet sink into a bed of moss and leaves. For two hours we walk thus, abreast, eyes down, following the forest's invisible paths, mushroom paths, etched across Reine's mind in an almost subliminal way. Every year since childhood she has followed the same tracks.

We don't find many – enough *girolles* for breakfast, and only one cep; it is too early in the year for ceps. We leave the woods and wade back through the grass, heading towards the children's cries. The sun is up, the light is limpid. We enter the dark warmth of the cottage and sit at the old table in front of the fire. Madame, Reine's mother, examines our finds and sets tiny cups of thick black coffee in front of us. The talk is relaxed and convivial. 'Did you go to such-and-such a spot? What! There were none under the fallen chestnut? My God! Do you remember the ones we found there the year before last?' It could be any day, any year, any century. We divide the spoils, sink a drop of *eau-de-vie* and I make my way home. It is only half-past ten. The day has begun well.

Eating and drinking in the Lot is not so much gastronomy, it is more a way of life. Simple pleasures like early-morning mushrooming result in gastronomic treats at meal times. The food revolves around the polyculture practised by the small *propriétaires*. Fruits are bottled, geese are stuffed, pigs are fattened, pâtés are tinned, ducks are turned into hunks of *confit*, and yellow chickens, dotted with butter and legs akimbo, are forced into ovens to emerge less than an hour later tasting simply sensational. It is a day-in, day-out, year-long occupation. *Tout es bou per sa sason*. 'To everything there is a season' takes on new meaning.

If you want to know about eating and drinking in the Lot, you should read Pierre Benoit's novel *Le Déjeuner de Sousceyrac*, a piece of writing in which is immortalized a rather dreary-looking hotel in the unprepossessing town of Sousceyrac. Today it has one Michelin rosette. In the days of the book, Mme Prunet surprised her uninitiated guests with the offer of a simple chicken. It was just that she forgot to mention that it would be preceded by foie gras of duck and little freshwater crayfish straight from the stream. Maybe she was being a touch mean, she wondered after the crayfish. Should she send the youngster to the *épicerie* for sardines? Then there was the trout and the dish of stuffed ceps followed by jugged hare and then the chicken, ending with a sumptuous *omelette au rhum*.

Eating in the Lot always has an element of surprise about it, especially in private homes, very small hotels or farm restaurants. It is hard to imagine just why one should be surprised, for even a most casual glance around the countryside reveals most of the unprocessed food that appears on the table.

The roads, for instance, are invariably lined with walnut trees, and in parts of the Dordogne valley you will come across whole groves of them. In spring, of course, they look wonderful, but come the nut season you can still see old women sitting out on their terraces cracking the nuts to extract the valuable oil.

Walnut oil, now such a delicacy and beloved of *nouvelle cuisine*, turning a couple of lettuce leaves into something unforgettable, used to be the staple oil of the countryside, used for cooking and lamp-lighting in an area which only serves butter with ham and radishes. (Don't be tempted to gather the roadside windfalls, by the way. This is not common land; the trees are highly prized and far from 'wild'.)

The staple food used to be chestnuts and there are still great forests of them. Nowadays, instead of being turned into rough black bread, they form part of the luxury food market, being made into expensive stuffings and *marrons glacés*.

Between the walnut groves, you occasionally come across a field of geese, a peculiarly medieval sight in the twentieth century. The geese are handsome striped birds with orange accoutrements, guaranteed to make any tourist reach for his camera. The *gavage* or force-feeding of the birds takes place for about three weeks before they are killed. The time-honoured way is to hold the bird between your knees and grind maize and fat straight into its gullet, stroking it down the while. This feed distorts and enlarges the liver of the bird until it can barely walk. Every time you tuck into a slice of foie gras (which for most of us is not often) you will have to bear this torture in mind. Certainly it is cruel. On the other hand, for the best part of their lives the geese graze freely in fields in a way which might make most British poultry feel distinctly envious.

In a world of subsistence farming, where everything and everyone is interdependent, a kind of equilibrium is achieved and sensitivities are kept at a distance. It is the twentieth-century commercial scale of the cruelty which is distasteful.

In the same way one could come to terms with the nurturing and fattening of a pig in the past; one pig, tended by a family too poor to eat much meat except on feast days. The pig, of which every last bit was used – preserved, made into pâté, roasted or stuffed – was finally killed amid much rejoicing on Mardi Gras or Carnaval by a special pig killer who travelled from farm to farm and knew exactly how best to cut its throat and drain the blood for *boudin* (black pudding) and cause it least pain. *Per cornobal se majo de car* (eat meat for carnival). Carnaval had very little to do with Christianity. It was a pagan festival abounding in masks and mystique, and as such fiercely suppressed by the Church.

The truffles you cannot see, as they lie hidden beneath scrub oaks and need a pig or a dog to sniff them out. Whether those of Périgord or Quercy are best is fiercely disputed, but the Lot has a big truffle market in Lalbenque. Commercialization of the truffle began in the fifteenth century. The prized truffles of the Lot are the Périgord truffles, not the white ones of Italy, nor even the black ones found in Britain. For mere fungi they have evoked many eulogies. Baudelaire, Brantôme, Dumas and Colette all wrote of them and Balzac was positively ecstatic: 'Quelques truffes à mon souper et c'est 10, 20 personnages de la Comédie humaine qui jaillissent sous ma plume.' 'Quelques truffes' today are only for the rich but you may get a few slivers in an omelette or a tin of pâté. A few slivers are usually enough, for they perfume and flavour everything they touch in a way which is indescribable.

Game is another obsession. 'If it moves, shoot it' seems to be the motto, and bearing this in mind it is unwise to go for a post-Sunday lunch walk over the *causse* after September. Rabbit, hare, wild boar, anything that flies, all are killed in such numbers that it is amazing that any of them survive to breed for another year. There are rules governing this annual slaughter but they never seem very apparent. The benefits appear on the hotel tables: roast boar, jugged hare, rabbit *en persillade*, pheasant, partridge.

In a land of rivers fish are plentiful, not just the trout and perch, the pike and now the Loire *sandre*, but also delicious freshwater crayfish, which arrive on your table in great steaming bowls along with bibs and finger bowls. There are numerous trout farms as well, where you can choose your own fish and have it hit on the head before your very eyes.

A land of plenty, indeed, with beef from the Ségala, *gigot* from the *causse*, every patch of earth cultivated to produce sweet young vegetables, fruit that is bottled, made into jams and syrups or dropped into your glass of *eau-de-vie* – peaches, apricots, plums and the famous strawberries of Caillac – but there is no sign these days of the saffron which used to be grown commercially in the Lot, although the fields are still high with maize from which the flour was made. There is no place in the Lot for the long *baguette* loaves, by the way; the peasant likes his big round loaves – *tourtes*.

I am not recommending hotels or restaurants in this book, or at least that was what I had decided until I met M. Labrousse. Tales of delicious meals eaten in charming out-of-the-way places at ridiculous prices have become something of a cliché. And the trouble with cheap, charming, out-of-the-way places is that once they are mentioned in guide-books, they cease to be cheap, charming or even out-of-the-way. Besides, chefs move on and there are a myriad of restaurant guides to help you make a choice. Better by far to discover your own private places, for eating is not always a question of feeding the body so much as the mind, and ambience or simplicity might be as important on some nights as food for its own sake is on others.

On my last visit to the Lot, however, I stayed the night at the unpretentious and charming Auberge de la Sagne, just outside

Cabrerets on the Pech-Merle road. The beamed rooms were warm and welcoming, for the rain lashed down outside, and the pretty dining-room was furnished with a big vase of wild narcissi. After a pleasant meal we fell into conversation with Mme Labrousse and her husband, who had emerged from his stint in the kitchens. We remarked politely on how well situated the hotel was, so near Pech-Merle. M. Labrousse was not impressed and a lecture followed on the problems of running small country hotels. It was not an unfamiliar lecture, for I had heard it from every hotelier I know. Nor do I doubt the problems, especially when you witness the standards that many small French hotels set themselves, and indeed are obliged to set in order to compete. The upshot of it all was that their position was no help at all, finished M. Labrousse.

Our platitude contradicted in that marvellously forthright way of the French, who have no notion at all of 'polite' conversation, we searched around for another. Word of mouth, we suggested, was probably the best advertisement. But at this M. Labrousse exploded with derisive laughter. 'You English,' he said, 'if you find a hotel you like you never tell anyone. You hate to find other English people. If there are two English families in this restaurant in the summer, they don't speak to each other. Word of mouth is useless where the English are concerned.'

So accurate an assessment was this of my own feelings that I felt ashamed when I thought of this chapter and resolved that M. Labrousse, at least, would receive a well-deserved mention. Elsewhere, in areas where I eat more frequently myself, I cannot bring myself to be so generous, unless I judge that they are the sort of places that would be well known anyway. One such I can certainly recommend is the Hostellerie de la Bouriane in Gourdon, where the Lacams will offer a warm welcome, a spick and span hotel, a great love and knowledge of the surrounding countryside, its culture and its history, good food with a regional flavour and a collection of cuddly dogs with English names. On cold autumnal week-day nights, when the hotel has been nearly empty, we have sat round the big fireplace in the dining-room, waiters, owners and clients together, swapping news and hearing tales of bygone days. Of such stuff are holiday memories made.

The plush Pescalerie's are a nice treat, and to sit on the terrace beside the river at Pont de l'Ouysse on a warm summer evening is enough to make food seem of secondary importance, but you will be no less satisfied at the simple farm restaurant nearby. These farm places live out the cheapness cliché, but are made for hearty appetites. A typical meal will consist of *tourin* (soup), home-made pâté, truffled if you are lucky, home-cured smoked ham with butter, a hot meat dish of rabbit or pork or a *confit* of duck, vegetables, served separately, home-made *cabécou* (goat's cheese), a dessert and coffee. There is rarely much choice, but no one will mind if you *'faire chabrol'* – pour a glass of wine into the remainder of your soup and drink it from the bowl, as is the custom. You sit with other guests around a long table, though it is not compulsory to talk to them. The family wait at table. You should book, and arrive at the appointed hour.

Most of the big hotels and restaurants offer very expensive gastronomic menus which include the specialities of the region: foie gras, *confit d'oie*, truffles and the like. As many of the local specialities also happen to be rather high-class tinned or preserved goods, you would fare far better if you were to indulge in these local delicacies at a farm restaurant, where they will be home-preserved and much cheaper. It is there too that you will find the ancient recipes – *la mique gourdonnaise*, a cabbage soup with wheatmeal dumplings; *lièvre en cabessal* (*cabessal* being the white turban that used to be wound round the head prior to carrying things), hearth cakes (*la fouace de Quercy*) and a curious dish common all over the south-west in various forms, *pastis*, where yard upon yard of very fine, layered pastry is filled with anything from apples to salsify. Usually in the Lot it will be sweet.

Of the cheeses the most commonly found are the *cabécous*, flat round little cheeses, which start off creamy and white, before developing a yellow crust, maturing slightly and finally oozing away ripely like Camembert. Then there is *Bleu des Causses* and Cantal, which creeps over the *département* border and is thought to be the oldest cheese in the world.

So what do you wash all this down with? What do Lenin, the Orthodox Church, the Tsars, Pope Jean XXII, Henri IV, Clément Marot and the Romans all have in common? The answer is the wine of Cahors. The Orthodox Church adopted it as its communion wine; the Tsars used it at official functions; Pope Jean invited Quercy wine growers to cultivate his new vineyard at Chateauneuf; Clément Marot called it '*une liqueur de feu*'; Caesar drank and exported it. The English liked it enough to make the wine-growers of Bordeaux feel so threatened that they started to operate a protection racket of taxes and constraints against the Cahors growers during the Hundred Years War and François I planted Cahors vines at Fontainbleau. A long and proud history which reached a milestone in 1971 when it was finally promoted to be an *appellation contrôlée* wine. Traditionally a black wine full of tannin, this is now being slightly modified for the wider market it is aiming at, which includes the USA and Japan.

In spite of the tannin it is good drunk young, when it is at its fruitiest, but it can be laid down, too, to develop into a full-flavoured, robust, purple wine, good with game and having a quite astounding affinity with the *cabécou* cheeses. The cradle of the Cahors wine is the area between Catus and Bagat, Soturac and the slightly Spanish-style village of Arcambal. The growers' aim is now firmly set at quality, and for this reason they stick together, even though there is a body of opinion which says that the best wine is grown on the slopes of the Lot valley rather than on the *causse*. But the generic appellation was hard won and they dare not split up and go it alone. Nevertheless probably the most interesting vineyard to visit does not hug the shores of the Lot. The Château of Haute Serre is found in the hills east of Cahors near Cieurac and it is here that as well as tasting the wine you can also have tours around the vineyards and see a video of the history of Cahors wine and Haute Serre itself.

At the end of the last century, in 1875, phylloxera all but wiped out the wines of the area. The *propriétaires* were advised to replant with American vines which were resistant to the disease, but these were expensive and many of the small farmers could not afford such a venture. Production fell dramatically, livelihoods were lost and it was in desperation that some turned to truffles. The slow climb back, therefore, has been all the more impressive. The big cooperative, which incorporates about 500 growers, is at Parnac, where a very modern plant is capable of bottling some 9,000 bottles per hour and produces 45% of the entire appellation. Those travellers staying in *gîtes* can buy direct from the Caves/Côtes d'Olt (Olt is the old name for the Lot) at very reasonable prices. There is also a wine tour taking in the main vineyards, soon maybe to add Mercuès to its list. You can get details of this from the Syndicat d'Initiative at Cahors.

Not all that long ago it was a common sight to see the portable stills being dragged round the *communes* by tractors, going from farm to farm as people distilled their year's supply of *eau-de-vie de prune*, a strong colourless liquid smelling strongly of plums. In an effort to stamp this practice out and earn a bit of money, the French government introduced a licensing system. Licences were issued to the head of a household for life only. As the men die off, so the right to distil the *eau-de-vie* dies with them, and soon the only *eau-de-vie* available will be that on the supermarket's shelves.

The other popular *digestif* is made from walnuts. *Eau-de-noix* is a dark brown and sticky drink, too sweet for me, although I quite enjoy its companion drink, an *apéritif* called *vin de noix.* This is made from walnuts too, but the fact that it is served with ice reduces the sweetness somewhat.

But it is the simplest meals that are sometimes the most enjoyable. A glass of Cahors and a *cabécou* and all seems right with the world.

Oun y a pa et bi Lou rey pot béni. ('Where there is bread and wine, a king may come.')

5

Architecture

Churches

Some people are châteaux people, but give me churches any day and give me especially golden-stoned, round-apsed, round-arched Romanesque, roofed in Roman tiles. Anything from Kilpeck to anywhere in Quercy will do. The Norman delights of Durham and Tewkesbury will assuage the desire for a while, but for a full fix I need the sun basking on a limestone wall and a tympanum from Toulouse.

For the south-west – and it is important to look at the Lot in its historical context of Haut-Quercy for a moment – threw up its own special school of Romanesque carving. The Languedoc School was based at Toulouse and branched out to Moissac (now in Tarn-et-Garonne) Cahors, Martel, Carennac and possibly Souillac. Then, too, there was the influence of the Périgord School, famous for its domed churches, which can be seen at Souillac and Cahors.

The Lot is fairly littered with Romanesque churches, easily identifiable by their rounded apse, their narrow, rounded windows and what Freda White described so aptly as their 'simplicity of mass'. There is something so immeasurably pleasing to the eye about these often small yet solid buildings.

Possibly it lies in the conjunction of straight and rounded lines; often it appears to have something to do with the roof and tiling. Perhaps it is merely the fact that, unlike exalted Gothic, you can actually see the roof. Nothing detracts from the lines; they are basic, and exude in their slightly crude way such a sense of history that you feel in touch with all things mystical.

In the golden age of the Languedoc, in the eleventh and twelfth centuries, when the arts flourished and were encouraged, there were not very many outlets for expression. The Church, as the only area of life where any real debate or learning went on, provided such an outlet, for it was the Church which sponsored all the art of the time, whether of monk or layman. Churches sprang up everywhere, meeting needs that were maybe not entirely spiritual.

These Romanesque churches are clearly modelled on the Byzantine ones that Crusaders must have seen on their travels, and certainly most Templar churches, including the one in London's Temple, have the same round apse. The dome was another feature copied from the Muslim world, and one which caught on in a big way in south-west France. Even the churches built without domes had uniform features – they had plain interiors and single naves and were built in the shape of a Latin cross with their chevets turned east towards Jerusalem. The ones which did have cupolas were usually nothing short of spectacular. Oddly, the cathedral at Cahors, firmly in Quercy, predated the other giant of the area, that of St Front in Périgueux in the Périgord, although it was by the latter name that the School came to be known.

From the eleventh century onwards vaulting began to be in stone, barrel vaulting at first, because the round arch was king and it was then, too, that sculpture began to be popular. This seems to have had its origins in the Middle East as well. How else to explain the similarities of the sculptures to the floriated columns of intertwined fronds and scrollwork so common to Celtic manuscripts? Aquitaine interlacing, this came to be called. But it is the historiated capitals depicting scenes from the Bible, and sometimes from everyday life, which capture the imagination, not forgetting the animals. Sheer, unadulterated fun was often had with the corbels. Great hungry monsters devour each other alive: allegorical animals, sometimes representative of the four Evangelists, in a tradition heavy with symbolism.

But all of this is surpassed by the tympanums. Whether a Christ in Majesty, or a Last Judgment, these simple, moving bas-reliefs, usually depicting a benevolent God amidst a frenzy of angels, evangelists and prophets, were carved from the heart by a skilled group of craftsmen. St Sernin at Toulouse has been destroyed, Moissac is a must even though it falls outside the Lot, Cahors is the stuff of conversions and Carennac and Martel are scarcely less impressive. It is said that the Toulouse School was responsible, in terms of influence, for the great west door of Gothic Chartres, certainly a *pièce de résistance*; but not, for me, so touching as the Languedoc tympanums.

The Lot had five big monasteries between 1040 and 1166 – Carennac, Marcilhac, Figeac, Souillac and Catus – and all of the abbatial churches, with the possible exception of Figeac, have good Romanesque work. But apart from these, it is the little country churches which have some of the best work, not necessarily in decoration but in sheer form.

South-west of Cahors, an excellent body was created in 1977 in the Association des Amis des Églises Rurales du Quercy Blanc. This group has done some really valuable work, carefully restoring the tiny rural churches of the area which had fallen into disrepair over the centuries. At Rouillac, for example, in the romantically named Comba del Mel (Valley of Honey), villagers freely gave their time, as did the fresco artist Michel Gigon. War and the passage of time had created havoc in these little churches, which were often used not so much as places of prayer but as places of refuge.

At Bovila it was the villagers themselves who burned the church down after the English had holed themselves up in it during the Hundred Years War. There are frescos at St Geniez, with its curious, roofed belfry wall springing up from the middle of the building and always putting me in mind of a Breton woman's hat. There are churches with traces of fortification and some with donjon towers, like the imposing one at St Pantaléon, or ones with the rather more ordinary elevated west façade, with round arches for the bells to hang in. A whole variety of little churches are grouped over the area. The northern Bouriane, too, has a collection of these small country churches in close proximity.

It was that enigma of a man St Bernard who put paid to all the wonderful monsters and animals and banned them from his own order, the Cistercians. 'For God's sake,' he wrote to the Abbot of St Thierry, 'if men are not ashamed of these follies, why at least do they not shrink from the expense?' St Bernard's influence was great. They died out everywhere. He has a lot to answer for.

A word, though, before we move on to the Gothic, about Rocamadour. It enjoyed the apogee of its existence in the twelfth and thirteenth centuries as a pilgrimage site in its own right en route to an even greater one, that of St James at Compostela. Although many of the buildings have been restored, there is still some Romanesque work to be seen, including some special twelfth-century frescos. And Rocamadour has another mystery; in the dimly lit Chapelle Miraculeuse, an ageing Infant Jesus on her knees, is a Black Virgin.

The cult of the Black Virgin was at its height in the twelfth century. She was seen as a promoter of fertility and patroness of childbirth, and she represented the power of the feminine at a time when the Virgin did not figure very much on the tympanums – her time came later. The Black Virgin legend is inextricably tied up with the Templars. She predates Christianity as Isis, the Egyptian mother-God, the black queen. Henry Lincoln and others, in their book *The Holy Blood and the Holy Grail*, quote *Le Serpent Rouge*, a book about Merovingian genealogy with thirteen prose poems corresponding to the zodiac signs. The poem for

Leo is interesting, for it seems to suggest that the Mother Goddess was represented not by the Virgin but by Mary Magdalene. Are the Black Virgins really Black Mary Magdalenes? Is this the secret of the smile on the crude statue at Rocamadour? Interested readers should read the Lincoln book and also Ean Begg's *The Cult of the Black Virgin*. Whatever the truth, powerful men worshipped at her black feet.

After St Bernard, pillar adornment occurred again only in Gothic form – leaf patterns and human figures; the animals had gone for good. Gothic in its pure, and generally northern, form was denoted by its evolution to vaulting that made use of diagonal ribs and pointed arches. Because this removed the thrust from the walls, windows could be used as a decorative feature. Gothic in its pure form is rarely found in the Lot, but rather something called Languedoc or meridional Gothic. It is a far cry from Amiens. Only the height is there, but the feeling of height is reduced by the main characteristic of this southern Gothic, which is the fact that the churches usually had a single nave with no transept, making the buildings almost as wide as they were high. You see examples of this at Gourdon and Martel.

From the thirteenth to the late fifteenth century, war put paid to building programmes, except for the *bastides*, where you can sometimes find examples of an Angevin style (akin to Early English). Churches, when they were built, were often fortified, like Rudelle or Martel. But the real work of the period was in statuary. Some sad *pietàs* formed the basis of an exhibition in Cahors in 1980, which typified much of the work found in Lot churches, although many date from later periods. Some of these *pietàs* are quite horrific in their naïve detail, with a tiny Mary struggling under the huge weight of a dead Christ, blood streaming down from wounds. They were the work, for the most part, of local craftsmen.

The Wars of Religion were the next hurdle to church building, indeed, it was an era of church destruction, with glass, of course, being particularly vulnerable to Calvinist hatred. This led in a curious way to the introduction of some Baroque, which is especially marked in the valley of the Lot, both east and west. This was a revolt against the austerity of Protestantism, but probably also reflected the growing links of the French monarchy to that of Spain. It was sometimes taken to extremes. At Cambayrac, for example, the rector of the parish, Antoine de Folmont, paid out of his own pocket for shiploads of white Carrera marble, along with rose and green from Prato. His plan was to decorate the whole church. One ship did not arrive so the nave remains unfinished, some might say thankfully, though this work was of a higher standard than the usual over-gilded altars offered as a kind of Catholic bribe to small churches. I have already nailed my colours to the mast, of course, but lovers of true Baroque will not be impressed by much of the tawdry work to be found here.

Finally the frescos; although these do not seem to have formed any sort of school or even a grouping, as do those in Berry. Nevertheless, many small churches in the Lot do have frescos, and many too are found in the Bouriane – Lamothe-Fénelon, Rampoux, Martignac, La Masse and St André, for example. They are not confined to this area, however, and, with the exception of a very few which are Romanesque, they all belong to the fifteenth century.

Châteaux

French château country is a sobriquet usually handed out to the Loire and it is true that for Renaissance architecture, especially, that area remains unsurpassed. In 1933, however, an American, Katherine Woods, wrote a book called *The Other Château Country* which dealt with the preponderance of châteaux in the Dordogne and its valley.

Lot castles on the whole – although there are a couple of

spectacular exceptions – do not belong to the Renaissance but to earlier times; they tend to be turreted, troubadour homes, feudal, fairy-tale affairs with more than a hint of refined Walt Disney about them.

But castles in the sense of defensive structures, which is what the early ones were all about, began way before the turrets. Somewhere in the Lot the oppidum of Uxellodonum lies hidden, or merely unrecognized, and there were other oppida, too.

To track down the very early fortresses, we have to rely on ecclesiastical history. The lives of the saints are useful here; clerics were among the few who could write at all, and from St Didier who was bishop of Cahors from 630 until 655, we learn that Mercuès must have been among the first châteaux, though hardly in the form it takes today of a much restored luxury hotel. From St Géraud writing in the ninth century we learn of St Laurent-les-Tours and from tenth-century records of Belcastel standing high above the swirling confluence of the Ouysse and the Dordogne. Then there is the testament of Raymond I, count of Toulouse, which refers to the castellum of Gourdon in 961 – castellum becoming castel in Occitan.

After the year 1000 the châteaux became far more numerous, and time and again you will come across the names of the big families of the area, the feudal families of the Lot and Quercy, those of Gourdon, Castelnau, Luzech, Pestilhac and Hébrard of St Sulpice, the Cardaillacs, the Calvignacs and, beyond our area but influential in it, the powerful viscounts of Toulouse. Although these families owned much land and property, their real power lay in their fortresses. The château, along with its lord, was the military post of the community, competing only with the Church for power, exercising that power over the people who lived and worked on the surrounding land, who would look to the château for protection in times of trouble and according to feudal requirements.

In order to offer this protection, the fortresses had to be built in strategic places; not always on high ground although this was easy on the *causse*. Sometimes they were built at river confluences, like Creysse; sometimes on top of cliffs above an important river like St Cirq-Lapopie; sometimes on mounds like Lamothe-Fénelon, which means simply the mound of Fénelon.

In those early days donjons or keeps kept watch over the countryside. These were purely functional buildings, massive, usually square towers with thick walls and spiral staircases, six storeys high. Their entrances were almost always on the first floor although Montcuq is an exception here. The towers had only very basic amenities, maybe latrines, or a sink, sometimes a chimney, but rarely all three. The important thing to understand is that they were used as merely temporary places of refuge. These keeps can be seen all over the Lot – Luzech for one – sometimes freestanding, sometimes attached with the passage of centuries to later buildings, but even in the thirteenth century the separation of military and domestic structures was still very marked.

Now, though, changes began to take place. The old fortresses were no longer isolated, for beneath the defensive structures houses were being built and quickly enfolded into the *enceinte* or surrounding wall. But defence was still the keynote. Battlements allowed arrows to be fired from a protected point. Knights' houses, like the ones you can see on the edge of the cliff at Flaugnac, hugged close in to the baron and his tower. But it was the knights who broke the mould. They started to move further afield and build *repaires*, or fortified houses. A thirteenth-century *repaire* was a simple affair: a tower, living quarters and maybe a moat or stake enclosure. They extended and complicated the feudal concept.

But it was not only the knights and barons who were building in the thirteenth century – everyone was at it, including the merchants of Cahors. Rich from their international trading, they looked around for ways of spending their money and came up with the novel idea of holiday homes in the country. These homes were called *bories* and were to be found mainly near Cahors, in places like Savanac and Polminhac. These allowed their owners an agricultural and economic outlet denied them in the towns (where they had been building too, of course) and although the violence of the times meant that they had to be defended, their role as leisure homes meant that they were quite often decorated as well. Because their style could not easily be incorporated into new buildings there are few extant *bories* today.

Knights, barons, merchants and the Church, that other great master of the people; they were all building castles. La Treyne was constructed with the funds of the bishop of Fréjus, and Roussillon had clerical connections too.

The Hundred Years War put a stop to all this and exerted an enormous toll on the existing châteaux. By the end of the War most of the big houses were uninhabited. Decades of guerrilla warfare, coupled with plague and appalling famine, meant that no fewer than 166 Lot *seigneuries* were completely abandoned, whole lineages wiped out and, even where distant relatives inherited, they inherited properties in such a state of disrepair that they were not worth restoring.

By the beginning of the fifteenth century, though, things were looking up. The population was on the increase and building began to blossom again, buildings erected on the rubble of a century of catastrophe. But the new-style lord of the manor had new ideas. He built a family home, fortified certainly, and enclosing a demi-hectare of land, so that in times of trouble all could be safely gathered in. No longer was the defensive building separate from the home. They joined together now, the machicolation giving a sense of uniformity to the buildings. To see how far we have come, compare the towering keep of Montcuq with the flowering Renaissance of Montal.

The donjons turned into cylindrical towers, staircases took on a new and decorative role. Gone were the spirals and crude ladders, to be replaced by flights. Noble life on the first floor (the ground floors were usually reserved for utilitarian needs) became more comfortable and luxurious. The chimneys showed signs of decoration, as, later on, did the ceilings; the bare walls were covered with tapestries, and there was more space now that the defensive towers had been turned over to rooms. The staked-out enclosure of the *repaire* was replaced by walls and turrets, in a complete fusion of defence and residence.

Quercy's Renaissance started a little in advance of the pure Renaissance of Montal and Assier. You see it in the sculptured fireplace at La Grezette near Caillac and the staircase at Clermont. Montal, of course, is famous in its own right. It is a jewel of a place, quite sober from the outside, which makes the surprise of the courtyard all the more impressive. And when you think that what is left standing at Assier does not represent even a quarter of the original building, you realize it was really a palace, built by one of the grandest lords of the court of François I. There is a certain recklessness and swagger attached to the image of Galiot de Genouillac, reflected in the bas-reliefs of his hero Hercules and himself, and in his enigmatic motto '*J'aime fortune*' or '*J'aime fort une*'. No one is really sure whether this is a declaration of love or a description of Galiot's luck.

Château architecture in the seventeenth century was often a case of rebuilding after the damage of the Wars of Religion, although it did produce one of my own favourites, Montcléra, and the monumental proportions of Grézels. All in all, though, the beginning of the Grand Siècle showed a decline in château building, which never recovered in this part of the world in spite of the classical elegance to be found at La Pannonie on the *causse* near Couzou.

The nineteenth century saw a revival which took the form of fake medievalism, a sign maybe that people were looking back to better times. Le Vigan, belonging as it does to the beginning of the Third Republic, is rather more honest, but in truth the days of Quercy were long gone, the New Age was dreams away and the riches of the Languedoc, both economic and spiritual, had become the spoils of war. The troubadour's song had died.

Rural domestic architecture

If you like the Lot at all, then it is almost certain that one of the things that endears it to you most are the *pigeonniers*, whose quaint towers dot the landscape and adorn almost every house. It is this marriage of architecture and landscape which is one of the Lot's most pleasing aspects. If you want to understand and learn about domestic architecture in the Lot, the best place to go is the new Open-Air Museum of Quercy (Musée de Plein Air du Quercy) at Cuzals; indeed, so new is it that unless they improve their signposting you may never find it at all, so I shall give you a clue – it is near Sauliac-sur-Célé.

The museum was the idea of that excellent local magazine and organization, Quercy Recherche, a body committed to the understanding and preservation of all things Quercynois. The museum takes itself seriously and is happily free of all the usual cheap tourist attractions. It is based on a village called Cuzals, which no longer exists. The old château, partly destroyed by a fire in 1943, has been converted into a centre, for the most part open to the skies, with pictures of village life and the inhabitants around the walls. Extant buildings have been left pretty well as they were, so some of the exhibits are 'real'. You will get a pretty good idea, for example, of the life of an agricultural worker in the nineteenth century by visiting the little farm on the estate, furnished as many still are today and with real food cooking on the open fire and real sheep and cows in the barn.

Wandering about, you will come across exhibits of old farm implements, of vine and strawberry production and tobacco. If you want to know how to build a *casela*, go inside and take a look; the instructions are all there. You will find out, too, what a *pigeonnier* looks like from the inside, how to draw water from the porous rock and how the oxen were yoked. You will see a fascinating glass beehive and gain a good understanding of the crafts that grew up around the local traditions. Take your own picnic or buy a simple but huge meal of locally cured ham, sausage and a *salade composé* to eat in the shade of the château. Cuzals is a good day out and there is even a very tasteful roundabout for bored children near the nature area.

But you don't have to go to Cuzals to see *pigeonniers*; they are everywhere. Even the tiniest, most modern farm cottage could boast a *pigeonnier*, and those which did not always had a place for the pigeons, even if it was only a hole in the attic. The reason for these pretty buildings was a practical one; it was, in a word, manure, which went by the nicer name of *colombine*. The high, arid *causse* pastures could not support cows, and manure, therefore, was short in the days before chemical fertilizers aided the vines. Pigeons provided so potent a manure that the dust, when collected, had to be diluted with rain-water so that it would not burn the seeds. So important was it that it actually figured in wills!

Where the dovecots were attached to the house they added the advantage of an extra room. Where they were separate, they were usually built at the limits of the owner's territory, in the hope that the birds would feed in the neighbour's land before returning home to deposit their precious load. This caused antagonism of such dimensions that it became known as *la guerre des colombiers*. It led to laws. In southern France, the seigneurial right to keep pigeons was replaced by the right accorded to all *propriétaires* to keep pigeons, as long as they had enough land to support their own birds and respect their neighbour's property.

The *pigeonniers* come in every shape and size. Detached, they can be round or square, some standing on very high legs, often with lantern-like additions at the top so that the birds could fly out from the highest point. Attached to the houses, the towers are usually square, with steeply pitched roofs, though further south the Languedocien type, with sloping flat roof, becomes more common. The *causse* of Limogne is the home of detached *pigeonniers*, which tend to be bigger, although size was not necessarily indicative of wealth. The peasant often built the *pigeonnier* himself, constructing it several storeys high so that grain or hay could be stored underneath. These charming buildings are the epitome of the Lot, and even today a new house is rarely built without the addition of a little tower, though these days one rarely sees a pigeon.

You do not have to go to Cuzals, either, to notice the little dry-stone huts that sit on the edge, or sometimes in the middle, of fields. The generic term for a hut of this kind is *gariotte*, a word you will not find used in the Lot very much except in tourist literature and estate agents' blurb. Terminology, indeed, can lead to confusion, but generally speaking they are called *caselles* or *caselas* in the north and *cabanes* or *cabanos* on the Limogne *causse* and in the south, 'a' being usually pronounced in Occitan as 'o'.

Freda White was puzzled by these little huts, but there is no mystery. They were built as storage places and shelters, and very occasionally as houses, in a land where the ground would have to be cleared of stones before any tilling could take place at all. What to do with these stones? Well, you built *caselles* or *pigeonniers* or dry-stone walls, or just about anything you could think of. The cabins are usually round, although very occasionally you may find a square one with a pyramidal roof. One at Sénaillac-Lauzès has tiny little steps running up outside for the hens to climb to a laying shelf; there is a trapdoor inside for collecting the eggs.

The interior of a *caselle* is the neatest thing imaginable. They were built on an *en tas de charge* system, which meant that the cone-shaped roof was formed by directing the major part of the thrust outwards and downwards. The larger and heavier stones went at the bottom and, as the cone rose and narrowed, the stones used became lighter and smaller. Inside them you just see rows of ever-decreasing circles, and I have to confess that it is still a mystery to me why they don't all fall in.

But it is the houses of the Lot that you will notice most; the plain, ordinary everyday houses, with their deep-pitched roofs and the way the corbelling makes them turn up at the eaves in a way faintly reminiscent of China. Honey-coloured stone and ochre houses that blend into the landscape, each lending something to the other; houses built to last, as Arthur Young noted in 1792. They vary slightly from area to area but are generally simply built, devoid of decoration, reflecting only the peasants' needs and the polyculture that they have always practised. Most are of limestone, although in the north-east, near the Cantal, they change to granite, which seems a bit gloomy after the sunny stone. They are wholesome, natural houses, built with the knowledge of generations. The limestone is chipped into blocks then discreetly joined with cement which barely shows, leaving a nice irregular line. Very often they are quite high and large for country cottages. This is because the beaten-earth ground floor, called the *cave* although it is not underground, is given over to farm needs. Here, in two rooms separated by a wall or partition, they make the wine, and the doors are huge to allow passage of the big wine barrels. Animals can be tethered here or tobacco hung from the ceilings.

Because it was thought unpleasant to enter the house through the *cave*, an outside stone staircase was built leading on to a little terrace, sheltered by a roof or, in very poor circumstances, by a vine or creeper. The combined structure of stairs and terrace is called a *bolet* and it is here that the women sit in the summer months, topping and tailing the haricot beans, while the men enjoy a glass of *eau-de-vie. Plus ça change*...

Off the terrace is the main room, kitchen, dining-room and living-room in one, dominated by a large fireplace and a huge table. In many houses in the Lot today things have changed little; the fire still burns, the chairs around the oilcloth-covered table are hard and rickety, it is dark and gloomy, and hens peer round the door. Nowadays these traditional features are juxtaposed with twentieth-century intrusions, so that, although Madame is cooking away on the fire, there will be an electric cooker tucked away somewhere. Jostling up against the chestnut *armoire* is a fridge, and although you may be sitting on the *salière* or salt-box in the inglenook, there will be a washing machine over by the stone sink, which empties directly outside through a hole the size of a child's fist.

On the outside, apart from the beautiful stone, you will see shutters, fitting flush against the wall so that the rain running from the eaves cannot penetrate the inside, and little ovals or circles cut into the attic to give light and air. The roof will be one of two types; either a steep, sloping Celtic roof in the north, covered with flat or *lauze* (stone) tiles or, in the south, a gently sloping Mediterranean roof covered with curved tiles.

As for local differences, you have only to drive around. You will notice that the Gramat *causse* houses sit flat on the ground and have no exterior staircase. This is because the poor pasture-land on the *causse* could not support beef; only the black bespectacled sheep, who live outside and do not need the shelter of the *cave*. Around St Céré there are many more mansard roofs. The *causse* of Limogne has free-standing *pigeonniers* in the fields and the *bolets* have stone roof supports, whereas around Figeac they tend to be of wood. In Figeac itself the *soleilho* or open attic is a feature. In Quercy Blanc the limestone is such that even bricks can be cut, allowing neat horizontal layers of stone to be laid, and the *bolets* are often incorporated into the house so that the roof continues down over the terrace. Around Catus there is a preponderance of *lauze* that puts you in mind of the Cotswolds. All of it is stunning.

Bastides

The best *bastide* is not in the Lot at all, but if you want to know what a real *bastide* should look like, then it is worth crossing the western boundary of the Lot into the Dordogne and winding your way up to Monpazier. The first time I ever saw Monpazier was on a hot, hot July day nearly 25 years ago, eyes and mind focused on the cluster of buildings at the top and the icy drink we hoped we would find there. Into the village at last, we drove straight under the cool gloom of the *cornières* and emerged from the arched shade into the glare of the sandy *place*. Maybe the old mongrel dragged himself slowly out of the way, maybe the scarlet geraniums spilling over the balconies swayed slightly as the car passed, but apart from that nothing and no one moved and Monpazier lay on, as it had lain for centuries, golden and drowsing in the afternoon sun.

The Lot has more than a handful of *bastides*, but none is so well preserved as Monpazier. You will find them all over the south-west, but the first was said to have been built at Montauban in 1144. Disagreements still exist as to the definition of a *bastide*. Received opinion is that they were a series of fortified towns, built at the instigation of the kings of France and England in the fourteenth century to establish land frontiers. Research, however, much of it undertaken by a body based at Villefranche-de-Rouergue, seems to indicate that this is not strictly true. New towns they certainly were, and free towns, too, but many were only fortified later on in the fourteenth century, almost certainly to cope with the ravages of the Hundred Years War.

Although it was not an entirely new idea, the building of *bastides* only became a real strategy after the Albigensian Crusade (1209-29), in a period which knew some optimism and some determination too to exploit peace. In the twenty years between 1250 and 1270 more than 50 *bastides* were created by the count of Toulouse. This building – and indeed *bastide* comes from the old French word *bastir* to build (or more directly from the Occitan *bastido*) – pandered to the new Gothic mood at large in the country, which in the north of France expressed itself in great cathedrals like Amiens and Chartres.

The new towns killed three birds with one stone. Usually built on fertile land or at some important crossroads, the towns were deliberately organized not around the castle or church as before, but around the market-place and town hall. One of the most important rights guaranteed in *bastide* charters was the right to a fair or market. There were other privileges too. The inhabitants could marry their children to whom they pleased and buy their own houses. There was no military service. The fishing was free.

People were even guaranteed against false imprisonment – so long as they paid. In fact, *bastides* were early recognized as a regular source of income and some of the local lords became very wealthy. In return for these rights the townsfolk had to undertake a series of commitments, which included the upkeep of the town and its defence in times of war. But generally speaking they were more than happy to pay for these privileges, which were often reflected in the names of the towns – Villefranche (free town, or Villafrancas as Bretenoux was called at first) is an example.

Thus was deliberately created a totally urban way of life which led to the slow demise of feudalism. Expanding economic prosperity had led to a positive renaissance of agriculture and commerce. Church, State and local nobility tried to tap this new wealth by grouping together the changing population into units which could be heavily taxed. The situation was further exploited by settling power on the shoulders of the burgeoning *bourgeoisie* and driving yet another nail into feudalism's coffin.

Bastides are usually easily recognized by their names: Villeneuve (new town), Villeréal (royal town) and so on (the Church went in for names like Sauveterre) and by their plan, which never varies. Forerunners of the modern American city by centuries, the towns were built according to a rectangular grid plan, with long straight streets crossed at right angles by shorter '*carreyrous*'. Narrow gaps divided the houses from each other, serving as fire breaks, and in the centre was the arcaded market square. The church was usually moved to a less prominent position away from the main square. The design made for very easy defence.

At the time when Quercy was divided by the Treaty of Paris, signed in 1229, there may have been a tendency to build for defence, and the best example of this is probably Labastide-Murat, built by Bertrand de Gourdon as La Bastide Fortanière in 1238 on the English front line, but followed as soon as was possible by Montfaucon which, although it passed into French hands later on, was planned by Edward II in 1292. Montfaucon is one of the prettiest *bastides* in the Lot, although for the best *cornières* (arcades) you have to go to Castelnau-Montratier, or maybe Bretenoux.

As for Monpazier, things have changed a bit. The market sells local delicacies labelled in English and the square is decked with postcards, but at quiet moments, sipping on a cool drink in the evening sun, life beginning to stir slightly – the mongrel has moved to a different place to catch the last dying rays – you look out over the golden square and its magnificent arches and reflect on the fact that Monpazier, too, was an English *bastide*. Seeing it like this, it does not seem very surprising that south-west France was considered such a prize and that the English fought so furiously to hang on to it.

PART TWO

In this, the second part of the book, the information is arranged geographically around the main towns. It is worth noting, however, that the Lot is a small depopulated *département* with only twenty places having a population of more than a thousand. Half that number have a population of over two thousand and even the capital Cahors can only scrape up twenty thousand. Inevitably, then, the vast majority of things to see exist in tiny villages or hamlets.

In an effort to be comprehensive and cater for every interest, I have tried to record most of these places, but the chapters are not arranged around any suggested route, merely as they turn up on the map. It seems slightly ludicrous to direct people twenty miles to a hamlet of 80 people, just to see a church which may be locked anyway.

Visitors, then, should invent their own routes or seek help from the Syndicats d'Initiative, or follow the many routes signposted by symbol on the roads – a *circuit*. Mostly people will probably want to choose a largish centre as their goal and slot in a few of the smaller places on the outward and return journeys. Few of the places merit long visits and determined tourists could easily cover each region in a day. But far and away the best way is simply to get into the car and amble. Pack a picnic and wander at will, following your own whim as to which tiny road to take next, making your own discoveries. The Lot is made for the independent traveller and inevitably your best memories will be of things you stumbled across accidentally.

As for the locked churches, there is no hard and fast rule, but generally the keys are kept in the nearest house. Don't be afraid to ask, people are generally extremely helpful.

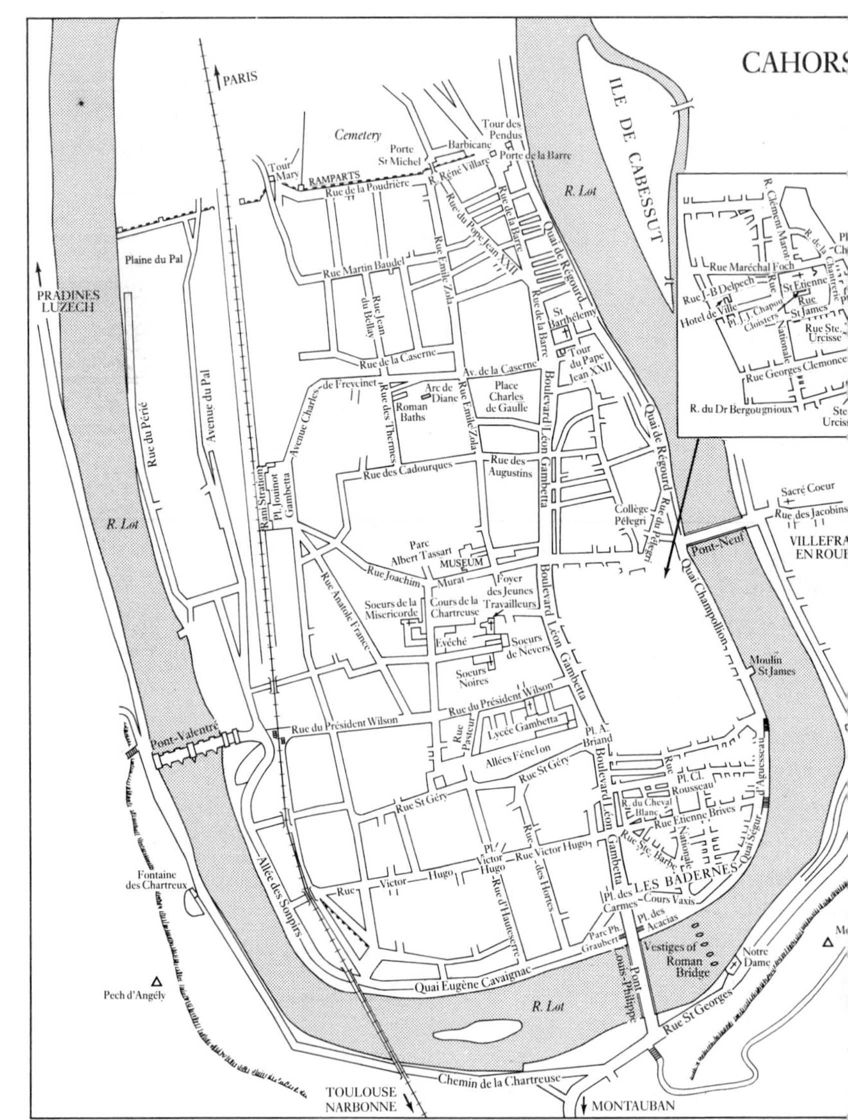
CAHORS
PARIS
Cemetery
Tour des Pendus
Barbicane
Porte St Michel
Porte de la Barre
Tour Mary
RAMPARTS
Rue de la Poudrière
R. René Villare
Rue du Pape Jean XXII
Rue de la Barre
ILE DE CABESSUT
R. Lot
Quai de Régourd
Plaine du Pal
PRADINES LUZECH
Rue Martin Baudel
Rue Emile Zola
Rue Jean du Bellay
Rue de la Barre
St Barthélemy
Tour du Pape Jean XXII
Rue de la Caserne
Av. de la Caserne
Avenue Charles de Freycinet
Arc de Diane
Roman Baths
Rue des Thermes
Place Charles de Gaulle
Boulevard Léon Gambetta
Rue du Périé
Avenue du Pal
Rue des Cadourques
Rue des Augustins
Quai de Régourd
Rue du Pélegri
Collège Pélegri
Rail Station
Pl. Jouinot Gambetta
R. Lot
Parc Albert Tassart
MUSEUM
Rue Joachim Murat
Foyer des Jeunes Travailleurs
Rue Anatole France
Soeurs de la Misericorde
Cours de la Chartreuse
Evéché
Soeurs de Nevers
Soeurs Noires
Pont-Neuf
Quai Champollion
Moulin St James
Rue du Président Wilson
Lycée Gambetta
Rue Pasteur
Pont-Valentré
Allées Fénelon
Pl. A. Briand
Rue St Géry
Rue Pl. Cl. Rousseau
R. du Cheval Blanc
Rue Etienne Brives
Rue Nationale
Quai d'Aguesseau
Quai Ségur
Rue Ste. Barbe
Rue des Hortes
Rue Victor Hugo
Pl. Victor Hugo
Rue Victor Hugo
Allée des Soupirs
Fontaine des Chartreux
LES BADERNES
Pl. des Carmes
Cours Vaxis
Pl. des Acacias
Rue d'Hautesserre
Parc Ph. Graubert
Vestiges of Roman Bridge
Notre Dame
Pech d'Angély
Quai Eugène Cavaignac
Pont Louis-Philippe
R. Lot
Rue St Georges
Chemin de la Chartreuse
TOULOUSE NARBONNE
MONTAUBAN
Sacré Coeur
Rue des Jacobins
VILLEFRA
EN ROUE
R. Clément Marot
R. de la Chantrerie
Rue Maréchal Foch
Rue J-B Delpech
St Etienne
Hotel de Ville
Pl. J. J. Chapou
Cloisters
Rue St James
Rue Nationale
Rue Ste. Urcisse
Rue Georges Clemonce
R. du Dr Bergougnioux
Ste Urcis

6

Cahors: 1

Hot and sultry, Cahors is a town of the Midi. You feel it the minute you drive down the long Boulevard Gambetta. The tall trees cast a cool shade in summer, but the southern air is there on rainy days too, something imperceptible. Maybe it is the light-suited businessmen who crowd the café tables in neatly ironed short-sleeved shirts and ties; maybe it is the way the roofs turn largely to Roman-style curved tiles now, and some of the surrounding *pigeonniers* take on a flat-roofed Provençal look; maybe it is the pollarded trees along the river bank. Whatever it is, it is there, intangible and tenacious, tempting you further south.

Cahors is practically an island city, caressed as it is by an all but all-embracing arm of the Lot, looping back on itself to leave only a narrow isthmus to the north. This should have preserved its ambience, for it is an old, old town, stretching back to Roman days, whose troops used to throw back the robust black wine with gusto, but sadly the town planners have allowed too much indiscriminate building. The railway station practically backs on to the medieval bridge of Valentré, for example, and even worse are the juggernauts, bound for Spain and Paris, which rumble up and down the Boulevard Gambetta, effectively dividing the town and making café conversations impossible as well as a health hazard.

It will take a determined effort to stop and look at the vestiges of the city walls. Indeed it takes a determined effort to stop at all, and if you do ease into one of the parking spaces which run at right angles to Gambetta, you will then be faced with the ordeal of backing out into the path of all the north-south traffic. So to the general cacophony is added the sound of screeching brakes and hands held firmly down on car horns. You can park more easily in the Allées Fénelon, close to the Syndicat d'Initiative.

For all this, Cahors is a friendly town with some elegant shops, and visitors will be able to pass a happy hour or two strolling in the old quarter of **Les Badernes**, where a huge and colourful market is held on Saturdays. Some of the streets here are less than two metres wide, some are arched, and every turn reveals a new treasure – an exquisite Renaissance window in the Rue du Docteur Bergounioux, a beautiful sixteenth-century door in the Rue Nationale, heavily laden with mouth-watering wooden fruit. Houses in this quarter can date from the thirteenth century. One from the Louis XIII period sports a memorable Toulousain staircase on the outside, later, of course, but very beautiful. Here at least the planners have acted with care and caution and this area is now the subject of a massive cleaning and restoration programme. The Syndicat d'Initiative will supply you with a leaflet detailing the sights.

The famous fortified bridge of Valentré lies on the westerly side of the Gambetta. Cross the bridge and turn left along the D8 and you will come to a spring called the **Fontaine des Chartreux**. In this land of limestone, of course, there is nothing very odd about underground streams and springs, but this particular one was worshipped first by the Gauls and then by the Romans, who called it Divona Cadurcorum after the local inhabitants whom Julius Caesar named the Cadourques. The spring, which still supplies the town's drinking water, travels from an underground well some twenty kilometres away in the *causse* of Limogne, although this was not realized until 1969.

There are still a few **Gallo-Roman remains** at Cahors, notably the baths in Avenue Charles de Freycinet, where there is also an archway reputed to be the entrance, and aptly called the Porte des Thermes, or the Arc de Diane. Extant remains of the large amphitheatre were plainly visible as late as the nineteenth century, as engravings clearly show, but today there is very little left, although excavations go on behind the Rue des Cadourques.

In spite of the initial resistance to Caesar, Cahors grew prosperous under the Romans, exporting linen and wine to far-flung reaches of the Roman Empire. The town became a kind of Roman crossroads, linking not only roads but river navigations also (Bordeaux was a Roman port). Vestiges of the allegedly Roman bridge can be seen near the Cours Vaxis, although there are some who claim that these are medieval remains and not Roman at all. But mosaic pavements of the period there certainly are (you can see examples in the museum) indicative of rich villas and the town's importance. There are, too, remains of an enormous aqueduct in the Vers valley, whose dimensions must have rivalled that of the Pont du Gard at Nîmes.

The second prosperous age for Cahors, notwithstanding the Albigensian Crusade, and of which there is ample evidence, came in the thirteenth century, when it established itself once more as a prosperous trading town. This reputation was enhanced by the arrival of the Lombard bankers, who increased its wealth until it became one of the financial centres of Europe, with popes and kings quite literally in its debt. The presence of the bankers, who were infamous usurers, attracted the Templars and other monastic orders, and their patronage too served to increase the town's importance. The Templars had in fact established themselves in the town as early as 1190 after the powerful lords of Vayrols had presented them with a gift of what is thought to have been 93 Rue du Cheval Blanc. Here they set up a hospital and chapel alongside the *commanderie*, but fear of epidemics spreading through the narrow streets from the many pilgrims who stayed there prompted the town consuls to ask the Templars to move outside the town. This they did, setting up home in the building which, since 1330, has been called La Chartreuse de Cahors.

Most of the sights of Cahors, then, belong to this second flourishing, and the most famous one of all is probably the **Pont Valentré**, still one of the most beautiful extant examples anywhere of fourteenth-century military architecture.

Construction of the bridge was decided upon in 1306, but it was not until 17 June 1308 that Géraud de Sabanac, a consul of the town, laid the first stone. Today the bridge has been much restored, although thankfully it has not gone the way of its companion bridge, the Pont Vieux, which had no fewer than five defensive towers and which was pulled down to make way for the age of cast iron. Valentré has a mere three towers and six pointed arches. Battlemented stairs lead to the first storey of the towers from bridge level. The limestone cliffs of the far river bank meant that the bridge could only be approached from the side, thus increasing its defensive properties, since a small castle commanded the road approach and was connected to the first tower. So impressive was the bridge that in spite of Cahors' troubled history there is no record of its ever having been attacked.

Augustus Hare, travelling at the end of the last century, found the restorations – then very new – a disaster and pronounced the bridge 'ruined from an artistic point of view'. Well, maybe, but you are unlikely ever to see anything quite like it again. And on a hot day, with the limestone cliffs behind it and the reflections rippling in the river, or at night, floodlit, it can look very romantic.

As with all good medieval buildings, there is a legend which concerns the ubiquitous Devil and the master mason, who was despairing of ever getting the job finished. So he made his pact with Lucifer: his soul in return for prompt execution of all his orders, so that the work would be finished quickly.

Things went well and the bridge was appoaching completion. Seeing that it was time to take some action, the mason sent the Devil off to the river to collect water – in a sieve. In spite of his speed, the Devil just could not reach the mason before the water ran away. Finally he had to admit defeat and so forfeit the mason's soul. Furious, he took his revenge, breaking off a stone on the summit of the central tower which since then has always been known as the Devil's Tower. Throughout the centuries and in spite of many attempts, this one stone would never remain intact. In 1879, however, determined efforts were made. During the course of restoration work, the offending stone was fixed firmly in place, and on its side, facing the town, was carved a little Devil trying in vain to pull the stone off again. So far, so good.

Back now to the east side of town to see the other famous sight of Cahors, the **Cathedral of St Etienne** in the Place Jean-Jacques-Chapou. One of the best ways to see the Cathedral, and indeed the rest of the old town, is to climb up the Mont St Cyr to the south-east. From there you look down on an exciting roofscape and can see quite clearly the loop or *cingle* of the river in which Cahors is enclosed. It also gives you a good view of the Moorish domes on the Cathedral.

When you come down the hill, make your way back to St Etienne and go straight to the north door, for this carved wonder of the Toulouse School is its treasure. Freda White thought the Ascension at Cahors even better than the Apocalypse at Moissac (Tarn-et-Garonne). I am not so sure. Moissac has those intricate pillars and that wonderful frieze of earnest-looking elders gazing up at their awesome Lord. Cahors is lighter in tone, but then again it surely scores in sheer design. There is the central figure of God, as always, but flanked this time by two angels of such grace and symmetry that one is amazed when one thinks of the one-dimensional, naïve paintings of the same era (1135). Above God, in a linked halo, the cherubim fly down to meet Him. On either side are scenes of the life of St Etienne and beneath God are the apostles, a rather more traditional crowd than the twenty-four Apocalypse men at Moissac. In the centre is the Virgin.

You will want to stand back and take a good look. Don't – you may get run over. Buildings crowd in on the church in a very medieval way, the street is narrow and dangerous and the doorway itself has sunk below the level of the pavement. It is a good idea to take binoculars to these spectacular doorways; that way you can see more clearly the detail of the faces. The face of God at Cahors is wise and moving, the face of a man who knows too much. The corbels, too, are worth looking at, especially the charming little naked man, clinging for dear life to the stone with a terrified backward glance at the ground.

Nothing inside can compare with the door, but the rest still merits attention. The cupolas make sense when one realizes that Bishop Géraud de Cardaillac, who built the cathedral in 1112 (a start had been made in 1080), had just returned from Crusade with Bertrand, count of Toulouse. Bertrand died in the Holy Land, but Géraud returned bearing with him the relics of Ste Coiffe. He decreed that the two domes be constructed. Thirty-two metres high, their dimensions were surpassed by none except those of St Sofia at Constantinople. Souillac, Agen, Périgueux and Angoulême looked on with admiration – and copied. Work on the west dome in 1872 revealed the early fourteenth-century frescos, depicting the stoning to death of St Stephen, his murderers, and eight prophets astride animals.

The nave is vast – 44 metres long – with a rose window. Two doors to the south lead to the cloisters, classed amongst the most beautiful examples of Flamboyant Gothic, with star vaulting throughout. There is also some good sculpture in the north gallery. The **Chapelle St Gausbert**, off the cloisters, has been turned into a museum after the discovery of some fifteenth-century paintings attributed to Canon d'Auriolles. It also contains the cathedral treasure, a modest haul, including the relics of Ste Coiffe. For real medieval, ecclesiastical treasure you have to go to Conques (Aveyron), but you will want to take a second look at the Last Judgment scene which entirely covers one wall of the chapel, and don't resist the temptation to go through the door in the north-east corner of the cloisters. It leads into a courtyard containing some of the best Renaissance decoration in all Cahors. One other relic may be of interest. This is a piece of linen in the Ste Coiffe chapel, said to have been wrapped round Christ's head during His burial and which once belonged to Charlemagne.

Fans of the Romanesque will take one last look at the door before moving on to **Ste Urcisse** at the bottom of Rue Clémenceau, where the capital heads on the sanctuary pillars are a delight. A very loving serpent twines around an apple tree half its size and Adam and Eve clutch at their vine leaves with a slightly half-hearted air. The other pillar shows a doll-like Christ with attendant angels.

Make your way, now, down to the river bank and the Rue Champollion, but keep your eyes skinned as you walk, for every street has something to recommend it; some are bridged, and there are decorated windows and doors, and curious corbels. The fifteenth-century **Maison Roaldès** is situated in Place Henri IV, which lends some credence to the unproven legend that Henry of Navarre stayed there during the siege of Cahors in 1580. The Roaldès were an old Quercy family who acquired the house in the seventeenth century. At the top on the south side is an old *soleilho*, an open attic found in some Quercy houses, but particularly at Figeac. Generally this would be used for drying linen, or sometimes skins if the house belonged to a tanner. This one has a wooden balcony, matching the criss-cross wooden beams of the building.

Cahors was a town of learning, with several illustrious establishments operating through the centuries, the most important of which was the University. The seat was founded in 1332 by Pope Jean XXII, a cruel man but one who, as the former Jacques Duèze, was a native of Cahors, a town to which he remained infinitely loyal and generous. He was, say some, the son of a cobbler who from an early age set his sights high, becoming tutor to the royal children in Naples. Subsequently he was appointed bishop of Fréjus, then of Avignon, then cardinal of Porto and finally pope in 1316. But Avignon had left its mark on him and in spite of a promise he had made to the Italian cardinals to return to Rome after his enthronement at Lyon, he didn't leave the country, becoming, after Clément V, the second Avignon Pope. In literal terms his promise was kept, for he had vowed not to mount horse or mule before returning to Italy, and in order to comply with this vow he sailed downriver to Avignon. At a time when war raged in Italy, Avignon seemed an attractive place for a pope, especially as John and his predecessor were both French; but, although they gave birth to an idea, they were well in advance of the schism that was to break out in the Church at the end of the century and lead to a breakaway group of anti-popes settling in the town. Cahors townsfolk were terrified of Duèze and this was not helped by his treatment of their bishop, Hugues Géraud, whom the Pope had flayed alive and then torn apart by wild horses on a curious charge of employing magical arts.

The University though, brought nothing but good to Cahors. Founded in the old Templar buildings of the Chartreuse, it had four faculties and attracted bright students (as many as 4,000 in 1500) who studied under the best teachers. It flourished until 1751 when, accused of being decadent, it was united with the University at Toulouse, which effectively suppressed it. Toulouse was delighted, for it had long planned for such a happening.

The students lodged in colleges which grew up in the town. One of them, the Collège Pélegri, the only one to survive, can be seen in the street of the same name. It was founded in 1368 by Raymond and Hugues Pélegri of Le Vigan and boarded thirteen students at the outset.

The other educational establishment of note was the Lycée, which still exists today. It was founded in 1605 by the lord of Thémines, senéchal and governor of Quercy, although it was a letter from Henri IV in 1604 which authorized the Jesuits to open a learning place. The school recruited from up to 50 kilometres away and by 1627 had some 700 pupils in its site near the Allées Fénelon.

The town walls and defences lie to the north, but stop *en route* for a quick look at the curious Saracen chimney in Rue Devia and the church of St Barthélemy, where Pope Jean XXII was baptised, although the present church dates only from the sixteenth century. Have a look, too, at the remains of the Pope's palace opposite the south door of the church, built for him by his brother Pierre. The tower stands five storeys high, with battlements at the top and twin, arched fourteenth-century windows.

The ramparts are at the end of the Rue de la Barre and it is here that you can see the St Jean tower or Tour des Pendus (Tower of the Hanged Men) in its commanding position over the Lot. The tower is open, on the town side, all the way to the ground. Alongside it is a building looking much like a baby château, the Barbican or Guardroom, designed to protect the once-adjoining Porte de la Barre. You can follow the ramparts across the isthmus, although only the Porte St Michel is worth a look.

In 1975, Nicole Haselberger was given the task of modernizing the **Cahors Museum** (in rue Emile Zola), which is housed in imposing buildings dating back to the fifteenth century and backing on to a pretty park. Here, if you can ever find it open, you will get a very good idea of Cahors' long history. It is a diverse collection which features, on the ground floor, some local archaeology, including Roman mosaics and a third-century Gallo-Roman sarcophagus. There is a valuable lapidary collection and the Renaissance is represented, amongst other exhibits, by two stunning slaves carved in dark wood, the eyes downcast and sad, though the figures remain immensely dignified. These moving statues are said to have come from the ruined palace of Assier. Upstairs there are paintings, ancient and relatively modern – Vlaminck and Dufy – and two rooms devoted to the famous sons of Cahors. Gambetta, the nineteenth-century democratic leader, he of all the avenues, streets and boulevards all over France, gets a room to himself. The other is devoted to Pope Jean XXII, and Murat (who has another museum in his honour at Labastide-Murat). Cahors produced two famous poets, Olivier de Magny, who died a young death at 30 in 1561 and was rather less well recognized than Clément Marot (1496-1544), known for his very beautiful translation of the Psalms. He wrote, too, of his native town:

> ...vers midy les haultz Dieux m'ont faict naistre,
> Où le soleil non trop excessif est;
> Parquoy la terre avec honneur s'y vest
> De mille fruictz, de maincte fleur et plante;
> Bacchus aussi sa bonne vigne y plante,
> Par art subtil, sur montaignes pierreuses,
> Rendans liqueurs fortes et savoureuses,
> Maincte fontaine y murmure et undoye
> Et en tous temps le laurier y verdoye...
> ...Au lieu que je declaire,
> Le fleuve Lot coule son eau peu claire,
> Qui mainctz rochers traverse et environne,
> Pour s'aller joindre au droict fil de Garonne.
> A bref parler, c'est Cahors en Quercy...

from *L'Enfer*

[Fate had me born towards midday, where the sun is not too hot, where a thousand fruits and many flowers and plants dress the earth, and Bacchus plants his vine with a subtle art, on stony mountains, yielding a liquor that is strong and full of flavour. Many springs murmur and meander there and at all times the laurel flourishes. At this place I'm talking about, the muddy waters of the Lot flow over and around many rocks to join the right-hand thread of the Garonne. In short it is Cahors en Quercy.]

7

Cahors: 2

The Lot Valley: west

Below Cahors the valley of the Lot belongs very certainly to the bishops of Cahors who worked and played along its banks, and to the vineyards of the black wine of Cahors. After Luzech, the rocky cliffs become a thing of the past, replaced by gentler slopes, and the river idles its way through the countryside in deep loops. Along the banks grow the vines, the wine from which would be sailed downriver to the Garonne and Bordeaux.

Mercuès, seven kilometres north-west of Cahors on the D911, has in recent years been famous for its château, a luxury hotel, standing on the edge of a promontory above the river. The site has long been fortified, however, as St Didier, bishop of Cahors in the seventh century, attests. The bishops of Cahors rebuilt it in the fourteenth and fifteenth centuries and in their hands it stayed right up until the act of 1905 which separated Church from State, serving as an excellent advance sentinel for Cahors itself. The name Mercuès came from the discovery of a Roman temple dedicated to Mercury on the same spot.

The château changed hands several times in the Hundred Years War and was besieged by the Calvinists in 1563. It was the seventeenth century that saw major embellishments and the

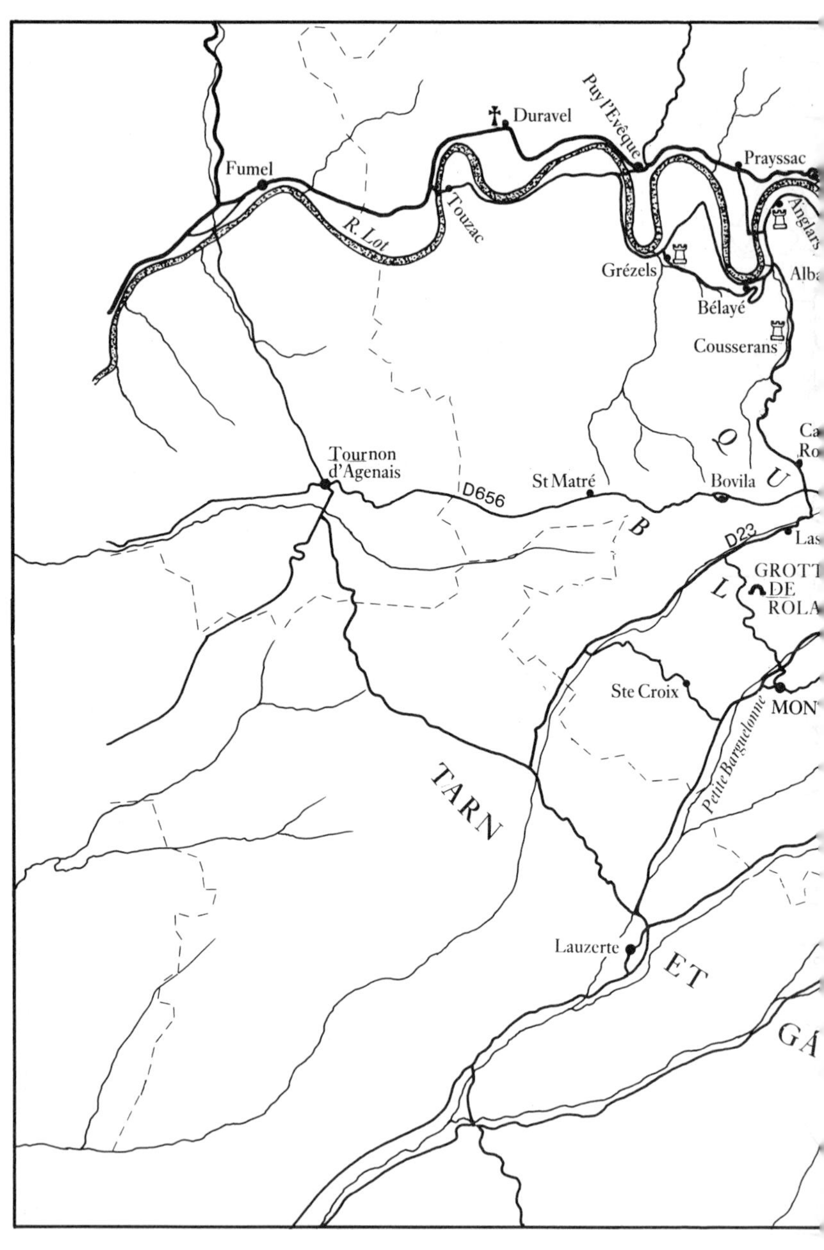

Duravel
Puy l'Evêque
Prayssac
Fumel
Touzac
R. Lot
Grézels
Bélayé
Cousserans
Tournon
d'Agenais
St Matré
D656
Bovila
Q
U
B
D23
L
GROTT
DE
ROLA
Ste Croix
Petite Barguelonne
TARN
Lauzerte
ET

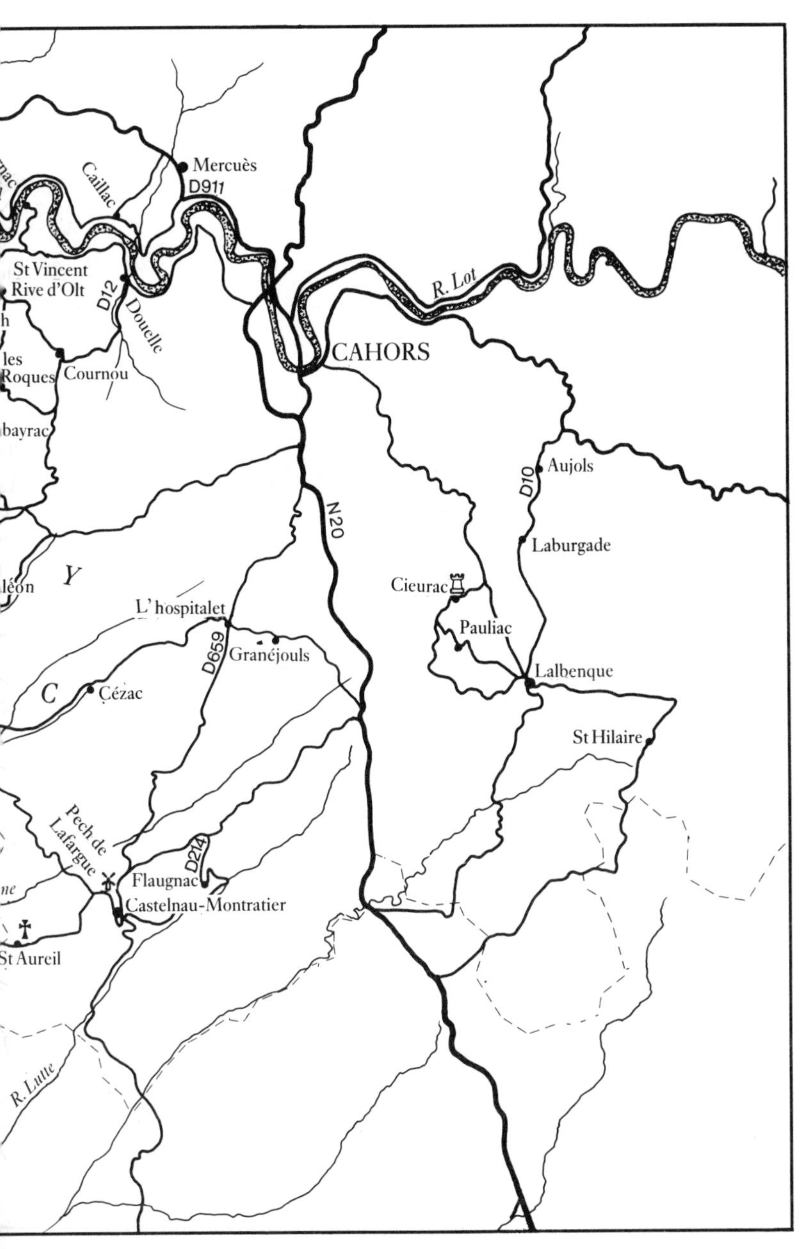
Mercuès
Caillac
D911
St Vincent
Rive d'Olt
D12
Douelle
R. Lot
CAHORS
les
Roques
Cournou
bayrac
Aujols
D10
N20
Laburgade
Y
léon
Cieurac
L'hospitalet
Pauliac
D659
Granéjouls
Lalbenque
C
Cézac
St Hilaire
Pech de
Lafargue
D214
Flaugnac
Castelnau-Montratier
St Aureil
R. Lutte

establishing of the gardens, which are still there, by Pierre Habert. A further 'restoration' in the nineteenth century by a pupil of Viollet-le-Duc proved little short of vandalism: all the architectural features of any note were ripped out, and only the shell with its heavy circular towers was left untouched.

From its vantage point you look down on the hamlet of Pradines, where the church is dedicated to St Martial, who was supposed to have lived in a local cave for a while. There is a sixteenth-century wooden *pietà* inside.

Douelle, on the south side of the river (D12), was an important ferry crossing and the seat of a barony at Cessac. A curious arrangement existed here, whereby the baron was awarded the somewhat dubious privilege of waiting on the bishops on the day of their enthronements. Leading the horse on which the bishop rode, the baron would then be required to wait on the table with uncovered head, bare right leg and right foot. In return for making such a fool of himself the baron was then allowed to walk away with the spoils – the horse and the dinner service used at the table. The latter, of course, was silver and worth a good deal of money. Perhaps they finally ran out of dishes, because the consuls had the château of Cessac pulled down in the fifteenth century.

All along this stretch of the river the vine reigns supreme and you will see this reflected time and again in lintels and doorways. In Douelle there is a particularly pretty door with two vines contained in panels.

Caillac back on the north bank has an Italian feel to it. On a flat, fertile part of the valley floor, the Romanesque tower of the church rises up beside the cedars, with the distant poplars as a backdrop. The church is a long, low affair with a porch running the length of it on the south side. Although the tower is beautiful, it is the Renaissance door of the church, sunk slightly below ground level, that is its *pièce de résistance*, covered with that fragile Renaissance carving so typical of the period. Curlicues, fronds, cherubs and Adam and Eve twine delicately around each other in an exquisite display. The nearby château of La Grézette is

Renaissance too, but shut to the public. It was built in 1562 by Massaut de Camburat, a Protestant captain who helped Duras capture Mercuès.

Parnac on the south side of the river is a must. This is real wine country, the straight lines of the vineyards obliterating all views from the car in places. Parnac is the home of the local wine cooperative and, although the modern building is rather ugly, you can see round it and buy some wine. Several of the Cahors châteaux are nearby and open for *dégustations*, Domaine de la Caminade at Parnac, for one, or you can bring a barrel and fill up from the pump with plonk at the Cave Coopérative.

The river's meanderings oblige you to cross and recross it many times as you work your way downstream, but at **Luzech** you will be obliged to cross it twice, for the town lies on an isthmus, much like Cahors, and is surrounded by the Lot on three sides: something which gives rise to traffic jams on market day.

The town is guarded by two hills, l'Impernal to the north and la Pistoule to the south. In 1840 a canal was cut to link the two branches of the river but now, because of the decline of river traffic, this has been filled in.

Luzech has been inhabited since prehistoric times and the Gauls had an oppidum on l'Impernal occupied and reinforced by the Romans until the second century after Christ, giving rise to speculation that it, too, might claim to be Uxellodonum. The first excavations were made in 1873 by Castagne and further ones were undertaken by Viré, unearthing a Gaulish wall from the last century BC and traces of even older ones belonging to the Hallstatt period of 900-300 BC. Tombs from the Barbarian era and a Celtic temple were also found. Still more recent work by Tardieu has revealed coins and other objects.

Because Luzech was such an important barony it came under attack from the English on several occasions and in 1188 Richard the Lion Heart ruled the citadel for a while. After the Albigensian Crusade the bishops moved in but the English were still a presence to be reckoned with, and in 1286 Luzech was one among 60 towns or châteaux contributing to the £3,000 that Philippe le Bel paid the King of England for getting out of Quercy. It was a waste of money. In nine years' time the Auld Alliance was signed between France and Scotland. The English would remain for nearly another 200 years.

The **keep** still stands on l'Impernal: a square, twelfth-century, no-frills building some 24 metres high. There are four storeys. You can walk up to it on foot for the view, or climb in the car up the V0 road north of the town. Down in the town, the Grand'Rue is just that, a wide street with a central bay for the market and plenty of the medieval still visible in the surrounding streets. The **Maison des Consuls** off the Grand'Rue has a little museum containing some of the archaeological finds, and windows belonging to the twelfth century. Nearby is the **Chapelle des Pénitents**, twelfth-century, with a small rose window and the remains of a fresco depicting hooded pilgrims on their knees. Even small towns like Luzech (1,500 inhabitants) had *quartiers*, and this particular one of Barry, around the Penitents' chapel, is one of the better bits of Luzech, especially the Rue des Balcons which has some picturesque houses.

Another pilgrimage spot is **Notre Dame de l'Ile**, set against a backdrop of cliffs, a lonely church which used to be cut off by an arm of the Lot (hence the name). The present structure dates from 1504 and was erected by a Luzech bishop, Antoine, but records show that the pilgrimage, celebrated on 8 and 15 September, existed in the thirteenth century if not before. The door is in the Flamboyant style and the niche above the altar shows Mary carrying not only Christ, but a bird, an apple and a rose as well. The town's main church, St Pierre, is fourteenth-century Languedoc Gothic and unremarkable.

More churches at St Vincent Rive d'Olt, only a couple of kilometres south of Luzech, but back on the south bank. One gets the impression that the whole countryside must have been on pilgrimage at one time or another, giving thanks for this or that. The oratory of Notre Dame de Bon Secours was erected in the seventeenth century after a particularly bad outbreak of plague. Les Roques was another pilgrimage spot, with a sundial above the door, and Cournou, with its gold-embossed altar, used to belong to an old priory. Both lie south of St Vincent. For a really pretty church, though, drive back through Luzech west on to the D9 and stop at **Camy**, an *église champêtre*, only big enough to serve the few villagers who lived locally. The round apse, the tiny belfry, the simplicity of it all and the cypresses standing alongside, taller than the actual church, form a perfect picture of rural tranquillity.

Cross back to the south side for the next stop. **Albas**, piled up above its weir, was, along with St Vincent and Luzech, one of the places that enjoyed a short interlude of prosperity thanks to its vineyards. In the middle of the last century the construction of railways allowed export of the wine beyond the traditional route downriver to Bordeaux. The wine on the banks of the Olt was supposed to be superior to that grown on higher ground. But the area's prosperity was short-lived. By the end of the century the phylloxera outbreak had ruined the outlook of many a Lot farmer, and it is only in recent years that a glimpse of that prosperity has been sighted once more, menaced still by the threat of disease.

The streets of Albas are very steep and full of steps. Seen from the north side of the river it looks pretty, with the church and town sitting on a cliff above the river; but once you are there there is a slightly scruffy feel to it all. Once again this was a bishops' town, fortified by Bertrand de Cardaillac during the Hundred Years War. He administered his diocese from the safety of his château, also defending the river when necessary, and after him two other bishops, Antoine de Luzech and Antoine Hébrard de St Sulpice, installed themselves in the same episcopal palace, today a private house, above the Lot.

Little of the old town remains. The nineteenth-century church replaced an old Romanesque one.

You have to cross back to the north bank to visit **Castelfranc**, a *bastide* of very straight streets indeed and a copy-book layout. The church is very defensive; a massive tower rises sheer above the west door, with no frills at all beyond a round window and a clock. According to the rules of *bastides* it stands at an angle to the main square rather than being centrally placed. This is one of the *bastides* founded by the Church and attributed to yet another bishop at the end of the thirteenth century. Unfortunately the market halls and the arcades have disappeared and so typical a *bastide* is it that it can appear a bit stark and uninteresting with its chequerboard layout. But as in most places, a wander round can throw up some interesting details, including a chapel just outside the main town erected to commemorate an extraordinary escape from the plague which had decimated so much of Quercy. The epidemic stopped quite literally at the gates of the town, symbolized by a small dead shrew found at the town walls. Shrews, of course, were particularly vulnerable to the disease, but although this unfortunate rodent fell victim, not a single person in the town did.

From Castelfranc there is a way-marked drive, one of many in the Lot, taking you round the Circuit Préhistorique du Causse, a misleading title, as we are nowhere near the *causse*. It leads you through Prayssac, another bishops' possession and once the home of Maréchal Bessières, whose statue adorns the town, then past the dolmens of Très Peyrou and Bertrandonne, 'the Armchair of Caesar'; but true prehistorians would probably find more of real interest on the *causses* of Gramat and Limogne.

Anglars, still south of the river but north of Albas on the D8, is an ancient-looking place by the side of a newly tarmaced road. It should more correctly be referred to as Anglars-Juillac to distinguish it from the Anglars by Lacapelle-Marival. The church is in the throes of being restored and the Romanesque apse is nearly finished, but it is the door on the north side which is most interesting, a badly damaged Renaissance one looking curiously out of place on the old church. Its sculptures, Christ and what seem to be two Marys, are practically three-dimensional figures and in dire danger of falling off altogether.

The château at Anglars is curious in having no angles. Each corner is slightly rounded and more curiously still, it is the twin of nearby Cousserans, near Belaye at the bottom of a loop of the Lot on the D8, with a good view over gentle countryside. You can cut across to another château, Grézels, which used to be called Château de la Coste. It had been given by Bishop Guillaume de Cardaillac to Bertrand de la Coste as a thank-you for help given in the Albigensian Crusade. Later on in the sixteenth century another lord of the castle, Jean II, served as one of only a hundred men in the French king's bodyguard. The castle is today the home of the Confrérie du Vin de Cahors. It is flanked by two square towers at the west side, but it is the round towers and the walled courtyard which represent the oldest part of the castle.

The prettiest place by far on this lower stretch of the Lot is **Puy l'Evêque**, and if all you want is a taste of the westerly part of the river, come here. The best view of Puy L'Evêque is from the south side of the river, although the town itself lies on the north. From here, you see it in all its beauty, rising up directly from the river in whose still waters it is reflected. Unlike so many of the Lot towns, Puy L'Evêque does not perch on top of a cliff; the town itself climbs the cliff. The lower houses, wistaria weeping over the walls, practically bathe their feet in the river's edge and the effect is quite spectacular. This perspective shows clearly the wealth of rich buildings climbing up to the church and the keep at the top dominated by a Lebanese cedar.

The name Puy is taken from *puech*, of which the local meaning is 'elevated site', and for many years the town was known simply as Puy. During the Albigensian Crusade it chose the Cathar side but was taken by Guillaume de Cardaillac, bishop of Cahors, which meant that it was within the bishopric in 1227, giving rise to its name of Puy L'Evêque. The English occupied the town on several occasions and it was they who altered the defences quite significantly and gave it the shape we see today. During the Wars of Religion the town was besieged by Caumont-Laforce, a lieutenant of Henry of Navarre. One hundred cannons were fired on the church and traces can still be seen of the damage, but the town withstood the attack.

The church, with its fortified belfry-porch, formed part of the defences. Little is left of the episcopal palace apart from the thirteenth-century keep. The Château de Lycheyrie, near the donjon, was the one-time residence of the clergy. Between the keep and the town hall is the Gruffière Esplanade from which you can look over the town and the river, or you could have a drink in the Hôtel Bellevue for a similar view.

Luckily, the other interesting village of the lower Lot is practically next door. To get to **Duravel** you merely follow the D911 westwards. Unfortunately, though, Duravel is not blessed with the same architectural elegance as its neighbour. It is one of those straggly villages ribboning the valley which seems, in its slightly crushed-up, down-at-heel air, to herald the industry which begins to blight the Lot at this point and totally wreck it around Fumel (Lot-et-Garonne).

But Duravel has its glory. Squeezed up among the houses is the Romanesque church of an important priory set up here by the abbey at Moissac. Diolidunum, or Duravel, had long been an important stop on the Roman road from Bordeaux to Lyon, which was probably why Moissac was glad to build the priory there. In the church they installed the relics of three saints, Hilarion, Poémon and Agathon, which had been given to Moissac by Charlemagne, and before long pilgrims started flocking to Duravel.

The priory had been founded in the late eleventh century but a church had existed on the spot since the fifth or sixth century. Although John Chandos and the English were resisted, the Huguenots caused the priory to disband after their attacks damaged both the building and Moissac's morale.

Today, the upper church has been greatly restored, but the frescos in the south transept are still visible, horrific demons lurking in wait for sinners and avidly devouring the ones they catch. A sarcophagus in the apse which, rather gruesomely, is opened every five years, contains the remains of the saints. The capitals are a Romanesque delight of monsters, martyrs and saints. But it is the **crypt** that people come to see, which seems to date from pre-Romanesque times. It is very small, about four metres square, with a low ceiling and four central columns. The capitals are all early Romanesque with the added touch of a coiled snake at the base of each, symbolizing death and resurrection. One has a peacock, too, symbol of the soul and an early Christian emblem. A niche which used to contain the saints is now a reliquary and you can see two angled windows for the pilgrims to look through when the crypt was too crowded.

Standing in the thousand-year-old crypt of Duravel, only the blue source of Touzac might tempt you further west. The pretty mill hotel alongside it is owned by M. Bouyou and his Welsh wife. The Lot *département* boundary is only a few kilometres away, and beyond that lies Fumel, mercifully out of the Lot altogether but a forceful reminder that you are back in the twentieth century.

The Lot Valley: east

Above Cahors the River Lot enters one of its most beautiful stretches. The *causses* of Gramat, Cajarc and Limogne crowd up to its banks and in many cases drop sheer into its waters. The river emerges mature and magnificent from its mountainous stretch above Capdenac, content now just to amble through the wide path it has cut for itself through the cliffs. But it is not tamed yet; that only happens after Cahors. There is a reined-in wildness about it still, which makes for some dramatic scenery.

The distance from Cahors to Capdenac, near the eastern boundary of the *département*, is about 80 kilometres and although you can jump banks with relative ease higher up, the first bridge lies at Vers, some 15 kilometres away. This means that a decision has to be made, on leaving Cahors, as to which bank to follow. You would be well advised, however, to follow the north bank, even though this will mean missing the dilapidated village of Arcambal on the D911, south of the river.

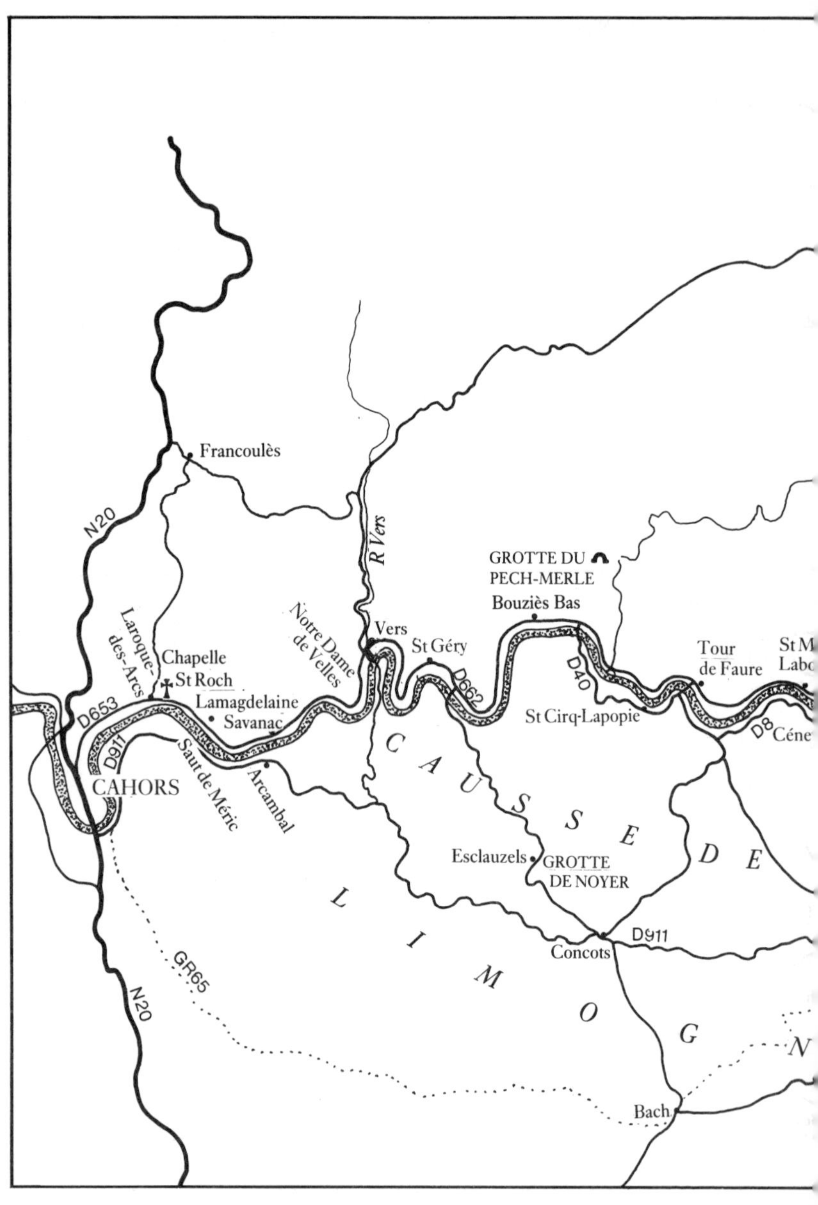

Francoulès
N20
R Vers
GROTTE DU
PECH-MERLE
Bouziès Bas
Vers
St Géry
Notre Dame
de Velles
Laroque-
des-Arcs
Chapelle
St Roch
Lamagdelaine
Savanac
D653
D911
CAHORS
Saut de Méric
Arcambal
D662
D40
St Cirq-Lapopie
Tour
de Faure
D8
C A U S S E D E
L I M O G N
Esclauzels
GROTTE
DE NOYER
D911
Concots
GR65
N20
Bach

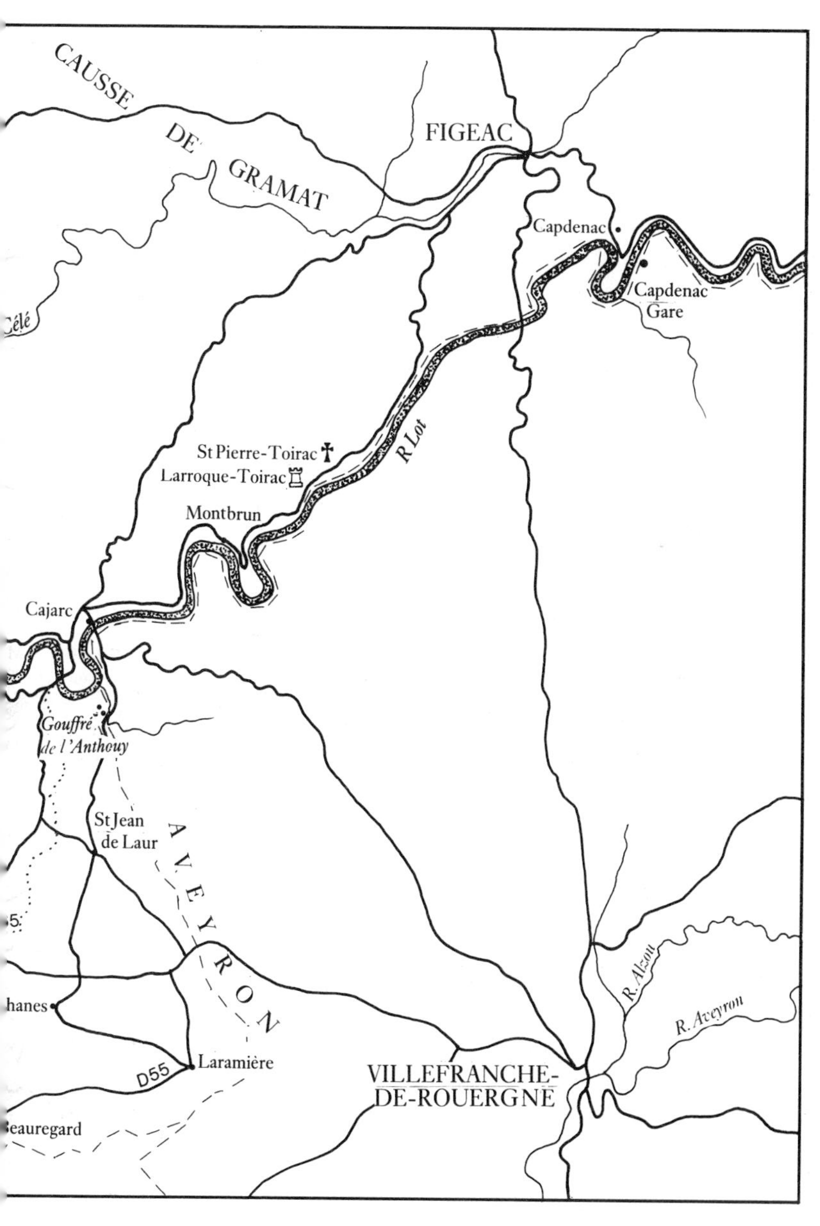
CAUSSE
DE
GRAMAT
FIGEAC
Capdenac
Capdenac
Gare
Célé
St Pierre-Toirac
Larroque-Toirac
R Lot
Montbrun
Cajarc
Gouffré
de l'Anthouy
St Jean
de Laur
AVEYRON
hanes
Laramière
D55
Beauregard
VILLEFRANCHE-
DE-ROUERGNE
R. Alzou
R. Aveyron

Arcambal is a centre for the Cahors wine trade, although it is hard to see it as a centre for anything. It stands on a hill, a little way from the river. I remember the first time I came across it, being unable to believe that such a place could exist so near the comparative sophistication of Cahors. It is southern Mediterranean in appearance with Roman *tuiles canal*, as the French call them, roofing all the buildings, most of which are firmly shuttered. There is a silence about the place and everything from the château to the houses is in a state of abject disrepair. The château has been in its day a fine old mansion, flanked with towers. A seventeenth-century terrace gives on to the valley and massive wrought-iron gates guard the entrance. Beyond its charming decrepitude, however, there is little of interest and visitors anxious to see it could easily slot it into a trip to the *causse* of Limogne, on whose edges it stands.

Leaving Cahors on the north bank, then, follow the D653. The first village, **Laroque-des-Arcs**, takes its name from the old Roman aqueduct which crossed the Francoulès valley in three tiers and took water to Cahors. Traces of the aqueduct can be seen at Pech de Clary and indeed in several places along the river, including Lamagdelaine. It was probably built in the first century and archaeologists believe it may still have been in use as late as the seventh century. Although unknown and unrecognized, this was one of the great Roman aqueducts of France, running down the right bank of the Vers some 31 kilometres to Cahors, and capable of furnishing the town with 200 cubic metres of water a day. The slope was carefully calculated at 1.2 mm per metre and it ran sometimes above ground, sometimes cut into the cliffs and sometimes in a tunnel underground to reach its destination; an engineering feat of spectacular proportions.

Near the Pech de Clary is the Chapelle St Roch, not a particularly pretty building but one with a commanding view of the river, shyer and less well known than the Dordogne perhaps, but just as beautiful. The old tower on the village outskirts dates from a time when the Lot was navigable (thanks, largely, to the engineer, Colbert) and tolls were exacted for sailing down it. Barges called *sapines* or flat-bottomed *gabares* ferried coal from Decazeville and cheese from the Auvergne, and lower down wine, of course, to Bordeaux and the sea. Once at Bordeaux the *gabares* were broken up and sold for timber.

> ...Dins la gabarra s'embraçavan
> E sus la riba l'aiga de l'Olt polit
> Dins la gaberra los breçava
>
> [Dans la gabarre ils s'embrassèrent
> Et sur la rive l'eau du Lot joli
> Dans la gabarre les berçait]

runs an old song above love on the river.

Lamagdelaine used to be called St Pierre Floirac and it is tempting to associate its name-change with a legend attached to a spot on the southerly bank opposite, the Saut de Méric, where the hoofprint of a horse is said to mark the place where a knight, in some kind of dire danger, invoked the name of St Mary Magdalene and was saved.

Savanac, next door to Lamagdelaine, back on the north bank, was famous for its *clairet* wine (which the English took to calling claret), and these days for its village bread oven as well, restored to working order by the proud locals and becoming once more a focal point of the village. Different *cantons* had different rules for these ovens, which were a vital part of everyday life. In some cases it was the client who paid for the wood to fire the oven, in others it was the *fournier* himself. In some cases the *fournier* was paid in kind, in others in money, in still others in a mixture of both. Sometimes the *fournier* collected the dough, sometimes the clients brought it to the ovens themselves, but no meal was eaten without bread and the evening meal was, and often still is, based on a thick and hearty soup of which bread forms an integral part. Nowadays, though, tourists might be more interested in the canoeing centre based at the village. Just before Vers you can stop for a look at the particularly pretty Notre Dame de Velles church of the boatmen of the *gabares*; twelfth-century with a round apse and squat tower and capitals inside depicting serpents and people intertwined. The nearby church of St Crépin is older still, first cited in 945.

Vers, nestling on the confluence of two rivers, the Vers and the Lot, was a Bronze Age site occupied by the Romans and has still more aqueduct remains, giving you an idea of just how enormous it was. Vers is classified as a first-category fishing river and has a representative of the Association de Pêche further up the valley at St Martin. The English made their home here during the Hundred Years War but, like all the villages near Cahors, this one lacks charm, compounded by the fact that the railway line now puts in an appearance on this side of the river. It continues to dog the Lot all the way up to Capdenac Gare, crossing and recrossing as necessary. As with some of the prettiest parts of the Dordogne it tends to spoil the scenery and in a car one is forced to judder over a hundred level-crossings. It does mean, however, that in France you can still reach fairly remote places by rail, and of course for the passengers it provides a picturesque journey.

The next village, **St Géry**, on the D662, the river road, is a Magdalenian site and there are said to be rock engravings in the Grottes de Pergouzet. Much of the prehistoric art along the Lot and Célé is in the hands of private owners, making sites extremely difficult to find even if you can gain access. You run the risk, too, of their being so undeveloped that you need torches and ropes to explore them properly. St Géry is named after the local eponymy for Didier, a seventh-century bishop of Cahors appointed by the Merovingian king, Dagobert. Didier was renowned as a brillant administrator and a man who did much good for Cahors.

After St Géry the road becomes much prettier and at **Bouziès Bas** you plunge through a succession of tunnels. If you look back after the first one, you will see a *château des anglais* or fortified cave, one of many used by our ancestors during the Hundred Years War. That the English left their mark on the place is indicated by the fact that this whole stretch is referred to as the Défilé des Anglais, or Pass of the English.

To reach **St Cirq-Lapopie** you can either cross the river at Bouziès and continue eastwards along the D40 on the south bank or carry on along the north bank, through the Défilé, to the Tour de Faure and cross the river there, in which case you will have to double back, westwards, to the village. It is hard to say which is the best way to approach this showplace of the Lot, from beneath or from above, but either way you will be unable to drive into the village itself. Parking is provided above the town.

St Cirq – the 'q' is silent – is undeniably picturesque. Photographs of it adorn every book and pamphlet on the Lot. Scenic views of its tiny steets, taken from every angle, grace nearly every postcard in the *département* to the exclusion of almost everything else, for the fact is that St Cirq deserves its reputation. It *is* exceedingly pretty. It *does* have a magnificent site. Because of this it attracts people, hordes of them, at the height of summer, who arrive by the coachload and disgorge into the village. Try, therefore, to pick your day carefully. If you are forced to holiday in August, at least try not to come at a weekend. The town has been beautifully restored but its real beauty is in the perspective as one rounds a corner, or the view from a cliff top across the river, and neither of these things can be enjoyed if you are queueing to get to the cliff's edge, or if every picturesque corner is milling with people. Inevitably people and postcards and souvenir shops take their toll and you may be left with the feeling that it is too pretty, too contrived. Nevertheless, St Cirq has been called the most beautiful village in France and there are days when its seems to merit the description.

St Cirq takes its name from the child martyr St Cyr, killed with his mother in Asia Minor in the reign of Diocletian. It is said that his relics were brought from Antioch to the area by St Amadour.

It should be no surprise, given its position, to learn that the clifftop has long been fortified, earliest records mentioning an eighth-century fortress. There are records, too, of Richard the Lion Heart trying – and failing – to seize it in 1198. The English made rather more successful attempts during the Hundred Years

War, capturing the town three times between 1341 and 1390. Up the flank of the rockface they came, using the passage still called the *'passage des anglais'* to take the castle 'by surprise and treason'. But it was not only the English who were interested in this strategic position, for ownership of the castle alternated between the leading Lot families of La Popie, Gourdon, Cardaillac and the Hébrard of St Sulpice.

In 1471, in the aftermath of the Hundred Years War, King Louis XI ordered the castle to be razed to the ground as punishment for Ramond d'Hébrard having taken the side of the duke of Guyenne against the king of France. This was a blow, but the ruins were still of sufficient strategic importance for the Huguenots to fight for them in the Wars of Religion. St Cirq had two lords during this period, a situation guaranteed to lead to trouble since one of them was a Cardaillac recently converted to the Protestant faith, and the other a Catholic, Jean de St Sulpice. At first an uneasy truce reigned and each side agreed that the partisans of the other must not take any action against the town. Inevitably the truce broke down and on 10 April 1580 the Huguenots moved in. In the event that was St Cirq's downfall for only months later, as the still Protestant Henry of Navarre evacuated Cahors, he ordered the château of St Cirq to be razed to the ground once more rather than return it to the Catholics.

You enter the village by the thirteenth-century gate of **La Gardette**. Every single street has something to offer; many have corbelled façades, mullioned windows and a wealth of exposed beams. Some of the houses are especially interesting and you should look out in particular for the Maisons Breton, Bores, Vaillat, Fréjaville, Daura and Leauzeau-Vinel. The **Maison Rignau** houses a museum with a peculiarly disparate collection of Ming China, lacquer work from Japan and some African art. Inevitably such a touristy village attracts tacky art work, but there has been a small revival of the old skill of wood-turning, a craft that once had a strong guild in the town.

The **church** has a sixteenth-century tower with a round

staircase turret attached but, although the apse is Romanesque with some historiated capitals and the remains of some frescos, the rest of it dates from considerably later.

From the highest part of the cliffs, where once the ill-fated Château stood, you can look out over the roofscape of the village and, with the aid of a telescope, away over the Lot and the *causse* of Cajarc. At the foot of the cliff, in a three-sided tunnel, runs the old towpath from pre-railway days.

Continue eastwards up the left bank of the river on the D8, to one of the few visitable castles of the Lot, **Cénevières**. Park outside and ring the bell on the big gate. The dogs sound fierce enough to put you off, even though they are on the other side. It must have been a bit like that in medieval times, too.

Cénevières enjoys a site almost as spectacular as that of St Cirq, perched on a vertiginous cliff above the Lot. Its history reaches back to Pépin le Bref, the eighth-century king, as does St Cirq's, but in the thirteenth century it passed into the hands of the Gourdon family. Scots readers might be interested to know that the owner believes there to be a Franco-Scottish link here, an early vestige of the Auld Alliance. 'Gourdon', he says, comes from the Scottish 'Gordon'.

The **keep**, with its great vaulted rooms and secret dungeons, is known as the Tour de Gourdon and dates from the thirteenth century, but Cénevières is chiefly known as a Renaissance château, not a thirteenth-century one. François de Gourdon had fought in the Italian wars and maybe came back with a few ideas. Along with his son, Flottard, he set about creating a Renaissance palace between the years of 1525 and 1585, using the best workers available in Quercy, many of them probably left over from work on the palace at Assier.

The château is protected by towers, walls and a drawbridge on one side and the river on the other. As you go through the door you see the seventeenth-century chapel built for the Protestant Antoine de Gourdon. Inside, the main hall, the *grand salon* and the dining hall are hung with Flemish tapestries and all have astoundingly lovely coffered ceilings, beautifully decorated with flowers. A small room is decorated with sixteenth-century mythological murals depicting scenes from the Trojan War, and an elegant gallery with Tuscan columns surrounds the courtyard. As with many of the Lot castles, it is Cénevières' position at the top of a cliff above the Lot that stays with you as a lasting impression.

Cross over to the north side of the river and **St Martin Labouval** if you are interested in *pietàs*. This one is seventeenth-century and shows an old and homely Mary carrying her son's limp body. Otherwise stay on the south bank for the pretty village of Calvignac, home of one of the most powerful of the Lot's barons. The church at Larnagol opposite has a modern Christ by Hairon.

At **Cajarc** the Lot boundary joins the river; south of the river and you are in the Aveyron. Cajarc is a fairly unashamed holiday resort, a busy place where shops display all the trappings of the French coasts: beach balls, inflatable whales and rubber rings. On the river there are pedalos, yachts and water-skiers. President Pompidou used to have a house nearby; he was introduced to the area by Françoise Sagan.

As with so much of the Lot valley, Cajarc belonged to the bishops of Cahors for a while. Unimpressed by this state of affairs, however, the townsfolk backed the Protestants in the Wars of Religion, leading to orders by Louis XIII in 1622 to dismantle the château. Little is left of it, then, beyond some thirteenth-century windows in a private property next to the church, which was built by Aymeric d'Hébrard. The church knew some prosperity thanks to the pilgrimage of St Sacrement, a saint popular in the Rouergue, the old province which became Aveyron. So popular, indeed, that a new bridge was built to deal with the influx of pilgrims, although it was later destroyed during the Hundred Years War.

It is a pretty, lively town of about 1,000 inhabitants, with its old buildings grouped in a circle round the church and château and some nice old houses down by the riverside where the water has been widened into a lake.

Montbrun has one of the plentiful Cardaillac ruins, dominating this pretty village high on a promontory facing the Aveyron's Saut de la Mounine (Monkey's Jump); the Cardaillac domain stretched far and wide. The legend attached to this graceful stretch of river is that the lord of Montbrun, angry at his daughter's love for the wrong man, ordered her to be thrown from the top of the cliff into the water. However, a hermit who lived in the area, hearing of the plan, was so appalled that he procured a monkey, dressed it up in women's clothing and hurled it off the cliff in the girl's place. The lord of Montbrun, seeing the monkey hurtling to its certain death, was overcome with remorse and, on hearing that his daughter was still alive, forgave her. As for the poor monkey, it must be marked down as a martyr to man's whims. I cannot help wondering just how easy it was to find a monkey in the Lot at that time; nowadays one could always go to Rocamadour, but I don't think they had a Fôret des Singes in the Middle Ages.

Continuing upstream you come across the cartoonist's castle of **Larroque-Toirac**, a seven-storey manor house of exaggerated features. The keep has a round tower abutting on to the main building, with machicolation at the top. Inside it has a spiral Romanesque staircase. Too tall by far, the keep was actually reduced in height from its original 30 metres in 1793. The castle is open to the public in the summer months.

It seems that the history of Larroque-Toirac began with a fortified cave on the site and grew from there; as early as 1233 there is mention of it in the records. In its early days it belonged to the Montbrun, and this allowed Pierre Duèze, brother of the Cahors pope, Jean XXII, to possess half the buildings as joint *seigneur*. After 1334, however, the Cardaillac got their oar in, as they did in most things around here, in their desperate attempt to rid the countryside of the English invaders. They were not entirely successful as far as Larroque-Toirac was concerned, for the castle did indeed fall into English hands on several occasions. At the end of the fourteenth century it burnt down, but the ruins were restored towards the end of the fifteenth. The pentagonal tower, the Cinq Cagres, was built thus to deflect any rocks which might be lobbed off the top of the cliff.

Inside, there are some fine chimneypieces, Gothic and Romanesque, and one of the lower rooms has some sixteenth-century art work depicting the arms of Larroque and the royal family. The nineteenth century saw a bizarre arrangement when the castle was lotteried off room by room, and it was only in 1923 that it was unified once more.

Larroque's neighbour is **St Pierre-Toirac**, a fortified, crenellated church erected in the twelfth century with nothing much to indicate its ecclesiastical origins. Rather like nearby Rudelle in this respect, though not in appearance, it is merely a keep, with only its polygonal Romanesque apse giving it away. Its history stretches back to 889, when there is evidence that a priory existed here, handed over to Figeac Abbey by the bishop of Rodez (Aveyron). The church was reconstructed in the eleventh and twelfth centuries and fortified during the fourteenth. The west door has a simple Romanesque tympanum. Inside, the nave has cradle vaulting and interesting capitals. The defensive room was above the nave and had the added benefit of a well, still in existence, which allowed people to withstand siege for some time.

St Pierre-Toirac can also boast a giant's footstep in the Gardet wood. Legend has it that this particular giant, feeling very thirsty, bent down for a drink from the river. In order to perform this difficult feat he placed one foot across the river at Balaguier (Aveyron) and one foot at La Plada in St Pierre-Toirac. Quercy is rich in giants' legends, popular tradition often referring to them as Gargantua. These were not giants stemming from any tradition of literature, but from the ancient, local and oral tradition of the Cadourques.

Capdenac, pretty well the last stop in the Lot and certainly the last place to have a feel of the *département* about it, is another Uxellodonum claimant, with golden stone and Quercy towers. It is very high, the view spoiled on the river side, however, since it gives on to the massive railway junction of Capdenac-Gare (Aveyron). There is no doubt that the Romans were here; excavations have been made, throwing up the remains of an aqueduct and coins and something optimistically called Caesar's Spring. Some of these remains can be viewed by the public in summer, although not at the sacred hours of lunch-time. There is a certain charm, I suppose, in the way things close down for two hours on the dot of midday, and grind to a total halt on Mondays, with only Sunday morning acting as a brief respite for shopping. When all is said and done, however, it is about as crazy and irritating as our own, soon-to-be-changed, licensing laws must be to French visitors.

After the Romans came Pépin le Bref and Henry IV, and of course this was long the home of the duke of Sully, the latter king's minister. Sully's son was governor here and Capdenac was a Protestant stronghold of some notoriety. Sully's château still stands.

The village is perfectly preserved, with ramparts and Gothic gates, a fourteenth-century keep and marvellously tiny streets winding up and down the hill which on a hot day seem to just drink up the sun. The two main streets, de la Peyrolie and de la Commanderie, have pretty corbelled houses and the belvedere at St Andrieu looks down on a stupendous view over the surrounding countryside. Although there is a museum at Capdenac, the famous statue discovered here in 1973, a plump torso of a woman dating from 3200-3000 BC, is now in the museum at Cahors.

Last stop on the Lot route is for *aficionados* only: the tiny hamlet of **Guirande**. So tiny, in fact, that it is not signposted, unusual for France. The church, however, is easy to find, a chapel near Felzin on the D31. No need to knock on house doors here, the key is in the electricity box on the north wall. The choir is covered with sixteenth-century frescos; Christ and an eagle in the middle, a dragon and a bull patrolling the walls on either side. The church is covered in white rough-cast, with the stones peeping through around the doors and windows. We are approaching the Auvergne. Already the stone has darkened. This is not a Lot church; the *département* seems far away, and beyond here the river is in its mountain stage.

Quercy Blanc

White stone houses on white-hot earth; Quercy Blanc lives up to its name. The houses are a different shape, great solid, square structures in white sculptured limestone, one long, Roman-tiled roof sloping gently over house and barn. Even the ochre tiles have a sun-bleached look to them. The *bolet* is enclosed to give shade. The slope is significant. There is markedly less rain here. Vines stretch over the hills, gentle rolling hills, in the neat, straight lines of all vineyards, drawing crazy patterns over the white soil. It is a heart-warming sight. Don't go to Quercy Blanc if it is raining.

Not all the grapes are grown for wine; this is the home of the sweet-tasting Chasselas dessert grape. Agricultural machinery grows tall and strange. Next to the vineyards march the armies of sunflowers. Long before France caught on to the dangers of cholesterol they grew sunflowers here. The yellow orbs bask in a slightly abandoned way, heads turned in uniform direction. Come the harvest, the heads bow and grow brown, wizened and ugly with age, and the fields seem strangely empty without their golden troops.

You could be forgiven for thinking you were in Spain. The houses have a Spanish air, there is a Spanish heat to the wind and the names are evocative too, Comba del Mel – and Bovila. Since I saw it, **Bovila** has become my ashram. On dreary, grey days in England I conjure it up in my head and ponder it. Not much to ponder. Bovila is little more than a lay-by off the N656 to Tournon d'Agenais (Lot-et-Garonne). Two, maybe three houses, ivy-leafed geraniums tumbling from the balcony pots – and the church. I am not quite sure what it was about this perfect little church which so impressed me. Suffice to say that if you have seen Bovila you have glimpsed the heart of Quercy Blanc. It is one of the many hereabouts restored by the Association des Amis des Églises Rurales du Quercy Blanc. A simple Romanesque affair that used to belong to a Benedictine abbey, an *église champêtre* now, set in its tiny raised churchyard with views across the white scorched countryside of the plateau of St Matré. And it is open. One of the joys of Quercy Blanc is that all the churches are open. No hunting half-way round the village for keys. You just stroll in and admire and stroll on out again, like the good old days.

The church, with its rounded apse, perfect in its simplicity, is not really white. It only looks that way when set against the profoundly blue sky and in comparison with the dark cypresses beside it, symbol of the south. Inside, the tiny cruciform shape is carefully restored, the stone cleaned and brilliant, reflecting the new glass of abstract muted shades, blue-grey and yellow, which cast a golden glow on the simple altar stone. The Spanish air continues with Moorish-style decoration round the choir window and on two historiated pilasters. At the west end is a small wooden gallery which you can climb for a new perspective. By the door are some postcards; rather amateurish pen-and-inks of the interior, but somehow fitting. It is an amateur's church, this, strictly for beginners. Inside and out it is very quiet.

It is a wrench to leave Bovila, but there are dozens of other country churches in the area, like Lasbouygues on the D23, little more than a cemetery chapel *en route* to Compostela; like Cambayrac; or the Templar church of Carnac-Rouffiac; or the little gem of Cézac. **Bagat**, slightly further south on the D185, lost in a valley, is equally well restored, but not so exquisite. The north transept holds a sad memorial to three members of the village: Lt Alain de Ginestet who died in aerial combat on 13 June 1940, Quartermaster Feliz Jargeau who died at sea on 3 July the same year and, saddest of all, Robert Ayrot who died during deportation. There is great use of colour here, with all the keystones in the roof painted blue and beige and a cheerful statue of what appear to be St George and the dragon.

On through the deserted countryside to **St Pantaléon**, off the D653 to Montcuq. St Pantaléon is big by comparison, thanks in part to its enormous donjon. Indeed, so defensive is the building still that although we parked in the square by the church it took us some time to find the entrance. In fact you approach the church from the street on the south side. A break in the ground floors of the houses reveals the arched entrance to a courtyard and a kind of presbytery opposite the church. This bizarre, tunnel-like approach conceals the simple Renaissance doorway. The place is alive with doves. Outside the huge tower and inside, too, they flap and coo quietly, high up in the roof. On the altar table, like an offering from the winged congregation, lay two soft, white belly feathers.

Drive back down the D653 to **Montcuq**, through the vines and the sunflowers, the cypresses and the sloping-roofed Toulousain *pigeonniers*, heat shimmering like a mirage on the road. Montcuq, about 35 kilometres south-west of Cahors, has a name guaranteed to make non-locals smirk, but in fact the 'q' is not silent and the name is derived from the hill on which the town stands, dominated by another enormous keep, 24 metres high, thought to date from the eleventh century. The keep came into its own during the Albigensian Crusade when it was continually attacked by Simon de Montfort. Montcuq was one of the few towns in the Lot considered a Cathar stronghold. Later on, during the Hundred Years War, the town was captured by the English, and then, during the Wars of Religion it kept up its reputation as the black sheep of the Lot by being a Protestant stronghold. Although there are still some old houses in the attractive town, which plays host to the Festival of Quercy Blanc every July and August, most visitors will find the walk up to the keep, and subsequent view over the valley of the Petite Barguelonne, its best feature. But Montcuq is also a good centre for exploring Quercy Blanc. The nearby church of Rouillac has the remains of a fresco in the choir depicting the Crucifixion and one of the most touching processional crosses you will ever see – a naïve carved Arab with huge nailed hands and sad black eyes. Nearby are the caves of Roland with 600 metres of galleries and formations reflected in a clear lake.

Ste Croix, on the D228 south-west of Montcuq, is another restored gem of a church whose enormous round apse has been badly damaged. The new windows by Mme Kinou Payen are three centimetres thick. These delightful churches of Quercy Blanc are a feature I keep returning to, for they are found round every bend in the road, along with roadside sanctuaries like that at Pont Cirq. They merit a detailed study, not least for the amount of work that a largely anti-clerical population has been ready to put into preserving its heritage. I cannot possibly mention them all here, but be on the look-out for them as you travel and you will not be disappointed.

There are Roman remains at **Castelnau-Montratier**; indeed, the remains here are amongst the few in the Lot that can actually be seen without too much difficulty, even though many of the finds have been removed to the museum at Cahors. You can still see the walls, baths and latrines of the Moulin de Sauquet, along with a whole water system. Castelnau-Montratier is famous too for its three windmills which stand on the Pech de Lafargue above the town, one of the better preserved *bastides* of the Lot.

The town, which was important enough in the thirteenth century to justify the name *cité*, used to be called Castelnau-des-Vaux, but it fell victim to an act of reprisal by the ubiquitous Simon de Montfort during the Albigensian Crusade. True to fashion, he completely demolished it. Not long afterwards the lord of Castelnau, Baron Ratier II, decided to found a new town, at the top of the hill this time, and nearer his castle, which had managed to resist the worst of de Montfort's excesses. The new town, built around 1250, was called Châteauneuf-de-Ratier or Castelnau-Montratier. The arcading is still very well preserved around the central *place*, as is the belfry on the *hôtel de ville*. There are several old houses like the Hôtel Rigal, with Renaissance doors and windows, but what utterly destroys the medieval feel of the place is the surprise you get when you follow the road to the bluff of the hill where the old church used to stand, for here is no medieval church nor even one of the Angevin style more commonly found in *bastide* towns. The church of St Martin could almost be called a basilica; an enormous, modern building, consecrated in 1921 and reminding you of nothing quite so much as Sacré Coeur. Somehow that anachronistic church of Castelnau-Montratier alters my whole perception of the town – for the worse.

There are old churches nearby, of course, more in keeping with the landscape, and they do not come much older than the one at St Aureil, whose crypt dates from the fifth century. And if you want a truly medieval town, take the D26 and travel east. You won't need to look for signs for **Flaugnac**. It towers above you away across the fields and up to a rocky spur. It is hard to find superlatives adequate for the site, or indeed sight. Don't attempt to take the farm road up to the top: there is a way through, but you would need a Mini with the properties of a Land-Rover, and turning to come back down again can be a perilous business, as we discovered. The easy way is along the D214.

Flaugnac is marked on the Michelin map with one of those signs which look like the rays of a setting sun and which denote a good viewpoint. But it is not the view from the top which is important (though how good do you want it?), so much as the view from the bottom looking up. From here you see the silhouette of the thirteenth-century Tour d'Estienne, huddling close by the presbytery and church, the Toulousain *pigeonniers*, the old fortifications and the farm.

From the top, and the road not surprisingly takes a long time to reach it, you see that the church is heavily restored and the village so deserted and discarded as to be depressing, though the knights' houses are rewarding and the pastoral views from either side not to be sneezed at.

L'Hospitalet, on the D659 north of Flaugnac, is a pretty village that used to be a stopping place on the Compostela route. The church choir was once joined to the hospital. It was at Bonnefont, near Granejouls, that a fourth-century mosaic was found signifying the wealth and size of the villa to which it must once have belonged. And even as late as the late eighteenth century, the *commanderie* belonging to the Knights of Malta at Granejouls could still be seen.

This ancient corner pressed up against the N20, with its Roman, Merovingian and medieval remains, is the last of the real Quercy Blanc. Strictly speaking the area continues on the easterly side of the main road, but the real feel of the place has gone now. Cahors is very close and there are signs of commuter living – rich houses and a few more people.

Lalbenque over on the east side of the N20 has a long history as a prehistoric site and there are many dolmens, both locally at Peyrelevade and at the dolmen de la motte St Simon, and in the area at large. Roman remains were found at St Hilaire and Les Bories and even Merovingian graves at Cammas. There is a medieval cemetery at Pech Peyrou and several châteaux. For all that, Lalbenque is today a dull place and famous for one thing only: Lalbenque is host to the world's leading **truffle market**.

Every Tuesday afternoon from November to April they come from all over Quercy, men with berets, dressed in black, each carrying a small wicker basket with a handle on top. Inside the basket a coloured handkerchief wraps the precious cargo. Black diamonds, the truffles are called, and the prices they fetch do make the description an apt one. Every year fewer and fewer truffles are found. Every year the prices go up and the market becomes smaller. Treat yourself if you can afford it. Buy just one – you pay by weight – and put it in a jar with some brandy. Before long that wonderful aroma will have completely flavoured the alcohol, which you can then use for cooking. In 1900, 1,030 tonnes of truffles were gathered in the Lot. By 1981 that figure had fallen to 5½ tonnes.

Leave Lalbenque north-west for **Cieurac** by way of the eighteenth-century carved cross that marks a crossroads on the outskirts of town. Cieurac is not famous for anything very much, but it is one of the best picnic spots around and for a small rambling village it is full of exceedingly lovely buildings. Almost the nicest is the farmhouse, with its splendid Toulousain *pigeonnier*. The sloping roofs of these dovecots are not so pretty, maybe, as the true Quercy *pigeonniers* on the Gramat *causse* further north, but this one complements the building beautifully. The *bolet* is supported on stone pillars and there are stone steps leading to the ground. Cieurac also has a splendid windmill complete with sails. The picnic spot, not far from here, is high on a ridge overlooking the vineyards of Cahors, which stretch away in lines over the hillside. Snuggling in amongst the juniper bushes, which smell strongly of gin, you feel immediately drowsy.

Cieurac has two châteaux. The château named after the village is not in the usual Lot style, hesitating as it is on the brink of the Renaissance. The staircase is the deciding factor – carved, as at Montal, most intricately on the underside, a fact that is lost on visitors since neither château is open to the public. Pauliac is more typical and barely rates as a château at all, being more of a *gentilhommière* of the late fifteenth century.

Descend to **Laburgade** with its traces of Roman road – Cami Ferrat – and its *chemin de puits*, an alignment of ten wells, then head for another straggly village further north, Aujols, on the D10. Nothing very spectacular here either, by Lot standards, except the enormous village pond in whose waters the buildings are reflected. From a distance it seems to have been thoughtfully provided with seats, until you realize that this is not a village pond at all but a *lavoir*, and the stone seats are not seats but scrubbing stones. As we got out of the car, unable quite to believe our own conclusions, an old lady trundled up pushing a wooden wheelbarrow full of sheets and solemnly immersed them in the plankton-filled water before spreading them out on the stones to scrub. It was hard to believe we were only a few miles from Cahors in the late twentieth century, but the image of that old lady, far on the other side of the pool, scrubbing away under the blue sky, was one that captured the charm and the rigour of Quercy Blanc perfectly.

The Causse of Limogne

The *causse* of Limogne lies in the south-east of the *département*, bordering on the Rouergue. It is an empty land without the feeling of height that you get on the Gramat *causse* and with many more trees and hedges enclosing its stony wastes. This makes it more palatable for some people, but it has none of the stark and dramatic beauty of Gramat, none of the rock faces or the green alluvial valleys and most of all it lacks the human habitation that one always stumbles across further north. Instead there are the scrub oaks and the juniper, of course, which reigns supreme here as it does on all *causse*-land, a peculiar plant whose berries take the best part of two years to ripen. Tourism hasn't reached this backwater yet, for all its proximity to Cahors and even to Villefranche-de-Rouergue (Aveyron), and many of the towns seem empty and neglected. One sometimes gets the impression that there are more dolmens here than there are people.

It is, of course, very poor, as is the rest of the *département*, and one gets so used to the prettiness of places further north that the eye and the mind have to make an adjustment to this somewhat flat, desolate region. It has its charm, nevertheless. On a hot day the larks soar, there is a whiff of lavender in the air reminding you of the Mediterranean, and on such a day its very emptiness can be its appeal.

You can get to the Limogne *causse* from the popular tourist haunt of Cajarc by foot on the Grande Randonné 65, one of France's enormously long footpaths, which winds its way from the Canal Latéral south of Moissac, through the Lot and into the Aveyron. Or you can leave Cajarc on the D146 and take the tiny road to the Gouffre de l'Anthouy. There is not much point to this route beyond the fact that it is exactly this sort of deserted farm track that makes holidaying in the Lot such a delight. As you wind up-hill and down-dale in dire fear of meeting a tractor round the next bend or of the road petering out altogether, you get a real sense of gentle expedition.

The **Gouffre de l'Anthouy** is not just an abyss; it also refers to the ruins of a convent called Lentouy or Anthouy, whose founding was attributed to St Namphaise, a saint who settled in the Braunhie. A sinister legend surrounds the convent concerning an order of nuns said to have been devil-worshippers. The *gouffre* is clearly marked on the tiny road alongside a rock fall. So clearly was it marked, yet so desolate the spot, that we decided the real action must be further on, thus losing our only chance for miles to park or turn in order to explore; so I am unable to tell you either about the *gouffre* or the ruins, leaving an enjoyable little adventure for readers so inclined.

St Jean de Laur holds the ruins of an old castle which in early times belonged to the counts of Rouergue, the boundary being about a kilometre away as the crow flies. From St Jean de Laur it is an easy route to **Limogne**, a workaday sort of place and the only town of any size on the *causse*. Even so, its population is less than a thousand. The surrounding countryside throws up the only two things that you find plenty of in the *causse* of Limogne – dolmens and *pigeonniers*. There are at least five dolmens nearby – Agarnel, Ferrières-Haut, Pech-Lapeyre, Joncas, Pajot – but most visitors will probably be more attracted by the *pigeonniers*, which take on spectacular proportions here. Habitation is so sparse and the land so poor that most of them are free-standing, mounted on legs with round or square towers, and all of them are exquisite.

If I had to pick one place in the whole of the Limogne *causse* for interested travellers it would be **Laramière**, a few kilometres south-west of Limogne. This is real lavender country with dolmens sprouting up amongst it. The area was totally wrecked by the Protestants, although at Promilhanes, on the way, you can still see the high walls that used to surround the home of the abbot of Marcilhac. Quite why it was that all the abbots of that abbey should choose to live so far from the village, I am not sure. Promilhanes seems to have been what estate agents today term a 'desirable location', as there are several old manor houses in the vicinity, and on the edge of the *commune* some ruins referred to as English forts; no doubt a reference to the Hundred Years War.

Laramière is a peaceful spot. Contained in this tiny hamlet of 250 people are all the ingredients that go to make up a perfect Lot village – a ruined mill or two, several *gariottes* in the fields, old bread-ovens, Roman remains at Cloup-Lestang, the second largest dolmen (Peyrelevade) in the *département*, weighing 25 tonnes, a very old *pigeonnier* and a really beautiful priory beneath which is the *gouffre* of Rausel. Why go further?

Only the south and east wings of the priory have survived the ravages of the Wars of Religion, but what is left can be viewed. You ring the bell and the owner, a correct and formal man, conducts you round the impressively restored interior. It was founded in 1145 by Bertrand de Griffeuile and attached to an Augustinian abbey in the Charente. Later on, however, it passed into the hands of the Jesuits, who restored it. The chapterhouse survives, with evidence of painting, and there is a little chapel; but the fact that the building is now an elegant home adds much to its charm and in the end one tends to wander from room to room admiring the décor as much as the history.

Leave Laramière, caught in a blissful time warp in its oasis of trees, and head westwards along the D55 to **Beauregard**. This *bastide*, instantly recognizable by its streets, straight as a die, was founded by the Church, the abbot of Marcilhac in this case and probably the one who lived at Promilhanes. There is a large square, with no arcading but a lovely fourteenth-century market hall roofed in *lauzes* and with the grain measures still in place. The town hall dates from the same century. The much-restored church has a relic of St John, which was greatly venerated by the locals and all who passed.

Varaire and Bach are short on real 'sights'. Varaire, like much of the *causse*, is Roman in origin; later on, the Cardaillac owned the *seigneurie*. The castle of Couanac has a machicolated donjon and very elegant windows, and there are still more dolmens to the south of town.

But holidays do not have to be a continual round of sights. Head back to the river through Concots on the D911 with its clock-tower and Esclauzels with its Grotte de Noyer, picnicking amongst the lavender and the larks, exploring interesting side roads, breathing in the feel of the *causse*, or perhaps stopping at a small hotel for a meal or a drink, talking to a few locals. Just because there is little to write about does not mean that you will not enjoy your visit.

8

Gourdon: 1

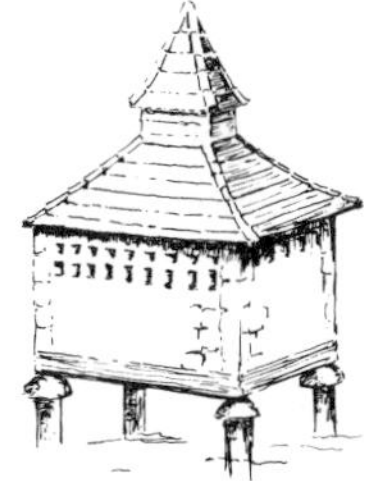

Gourdon's appearance, a golden town perched atop its little hill overlooking the valley of the Bléou, seems to owe more to the landscape of Tuscany than that of France.

The best approach is probably from the Sarlat road, where the town rises dramatically in front of you. The tall pine trees in the cemetery, the tiered houses, the ruined château ramparts, and finally the huge church towers of St Peter, pile up like profiteroles, one on top of the other. There are, though, several other approaches and a thousand different views that are nearly as good, for the hill is higher than it looks – 269 metres – and delicious glimpses can be seen for miles around in quite unexpected spots.

Hardly anything, though, can compare with the view from the top of the town and the château esplanade. As a teenager I scrambled up to the old ruins along *la route des amoureux*, clutching at branches and rocks and boyfriends' hands to aid the ascent. In those days it was a secret spot; now most people can manage the neat terraced steps. Secret or not, the view is just as good: a circular view, a view with distance, a view with immediate local interest. This indeed is a land of views. The *pointe de vue* on the Reilhaguet road to the east is impressive; the view of the River Dordogne from the N20 just after Souillac is dramatic; the view from the *bastide* of Domme (Dordogne) is peaceful and beautiful, with the river snaking its silver way through lush meadows; but none can touch Gourdon for sheer range. Almost level with you are the fortified towers of St Pierre, below you the town roofs – pantiles, *lauzes* old and new and every differing shade of red. Beyond the town and the hustle and bustle of trains and cars and everyday living, the rich Bouriane countryside undulates; and beyond that, eastwards, the *causse* of Gramat stretches away towards the Cantal and the Massif Central.

There is an elaborate orientation map to guide you and one of those franc-in-the-slot telescopes, but it is almost too good to waste time with all that. Choose a good, clear day and just look. So little remains of the château that it is difficult to realize just how majestic and important it was.

This little feudal city used to be dominated by two massive towers, the Tour de Brune in the north and the Tour del Miral in the south. So vast were these towers that an early inventory could only describe them as *'grandes, horribles et épouvantables'*. First mentioned in the will of Raymond I, count of Toulouse in 961, it played host to popes and kings, like Pope Calixte II, in 1119, and Richard the Lion Heart, who overran it in 1189 during the course of a Quercy campaign. Indeed, it is said to have been one Pierre Bazyle, companion-at-arms to Bertrand de Gourdon (lord of the castle) who, as an act of revenge, shot that secret weapon, the crossbow, and mortally wounded Richard at Châlus (Haute-Vienne). Anyone who has seen the distance the arrow was required to travel might doubt that story, if not the identity of the assassin.

Bertrand, though a lord, was a troubadour in the Languedoc tradition, but his singing and poetry came to an abrupt halt in 1241 with the cruel Albigensian Crusade. The inquisitor, Pierre Cellani, accused Bertrand of sheltering some heretic Cathars in the castle and Bertrand's son, Fortanier II, founder of nearby Labastide-Murat, was even said to have participated in the Cathar ceremony, the Consolamentum. Bertrand and Fortanier managed to escape punishment, but 138 inhabitants of Gourdon were not so lucky; some ended up in the Holy Land fighting the Infidels for their sins.

During the Wars of Religion the castle belonged to Pons de Lauzières-Thémines, one-time *maréchal* of France, whose family had acquired the *seigneurie* around 1250 when Hélène de Gourdon-Salviac married Gisbert II of Thémines, a propitious match which brought the Bouriane to the Thémines family. The Lauzières-Thémines were associated with the château right up to the Revolution, apart from a period when it passed, via Jean II of Armagnac, to the French Crown, and another brief excursion into the hands of the Estrée family later on.

After the Hundred Years War and the Wars of Religion, the château was in such a state of disrepair that Pons de Lauzières-Thémines, although his preferred home was Milhac, eight or nine kilometres away, embarked on a restoration programme. His plans, however, fell victim to local squabbling and, more seriously, to his own temporary fall from favour with King Louis XIII, which came about because he had taken the side of Marie de Médici against the king. He was thus unable to prevent the orders of the duke of Mayenne, governor of Guyenne, to dismantle his château. The orders were carried out on 12 May 1619 and the noble castle of Gourdon was no more.

Although the château restoration was a failure, the recent restoration of Gourdon itself has been a resounding success. The ochre houses have been cleaned and tidied up. The tiny radial streets climbing up to the church, streets with wonderfully evocative names like Zig-Zag, have been retiled. Walls in danger of collapse have been reinforced and neatly capped with tiles. New shops and restaurants have sprung up, although they only ply their trade in the summer months, and a music festival has been established in July and August. But for all this, Gourdon seems to get its priorities right. So far it has not succumbed to tourism and it remains very firmly what it clearly is, a market town.

The **market** is held every Tuesday and Saturday up by the

church, but twice a month or so it becomes a real *foire* and the whole town is given over to it. Built on a hill, the town is encompassed by a circular road near the base, the original *fossé*, or moat, and it is mainly here that you will find the stalls. Come early on the appointed day or you won't find a parking space. Cows are tethered under the town walls. Pens of sheep are crammed next to boxes of geese and goslings. Ducks, chickens and rabbits vie for a place with farm machinery, pots and pans, clothes, carpet-sellers from Morocco and local craftsmen selling wooden baskets and rush chairs. Rows of espadrilles and aprons crush up against stalls selling *merguez* sausages or slightly suspect herbal cures that look like witches' potions. Non-local craftsmen sell some very ordinary-looking jewellery.

The restaurants prepare the day before. Tables are set outside for the overspill of people if the weather is fine and on the day the raucous babble of patois-speaking *propriétaires* discussing prices and pigs echoes round the town. (The pigs used to be penned up outside the Hostellerie de la Bouriane, as residents who woke to their squeals would discover, but now they have been moved to the outskirts.) The cafés are full to overflowing and the waiters and waitresses run hither and thither with a *pastis* and a *rouge* here and a coffee and a *muscat* there.

Up by the church, in the square in front of the great west door, where in 1317 young Guillemette Robert was burned to death as a *fachillera* or witch, the vegetable stalls are laid out alongside the fish and (dead) poultry. Nearly all the produce is local – jars of foie gras and home-made *cabécous*, most delicious of all goats' cheeses, *girolles*, strange yellow mushrooms, *ceps* if you are lucky and piles of fruit according to season.

By midday it is pretty well all over. The sheep are loaded, somewhat unceremoniously, into vans, the remaining fowl are battened down into their boxes, and the rest of the day is given over to food. Lunch-time today is electric, with toothless old farmers in overalls spilling out of every available café and restaurant. The talk is age-old talk of land and beasts, weddings and deaths.

If you are planning an evening meal and don't want a heavy lunch, this might be the time to stroll up to St Pierre, although it can also be fun to go on a Saturday afternoon and watch the brides queuing up outside the arcaded Hôtel de Ville for the civil part of their marriage ceremonies.

There was originally a fine Romanesque church on the site, a dependent of the abbey at nearby Le Vigan, but it fell into such a state of disrepair that towards the end of the thirteenth century the authorities ordered another church to be built. Gourdon was then at the apogee of its importance as a fortified town of some 5,000 people; a huge population when the entire kingdom of France only numbered 15 million.

Accordingly, a Frenchman from north of the Loire was hired to build a Gothic structure; a style considered indicative of the town's importance. Work began in 1302, but progress was very slow indeed, with minor hitches such as plague and the Hundred Years War intervening, and the result is very much a Quercy or Languedoc interpretation of Gothic, rather military and austere, with massive, asymmetrical towers rising a sheer 35 metres or so. The only light relief is the pretty rose window, though that has battlements beneath, and the large, decorated west door with stylish archivolts. Standing to the left of the south door is a curious statue of a hooded monk carrying a sundial. Inside the style is again of the Midi – a huge nave with ogive vaulting, 23 metres high; no proper transept but lateral chapels leading off. Behind the altar is a seventeenth-century frieze of gold-embossed wood panelling representing scenes from the life of the Virgin; not my favourite but rather unique for all that. Frankly, if you stopped at Chartres on the way down, you will not be impressed with St Pierre.

Those in need of exercise can now walk round to the north side of the church, or to the little square on the east, thick with fallen chestnuts in September, and climb up to the castle view. Whatever you do, though, do stop for a peep at the very beautiful eighteenth-century doorway on the **Maison Cavaignac** at the top of the rue du Roc, overlooking the chestnuts. Jean Baptiste

Cavaignac was one of Gourdon's famous sons. Born on 23 February 1762 he rose via the parliament at Toulouse to great heights, finally ending up in the court of Naples, where he served with his friend Joachim Murat from neighbouring Labastide-Murat. Banished by Louis XVIII for voting for the death of Louis XVI, he died in Brussels alongside another Gourdon compatriot, Alexandre de Lauzières-Thémines, bishop of Blois, last *seigneur* of Gourdon before the Revolution. Exiled to England for refusing to swear the constitutional oath, the latter died in Brussels in 1829.

If you visit Gourdon in July and August for the music festival, some of the concerts you attend are sure to take place in the only other church of any importance in the town, **Les Cordeliers**. This ancient and lovely church was originally the chapel of a monastery, Les Cordeliers, founded by Gisbert II de Thémines and Hélène de la Bourianne after their marriage in 1251. They were aided by Christophe de Ramondiola, a disciple of St Francis and creator of Les Cordeliers at Cahors. St Louis, too, favoured the Franciscan and Dominican orders and himself founded Cordelier monasteries as far afield as Jaffa. The name 'Cordelier' comes, of course, from the cord the monks wore round their waists in place of a belt.

Les Cordeliers at Gourdon rose to importance in the first half of the fourteenth century after two monks, Fortanier de Vassal and Guillaume Farinier, held important positions within the order and went on to become cardinals. With the Hundred Years War the monastery declined, but the *coup de grâce* was really the Wars of Religion. The Calvinists, led by the infamous Symphorien de Durfort, lord of Duras, chose Gourdon as their rallying point *en route* to unite their army from the Languedoc with that of the Quercy Huguenots to the north of the town. Duras stayed in Gourdon, a town largely faithful to Catholicism, for one month, during which time he wreaked havoc upon it. He paid special attention to the rich monastery, which he set on fire and pillaged, torturing and disembowelling the monks. Leaving

Gourdon in ruins, he made his way to Orléans where he was killed defending the city against the Catholic army of the duke of Guise.

Although there were a few converts to the new faith – Louis Labrande preached the Reform at nearby Salviac – Gourdon's experience at the hands of the Calvinists had been so memorable that it remained a predominantly Catholic town in spite of a visit by Etienne Gragnon, sent by Calvin himself. Religious confusion, however, reigned in the town for a good few years until the Edict of Nantes in 1598 heralded the return of a brief peace.

It was during the Revolution that Les Cordeliers came under attack once again. On 8 September 1793 the archives were burnt. The wood panels and other finery were all wrecked or stolen and the monks dispersed, in spite of a plea to the Assemblée Constituante to spare both monastery and church, which soon afterwards lost its sanctity and became a public meeting hall.

The church as we see it today has been spoiled by careless restoration, most notably the square tower, which was rebuilt in imitation of those of St Pierre where previously it had had the typical Quercy flat-fronted bell tower. Inside, though, the windows and nave have great purity and the few naïve stone carvings are direct and moving. A hand hovers above your head in the nave offering a blessing and in the sacristy the serene face of God looks on – probably today at the artistes dressing for a concert. Another true glory remains, in the fourteenth-century polygonal font, which shows Christ blessing the disciples.

All that remains of the ancient chapel of **St Siméon** is the tower and a small room to the left of the new church. The chapel was a dependency of the abbey at Sarlat (Dordogne), but the real reason for the visit here is to see one of the few surviving relics from Les Cordeliers – a magnificent sculptured wooden chair, badly needing some woodworm treatment, propped up by a kneeling man dressed in lion skins. It was made by Tournier, a local sculptor.

St Siméon's adjoining twelfth-century hospital was a

foundation of the Le Vigan abbey, though happily there is a more modern building on the outskirts of the town, towards Salviac.

If after all this church history you feel in need of a drink, stroll a few yards up the hill to either of the two cafés in that direction. The Café de Paris is directly on the road, noisy and somewhat wasp-ridden owing to the existence of an impossibly irresistible pâtisserie next door. My own favourite is the Divan, where the chairs are set well back from the road and there is a view of the fortified gateway to the Rue Majou and the pretty balconied houses.

It was at the Café-Hôtel Divan that Nancy Cunard, the poet, rebel, heiress, flapper-girl and lover of Louis Aragon, began her autobiography in a blue-covered notebook of that squared paper so commonly sold in France, which she probably bought at the Maison de la Presse across the road:

> Begun this day of rain, Monday October 29 1956 in the Café Divan, Gourdon, Lot, France. NOTES for the makings of the MEMORIES Book of the Writers and Artists one has known throughout life – chronologically. (These fragments have I shored against my ruin.)

Ms Cunard had set up home at Lamothe-Fénelon and the Divan was obviously a regular watering hole for her, for when she developed emphysema in September 1963 she went to hospital in Gourdon, and on being discharged moved into the hotel. Burkhart, who visited, described it thus: '...downstairs a salon café of pinball machines, local youth and nervous young proprietor; upstairs, tiny rooms furnished and panelled in raw orange pine...when Nancy was able to leave her raw orange cubicle she descended and sat in a corner of the pinball salon, writing her letters, drinking rough red, which she would occasionally ask one of the boys to share a glass of, catching her breath between Gauloises.'

Near the hospital and opposite the supermarket on the outskirts of town is a tiny thirteenth-century chapel called

La Maladrerie. This was a leper hospital; the lepers being housed here under strict rules that because of the risk of contagion they must not consort with the local population. In August 1313 a leper called Etienne Estèves, whose wife was also at the hospital, apparently broke these rules to his cost. He was accused of committing adultery with Bertrande Lacaze, who was not a sufferer. On 4 September, Estèves was condemned to be burned alive.

Take a stroll around the picturesque and winding streets of the **old town**. In Rue Cardinal Favinié there are ancient houses with turrets and mullioned windows. Rue d'Anglars has a sixteenth-century gate. Rue Alfred Filnol has seventeenth- and eighteenth-century façades, and the Maison d'Albert. Turn any corner and you will find a pretty view. There were four principal gates to the old medieval town: Roc, Ségur, St Jean and Majou, with *quartiers* of the same names. Rue Majou (Major) was the main commercial street, and today it is beautifully restored, with corbelled houses and the Maison d'Anglars, the house of a renowned Gourdon family. On the other side of town the important trading gate of Mazel is still quite well preserved and vestiges of the original town walls are still visible. As you walk around the streets you will see tantalizing glimpses of sheltered courtyard gardens, the sun glinting on the limestone walls and casting long shadows.

Through the fortified gateway of rue Majou, on the right as you descend, you will see the old chapel of Nôtre-Dame-du-Majou. This tiny sixteenth-century chapel was a place of pilgrimage, though it was barely complete before it was pillaged by Duras. Restored in the seventeenth century, it suffered again in 1790, when objects were stolen and the precious crown from the Virgin's head was removed and sent to the Hôtel de Monnaie at Bordeaux, undergoing further restoration in the nineteenth century. Thanks to the women of Gourdon, who protested vigorously on hearing that the chapel was to be demolished, it has survived to the present day.

SOUILLAC
le Roc
SARLAT
Nadaillac-de-Rouge
Lamothe Fénelon
Masclat
R. Dordogne
N20
Loupiac
Fajoles
Milhac
Domme
Payrac
Rouffilhac
Anglars-Nozac
Prouillac
Reilhaguet
B O U R I A N E
Cougnac
St Projet
GOURDON
Le Vigan
N.D. des Neiges
R. Bleou
DORDOGNE
B O U R I A N E
Pont-Carral
l'Abbaye Nouvelle
Salviac
R. Céou
Ch. de Clermont
St Pierre du Grand Roque
Dégagnac
Frayssinet
Marminiac
Concorès
Labastide Murat
Cazals
Rampoux
Lavercantière
St Germain du Bel Air
Montcléra
St Caprais
Villefranche au Périgord
Frayssinet le Gélat
Dégagnazes
Thédirac
St André
Les Arques
GIRONDE
La Thèze
Goujounac
Uzech
Lherm
Montgesty
Salvezou
Gigouzac
Mechmont
Pomarède
Cassagnes
Canourgues
R. Vert
St Denis
R. Thèze
Catus
Ch. de Bonaguil
Montcabrier
Les Junies la Masse
St Médard
N20
R. Masse
Crayssac
R. Lot
R. Lot
CAHORS

9

Gourdon: 2

The Bouriane

The area surrounding Gourdon is called the Bouriane; a fertile, bosky land of rich red soil and the fan-spray leaves of the sweet chestnut. The name comes from *bourie*, the word used to describe the many small farms of the area. The north-westerly reaches of the Bouriane border on the boundaries of the Dordogne *département*, so it is not surprising that the land has a look of the Périgord about it; neat fields and hedgerows and a tidy sort of air.

If you are staying at the Hostellerie de la Bouriane in Gourdon – and why on earth would you stay anywhere else? – you can get your first real taste of the Bouriane by walking off your Sunday lunch. Replete with *cailles aux raisins* and other delights of the Lacam kitchen, walk out of the hotel and straight ahead, past the men playing *boules* and under the railway bridge. Follow the road downhill for a couple of kilometres or so until you reach the valley floor. Ignore the dogs, whose barks are worse than their bites. Easier said than done, perhaps, and there is no doubt that in this country area one comes across them frequently and they can seem menacing. Carry a walking stick if you are nervous.

As you reach the bottom of the hill, you cross the bridge over the Bléou and come across a group of buildings – an old water-mill, a couple of houses, the public washing place *(lavoir)*, and **Notre Dame des Neiges**. It is a magic spot on a hot day. Trout bend their silver-smooth way through the water, red geraniums spill from the mill balcony, dragonflies dart blue-green across the stream, pied wagtails agitate along its edge, the brook babbles into the washing place, and the little church of Our Lady of the Snows nestles snugly into the hillside.

It is a gem of a church, this one, but whilst the mill is cited in an act of 1233, no mention of the chapel can be found until 1323, though it is clear that it had existed for some time by that date. The dedication – Nostra Dama de Nevejo, as it used to be – was made in memory of the miracle of the snow which happened in Rome in AD 352. The Virgin appeared to Senator Giovanni and the pope, and the next day, although it was the height of summer, the spot on Mount Esquiline where she wished a church to be built was found to be covered in snow.

The building is simple and pleasingly squat, though only the Romanesque apse remains of the original church. What strikes one immediately is the west door, dating from the restoration and enlargement which took place in 1646 in the hope of reviving what had been a popular pilgrimage spot. It has little in common with the rest of the church. Nevertheless it is a charming anachronism, covered with a long Latin inscription and giving us a little history of the church, its pilgrimage and its miracles. The spring which flows from the church, and from which the miracles arose, can be seen by asking for the keys at the next-door house. Inside, there is an altar by Tournier, the local craftsman, who appears to have been a prolific worker. This one was made in 1698 and represents the principal mysteries in the life of the Virgin. There is, too, a little fourteenth-century Virgin, typical of many found in Quercy from that time.

Those energetic enough or still feeling full can continue on foot to Le Vigan; otherwise return for your car and take the direct route along the D673.

Le Vigan is a working village, unknowingly familiar to those who have seen the film *Un Si Joli Village* and, although it lacks the charm of some of the prettier *causse* villages, it has a good deal of character. I must admit I feel a special affection for the spot.

Le Vigan was my first proper introduction to the Lot. Here we stayed in the halcyon days when Mme Mezon ruled the only hotel. Rooms and meals were eight francs apiece. There was no menu. Each evening you sat at the oilcloth-covered table in a state of slightly nervous anticipation. Mme Mezon's cooking was far from orthodox, but the meals were the expression of an artistic and imaginative woman. Dishes appeared in bizarre order – fish following meat, vegetables thrown in between all courses, as if she had suddenly remembered the haricot beans picked yesterday morning. Toothless, dressed always in black, legs swollen like balloons, she toiled endlessly with unfailing good humour.

There were never fewer than six courses, eight was not unusual. No *nouvelle cuisine* here; it had not been invented. Saturated fats were the order of the day. The food was cooked in pork fat and the pâtés came surrounded with it or coated in bright yellow duck grease. Wine, a litre of Caves St Antoine – the label indelibly fixed in my mind – came with the price of the meal.

Steak days were the only 'treat' we came to dread. Great lumps of inedible, unchewable meat which had to be concealed in pockets or handbags rather than offend her. With seven other courses it scarcely mattered. There were far more exciting dishes to try, in any case. The days we looked forward to most were *les noces*, when hotel guests fared as well as the wedding guests themselves and usually ended up by being invited to join the festivities.

Day and night the place was full of people – villagers, farmers, road-menders – drowning the place in a cacophony of noise – the men teasing the women, Reine and Michel shouting to (and at) each other as yet another kitchen crisis arose. Everyone knew everyone else, and soon everyone knew us too, and it was in Le Vigan that I formed some lasting friendships.

In the quieter moments I would be taken to collect the potatoes from the farm or pick up the bread from the old baker round the corner. The bakery was dark and ancient, and the loaves came out of the log-fired ovens long, round, oval – every shape and size, but always hot and crusty. In the evenings we would crowd into cars and go off to the local village fêtes, where all the courting was done. Armed with bags of confetti, we would stalk each other round the backs of dim buildings, faintly etched against a starry sky. The nights were always clear, just as the days were always hot. Confetti in your mouth, in your eyes, in your ears; in every pocket and spilling from your shoes. Up and down the village streets we would dance, pausing to watch the two old brothers, who grew and smoked their own tobacco in thick, crude cigarettes, dance the *bourrée* together. One would be staggering from drink, the other from Parkinson's Disease, but oh, the smiles on their worn faces. And so to bed and in the morning a mock scolding from Reine, as she swept up still more confetti which had fallen from your clothes as you undressed.

Today things have changed, Mme Mezon and even her son, Michel, are dead. Reine has married and moved to Montauban, but friendships endure. There is still the fête in October and *méchouis* on 14 July, with a service round the tiny war memorial and aperitifs in the Mairie afterwards. Apparent strangers still approach you with warm invitations to stop by for a drink or a meal and enquire after your family. This open generosity typifies the Lot, it would seem, and makes a complete nonsense of that English myth and cliché that the French never invite you into their homes.

Despite its workaday image of post office, shops, school and a few modern houses, Le Vigan has its glory and one that is difficult to ignore, for dominating this fast-growing village of eight hundred inhabitants is the **abbey church**. The priory was founded in the eleventh century and was a dependent of the big abbey church of St Sernin at Toulouse, given to the latter by the bishop of Cahors, Géraud de Gourdon. It was the canons of St Sernin who undertook the construction of the collegiate.

The heyday of the church, however, came in the thirteenth and fourteenth centuries, when it grew strong under the protection of kings and popes and the archbishop of Bourges alike. It is interesting to note that Raymond de Pélegri, one-time canon of Le Vigan in the fourteenth century, was also canon of Cahors, Salisbury and London. Privileges were showered upon the priory, and it seems to have been fairly stuffed to the hilt with relics of one sort or another; a papal bull from the end of the eleventh century mentions Ste Charité and Ste Foi (although these are more usually associated with Conques), Ste Espérance and Ste Sophie. The relics of St Gall, patron saint of fishermen, were transferred here in 1384. The church's prosperity, however, did not survive the Hundred Years War and the English pillaging of the priory, although the relics of St Gall did. It is a powerful building with a massive belfry and some very good fifteenth- and sixteenth-century glass, beautifully set off by the restoration work now being undertaken and long overdue. There are also Romanesque capitals and seventeenth-century wood panelling.

Above the village is the much-restored château, shut to the public but scene of some hot, September, Proustian memories for me – the men on ladders gathering grapes from the vine on the wall; the children inside, sliding along the marble floors, giggling helplessly by the piano, creaking open the big shutters to admire the view over the Céou – for the lake did not exist then.

Follow the road that runs through Le Vigan, keeping the *plan d'eau* (man-made lake) on your left, and you arrive at **St Projet**. Strictly speaking, St Projet belongs to the *causse*, and you will notice the land rise as you approach the N20. The village has an *auberge* which does not serve meals, but whose red-checked tablecloths are always maddeningly and invitingly spread for lunch, glasses and cutlery piled on top. It also has a curious monolithic cross with naïve carvings. In a land where one can dismiss Romanesque churches as everyday, the church holds little of interest, though the bell tolls mournfully for the few faithful. St Projet also has the best butcher's shop for miles; to watch Madame prepare a *rôti de porc* (first catch your pig) is to watch a work of art.

On now north up the N20 to Payrac, a pretty village though somewhat spoiled by the main road running through it, then turn left and follow the signposts to the twilight-sounding name of **Lamothe-Fénelon**. The old name was La Mothe-Marsaut, but the seigneurie passed to the Salignacs, who were seigneurs of La Mothe and Fénelon, and so the two names were linked. The Salignacs were the family of François de Salignac de La Mothe Fénelon, archbishop of Cambrai, and better known simply as Fénelon. The château, his childhood home, lies just over the Dordogne boundary, but the man himself will crop up again at Carennac.

This village was also the unlikely home of Nancy Cunard, whom we met in Gourdon. She loved the area and so did her visitors. Irene Rathbone found it 'hot, peaceful, delectable . . . Fields shimmered in the heat: walnuts one length of the road cast shade.' As for Nancy herself, she wrote to Cecily Mackworth in spring 1950 '. . . I adore it and adore this region . . . Had I lived down here from the start the whole of my life would have been different and I should not have lost everything.'

The church at Lamothe-Fénelon is particularly appealing with a typical flat-fronted Quercy belfry, fourteenth-century and very defensive-looking.

On now to **Masclat**, a truly beguiling village with an ancient church adjoining the sort of château one dreams of owning. Two tall palm trees stand sentinel outside, though these suffered badly in the frost of 1984/5. The seigneurie was divided between three families, one of which was the family of Blanquefort, or Blanchefort. Bertrand de Blanchefort, founder of the Knights Templar, belonged to the same family, but although there are records of Bertrand being *seigneur* here, fans of that best seller, *The Holy Blood and the Holy Grail* (more interesting for the light it throws on the Templars than almost anything else) will be disappointed to learn that the church is not dedicated to St Mary Magdalene.

This bit of land, the northern Bouriane, is a charming backwater and one can wander the tiny roads for hours. Old ladies in straw hats, bent double over the fields, take the opportunity of a passing car to stretch their muscles and view the distraction. You can still see horse-drawn ploughs, though very rarely, these days, oxen. In June the fields are neatly planted with ripening wheat, barley and maize. In some the broad leaves of the tobacco plant are in evidence and all along the road is the ubiquitous walnut tree.

Wander in and out of Fajoles, perhaps; it is scruffy and deserted but the crumbling church has a particularly lovely south door. Tiny pillars with decorated capitals are alive with naïve figures climbing up them. The church was mentioned in 1143 as belonging to the monastery at Le Vigan. It is difficult to get a glimpse of the château at Nadaillac-de-Rouge because of the high walls and the proximity of the track to the castle. A better view of it can be had from the churchyard, in the same style as Lamothe-Fénelon. Le Roc, even nearer Souillac, was an Iron Age site; Loupiac has a seventeenth-century castle which belonged to the Estresses family

Rouffilhac has a Romanesque church and was yet another village belonging of the powerful Thémines family, whose main residence was the lovely **Milhac**, ancient *chef-lieu* of the Bouriane and a gem of a place, well kept and clean, with flowers spilling from every balcony and step. Approaching Milhac from Gourdon, you see the cliff on which the château was built, with a commanding view over the Bouriane. Approaching from the other side, you come through the delightful village and your view of the château is slightly obscured.

Prouillac is worth a quick look for the curious Latin inscription above the door to the sacristy in the church: *'Qui non intrat per ostium in ovile ovium sed ascendit aliunde, ille fur est et latro'* – apparently a warning that anyone who enters the church by unorthodox means shall be considered a thief and a brigand.

Anglars Nozac has a Renaissance château and a Gothic church, but make your way across country now to Cougnac.

There is something rather charming about the caves at **Cougnac**. *Aménagement* is down to a minimum. There are two caves; one full of very fine, white needles of stalactites and stalagmites and discovered in 1948, and the other, more important, full of paintings and only discovered in 1952. Abbé Breuil pronounced the latter cave important and interesting. As at Lascaux, the entrance was blocked for many years, thus preserving the pictures, which are renowned for their exceptional freshness and clarity. All the art in the cave is thought to belong to the Aurignacian-Perigordian period (i.e. dating back to 20,000 BC and beyond), though in style it resembles that of Pech-Merle more than that of Lascaux.

The paintings are all in profile, and whilst there are the usual collections of animals – deer, ibex, mammoth and the like, some in red with a black outline – what makes Cougnac so special are the human figures, so rare in cave art. Some of these human figures are pierced with lances or arrows, but who they are, or what they represent, no one can be sure. There are also some fingerprints, the fingerprints of Stone Age man, and quite startling it is to stand before them contemplating the fact.

The paintings are inclined to make you forget the natural wonders of both caves, which are significant, and the guides finish with a very sweet little *pièce de théâtre*, slowly switching the lights off to show you the cave lit by its own phosphorescence.

The two caves are set in woodland and you walk from one to the other, a pleasant shady stroll if it is a hot day. It is a curious feeling one experiences after a cave viewing, a feeling of one's sense of balance having been slightly disturbed, linked with an imperturbable sense of relief; or is it despair?

The Bouriane to the south of Gourdon is the real Bouriane of sweet chestnut woods, with logs piled in neat stacks by the roadside like brown abstract paintings, pleasing for the warmth and variety of their colours. The hills are gentler than those of the *causse*. Small streams and brooks trail along the valley floors.

Some communes like Frayssinet, Catus and Cazals have flooded their valleys, the resulting lakes serving the leisure needs of locals and tourists alike. It is difficult to become reconciled to these lakes, too round or too square as they are, out of place in a limestone land of rivers which flow above and below ground, where after a heavy rainstorm roads drain in a matter of minutes; yet they undoubtedly give pleasure to all who use them, in an area far from the leisure facilities of the coast or a big city.

This is also the country of what I like to call the painted churches; that is, churches with frescos painted on their walls, some of them newly discovered.

It is a difficult piece of country, nevertheless, to get to grips with in one excursion without trailing back and forth and, whilst there is nothing to see of outstanding importance, it is an area rich in history, much of it tied in with English history. I would, therefore, be tempted to tackle it in two journeys.

Taking the Salviac road (D673) from Gourdon, you pass the ruins of what is rather quaintly referred to as the **Abbaye Nouvelle**, near Pont-Carral. This abbey (as opposed to an earlier one at St Martin-le-Désarmat) belonged to the Cistercian order and was founded in 1242 by the big Aubazine abbey in the Corrèze, as were many of the ecclesiastical sights around here. However Léobard, as it is sometimes called, never achieved the same importance in the area as the abbey at Le Vigan. The ruins are imposing, not to say glowering, and covered in creeper, with enormous buttresses supporting what seems to be a very tall edifice indeed, the height accentuating the fact that only half of it is still standing.

Salviac itself used to be a neglected, seedy-looking little town, but the signs are that attempts are being made to clean it up and accord it some sort of status as *chef-lieu de canton*. The sturdy Gothic church, belonging largely to the late thirteenth and early fourteenth centuries, is in the middle of a one-way traffic system.

It contains fragments of fourteenth-century glass in four windows, which instruct us in the martyrdom of St Eutropius, first bishop of Saintes, an interesting town in the west of France. Eutropius is said to have suffered martyrdom because he managed to convert Eustella, the daughter of the Roman governor.

The château with pepper-pot towers is called locally the Château des Templiers, although there does not appear to be any record of a *commanderie* here. The town was built on a prehistoric site, but there are few traces of anything nowadays apart from the dolmen of Pech-Curet and a cave with some paintings of doubtful authenticity.

During the Hundred Years War, Salviac was taken and retaken by the English, who roamed the area causing havoc. There are some nice old houses in the town and, to the north, the little fifteenth-century chapel of Notre-Dame-de-l'Olm has a gold-embossed wooden altar and a seventeenth-century Virgin.

Marminiac is a tiny place which also has English connections; for it was the English who occupied it and destroyed the château of Bonafous. Roman remains have been found too – a few medallions were excavated from some tombs and there are still traces of the Roman road which ran between Cahors and Périgueux. The church is a much-restored edifice with little to see, but there is some modern glass by Bissière in the windows of the Chapelle Boissierette.

More English connections at **Cazals**, back on the D673. It was the seigneurs of Gourdon who built the château of Cazals, which is mentioned in a treaty of 1193 between the count of Toulouse and Richard Coeur-de-Lion; and a further link exists with the Cazals charter, granted to the citizens in 1319 by the *senéchal* of Quercy on behalf of the king of England. The name Cazals comes from *casa* (house); *cazals* themselves being the little properties cultivated by serfs who were dependent on the seigneurie of Gourdon and who lived along the old Roman road. Cazals boasts another *plan d'eau*, slightly better than most of the others by virtue

Tympanum, Cahors Cathedral.

Lauze cupolas on the abbey church at Souillac.

The Virgin and Child,
Castelnau-Prudhomat Church.

The dancing Isaiah of Souillac.

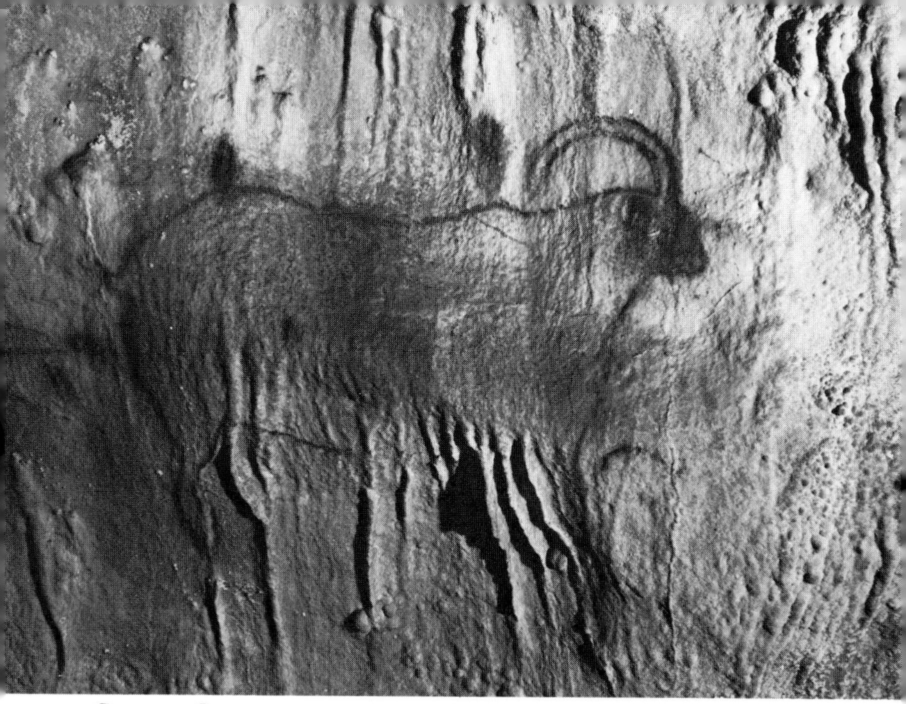

Cave art at Cougnac.

A typical farm in the Ségala.

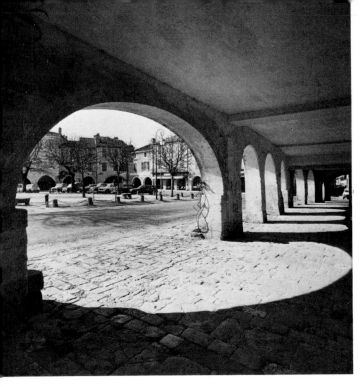

Typical *cornières* at the *bastide* of Castelnau-Montratier.

A free-standing *pigeonnier* at Castelnau-Montratier.

The Pont Valentré, Cahors.

Château de la Treyne above the Dordogne.

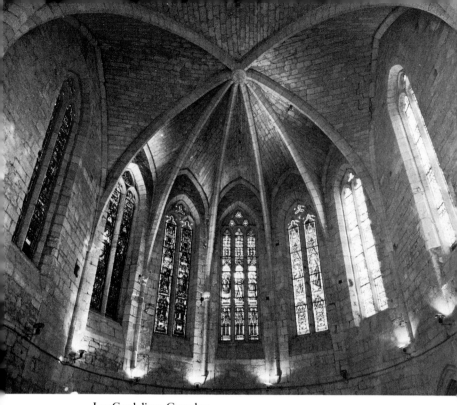

Les Cordeliers, Gourdon.

The abbey church at Le Vigan.

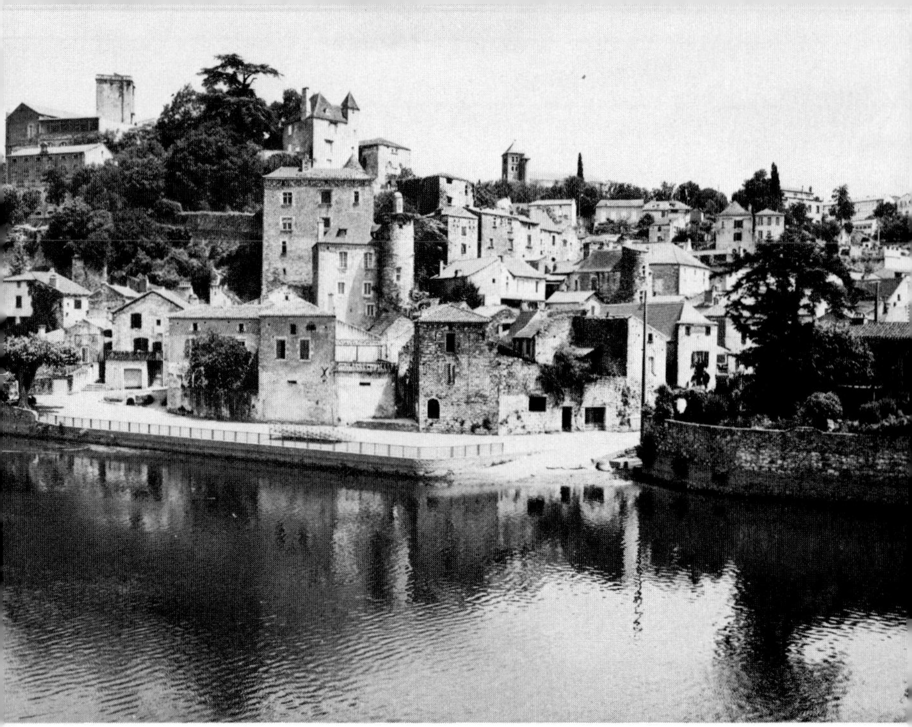

Puy l'Evêque.

A richly carved door, Puy l'Evêque.

The church at St Cirq-Lapopie.

Castelnau-Bretenoux.

Roofscape at Carennac.

Martel.

The priory at Espagnac.

of the fact that the hill on which the town stands rises above the water, giving it a rather more landscaped air.

The church is much restored and from a distance looks quite modern, although it was in fact an abbatial church and there remain some charming Romanesque capitals depicting the Last Judgment in that wonderfully naïve style which so typifies the Romanesque.

Close to Cazals is the utterly disarming château of Montcléra, home of the Gironde family, although in the years preceding the fourteenth century it was the fief of the powerful family of Guerre. A dream of late fifteenth-century architecture, the château has towers of all descriptions jostling for position and even little baby ones sprouting from larger versions. There is a fortified gateway, and houses and church cluster close by; the whole ensemble stands in wooded parkland looking like an illustration from a book of fairy tales. Unfortunately it is closed to the public.

St Caprais, at the limits of the Lot boundary, has a menhir and a dolmen at Pech Sauvage (called locally Pierre de Loup), and the ruins of an old Huguenot chapel perched on a rock.

Another menhir with the wonderful name of Peyropincado can be found near Frayssinet-le-Gélat, where the monument *'Aux martyrs de la barbarie allemande'* bearing fifteen names recalls Nazi atrocities in the village during the last war. The church is a disappointment.

La Thèze, near Frayssinet, and **Montcabrier** are both *bastides*, although the former is nothing but a tiny hamlet which belonged to the archrival of Montcabrier, Pestillac. Montcabrier scarcely ranks as one of the best or prettiest *bastides*. The plan is there all right – nine square islands constitute the original town. The oldest houses are in the central square and some are as early as the thirteenth century, but the arcades, sadly, have all been filled in.

The town was founded by Guy de Caprier on a hill belonging to the lords of Pestillac, a neighbouring village, an act which led to a long dispute between the two towns, finishing in Montcabrier's favour and leaving Pestillac in ruins. The twelfth-century donjon can be seen on the opposite hillside, as can vestiges of a church of the same era. The church at Montcabrier is solid and defensive-looking, as many *bastide* churches are, the front wall rising up sheer to form a five-bell belfry, although there is a nice Flamboyant doorway. Inside, things get too ornate for my taste, but the wooden altar and the statue of St Louis in the side chapel are worth a look. There are also some frescos in a very bad state of repair.

At Montcabrier you are only a few kilometres from the spectacularly beautiful castle of Bonaguil which, although it falls just outside the Lot boundaries, is definitely not to be missed. There are some interesting graffiti.

Heading back to Gourdon, now, take the D189 and go through Cassagnes, a chalcolithic site and the home of one Timothée O'Donovan, an Irish curate in 1793. Then on to Goujounac via Pomarède, with the ruins of a Benedictine convent. **Goujounac** is a tiny village with the ruins of a château destroyed by the Huguenots in 1590. The church was similarly set alight, but the Romanesque apse remains. So does the south door, tumbling down and bricked up but sporting a beneficent long-haired Christ sitting in glory, and encircled by the symbols of the four Evangelists. It is small fare compared to Carennac or Cahors, but all the requirements are there. One imagines that the local craftsman must have had Beaulieu in mind when he created this exquisite miniature.

Les Arques on the D150, six kilometres south of Cazals, is a sad little place full of architecture signifying a rosier time. Most of the village seems to be in a state of collapse. A tall *gentilhommière*, with round tower and sentinel palm tree, stands guard above the church with Moorish arches which is undergoing expensive restoration egged on by the discovery of the crypt. Les Arques was a Gallo-Roman site and later on had a priory, founded in the eleventh century by the abbey at Marcilhac. It is quite possible, therefore, that the excavations will reveal some treasures, although the old woman we met outside seemed far from pleased about the 'millions' of francs already spent. She was talking, of course, in terms of old francs, as many of the inhabitants, old and young, still do. Outside there are some sarcophagi.

Near Les Arques, in the valley of the Masse but not to be confused with it, is the Romanesque **Chapel of St André**. This tiny building is sited in the middle of a cricket-filled field and is another building of the 'first catch your person with the key' variety. The charge, once we had found them at the nearby house, was three francs. The paintings in the apse are of the late fifteenth century and were discovered in 1954 by the sculptor Zadkine, though humidity, amongst other things, is unfortunately destroying them. They are nevertheless of very good quality, depicting the apostles and their attributes, six to the right and six to the left – Peter with his keys; Andrew with his cross. Matthias and Matthew are worn away, but the others on the left are clearer. On the roof is a Christ in Majesty, His right hand raised, His left resting on a globe surmounted by a cross. The pillars, too, are decorated.

Pick your way back across the field and head for **Rampoux**, where once again you must play hunt-the-key, although this could be a temporary measure while the church is being restored. Again, too, the frescos belong to the fifteenth century, and the scenes include Judas kissing and betraying Christ, a large Crucifixion and a moving *mise au tombeau* of simple lines.

Lavercantière was ravaged by plague in 1506, and the little chapel in the town is thought to be the hospital chapel. Like so many of the tiny villages and small towns in the Bouriane, Lavercantière is so surrounded by the ruins of abbeys and convents that one's impression is of an earlier population made up entirely of monks and nuns.

Dégagnac to the north, on the D6, was evangelized very early on after the passage of St Martin, though before him came an earlier religion, as the standing stones of Peyrolevado possibly bear witness. There are old houses to be seen, the remains of the ramparts and the ruins of the priory of Lentis.

From Dégagnac you can either head for Gourdon on the main roads or cut across-country to St Clair to finish off the north-east corner of the Bouriane. St Clair's church was another old priory linked to Le Vigan. The little church at Souillaguet has two seventeenth-century wooden altars worth looking at before you head for home.

The rest of the Bouriane is best toured using Catus as a base. **Catus**, which lies sixteen kilometres north-west of Cahors in the valley of the Vert, has another *plan d'eau*. It is *chef-lieu de canton* and owes its former importance to the existence of an abbey founded in the eleventh century by the abbey of Cluse in Piémont. The **church** today has a three-storeyed bell-tower, but it is to the wonderfully detailed capitals, in the style of Moissac, that you should pay attention. Twelve pillars are decorated, top and bottom, alive with curious symbolic carvings and some that are more easily decipherable, such as the Last Judgment. The town, which used to be fortified, has some lovely old **houses**, notably the fourteenth-century one belonging to the seigneur of Savanac and the sixteenth-century one which used to belong to the family with the wonderful name of Clermont de Toucheboeuf. The **well** of St Barnabas (whose head is in the church of St Sernin at Toulouse) was an old pilgrimage spot. Of the buildings around Catus in the countryside, many retain their traditional *lauze* roofs, including a famous and much-photographed farm which appears in all the postcard shops. The stone for these roofs, similar to some found in the Cotswolds, was quarried at nearby Crayssac, though gradually tiles became more popular and, of course, cheaper.

Making a circular trip to the west of Catus, head first through St Médard to **La Masse** on the D37, notable, so all the guide-books tell you, for its octagonal, thirteenth-century Saracen chimney at the Maison de Cavaille. What they tend to leave out are the murals in the tiny church. We managed to get the key from an unusually sullen and monosyllabic woman who trailed slowly and resentfully up the path to her house and back again; though it has to be said that she brightened visibly on being offered a generous tip. The church, once opened, is simple, small, damp and in a dire state of disrepair. The left wall has the standard religious scenes one would expect, but those on the right are far from orthodox. Striding across the wall, a laughing sneer on his evil face, is a brilliantly alive Devil and a retinue of other menacing pagan creatures. Curiously, there is something jolly about these devils dancing across the wall of the little church, and one is tempted to choose the wrong side. One hopes the paintings will be restored before they and the church fall apart. They are well worth the effort of finding the key.

The rest of the trip is a gentle meander through small villages, arriving first at Les Junies, through which ran the Roman military road from Agen to Clermont Ferrand. The land on which the château stands was offered to Bertrand de Jean by the bishop of Cahors as a gift of thanks for his help in the vicious Albigensian Crusade. The present building, set among trees, is built to a simple rectangular plan flanked by three round towers, and dates from the fifteenth century. During the Hundred Years War it was taken by the English, though access is now denied to all. Les Junies used to be the seat of a Dominican priory founded in the thirteenth century by Gaucelin des Junies. The church still stands, strongly fortified but pretty for all that and softened by the trees which press round it.

Prehistorians should note the cromlech of Roquebert, but modern historians should head for the ancient Romanesque church of La Canourgue at Canourgues, then on to Lherm, a village notable for nothing at all beyond some very lovely local architecture. Thédirac boasts another fortified church, and the prehistoric site of Montgesty has a menhir and the remains of a Roman villa at Mas-de-Rieu.

Exploring to the east of Catus you arrive first at St Denis.

Various excavations here have discovered funeral vases in the cemetery, sepulchres belonging to the Middle Ages in the presbytery of the church, and money at Py, where there is also a restored mill, the only extant building of a grouping which used to include château and chapel as well.

Mechmont has an old priory church and several mills, which are common hereabouts because of the preponderance of streams and rivers. The church at **Gigouzac** was connected to Le Vigan. Today it is much restored, but there is still a *vierge de pitié* belonging to the seventeenth century. Again, there is some lovely local architecture in the town; notably a beautiful house with *pigeonniers* and a very fine seigneurial mill with an arched entrance.

Uzech was an old pottery centre with ten factories still standing in the early 1880s. Pottery was an important industry, of course, in the days when all cooking was done on an open fire in pottery vessels. Montamel has a different sort of mill – a windmill. And the fourteenth-century church at Puycalvel and the very lovely bell-tower on the church at Murat take us to the limits of the Bouriane, which for the purposes of this book we shall regard as the N20.

North now to St Germain-du-Bel-Air on the D23, where the castle of Septfonts used to belong to the *commanderie* of the Templars of Peyrilles. The castle at Peyrilles itself was mentioned in the Treaty of Issoudun between Philippe-Auguste and Richard the Lion Heart, though it was destroyed during the Revolution. **Concorès**, to the east, is almost entirely in ruins; the ruins of the ramparts, the ruins of the priory of Lentis, and the sad ruins of the castle of Clermont, ancient home of the Toucheboeufs we met in Catus, though with the *lauze* roof of its pepper-pot tower still intact. Then there is the pilgrimage church of St Pierre de Grand Roque, appropriately enough at the foot of a cliff. The town has many old houses – one lintel reads 1696 – and the castrum used to belong to Richard Coeur-de-Lion. Nearby are the château of Veyrières and an old boundary stone at

Peyrelevade. All this in a village of some three hundred inhabitants! It is not that any little English village cannot produce a historical pedigree, but the charm of the Lot (and indeed France in general) is that so many of the buildings are still standing and still largely untrammelled by the trappings of the twentieth century.

Return to Catus by way of the churches of Degagnazes and Salvezou, thus completing your tour of the Bouriane; a land ravaged by plague, war and the English, and with nothing special to show for itself beyond one of the world's great painted caves, a few menhirs and dolmens, a couple of *bastides*, several châteaux and some fairly good ecclesiastical architecture – and of course the painted churches. These simple charming church frescos are a forgotten feature of the Lot, though they are certainly not exclusive to it. They may not merit a visit unless you are staying in the area for some time, but I would single out St André for its position and La Masse for its dancing devils as both representative and worth seeing in their own right.

10

The Gramat Causse

The *causse* of Gramat is the very heart of Quercy, the largest and wildest plateau in the Lot and the one which typifies it most. Eyes are stretched by horizons that continue into infinity, nostrils fill with the scent of the purple-flowered thyme that hugs the stony soil and the intoxicating smell of juniper. In late spring and early summer the honeysuckle trails and tangles along the hedges and scrub, smelling sweetly. Larks and grasshoppers rise at every step and hawks cruise idly by on air currents far above.

On a wet day it could be thought desolate, perhaps, though on a wet day the clouds roll round a sky that seems within touching distance and the lightning streaks along the ridges in a dramatic, unhindered fashion. On days like this the *causse* farmers stand prepared, for fire is feared in these isolated parts. But on sunny days the desolation feels far away. The sun bounces off the blistering rock and the land heats quickly as the water drains away. Oases of cool, green meadows and slow streams lie beneath cooked, cracked rock fissures. In June the wooded slopes of scrub oak and maple are green and furry, but by September they are burnt red-brown and parched and the streams have dried up. A noisy, almost tangible silence prevails, emphasized by the crickets and the rustle of snakes and lizards as they ease through the crisp, dry leaves.

So neatly, so perfectly do the *causse* villages fit into this landscape that they barely seem man-made at all. Straddling the ridges, undulating with the land, they crown the crests defiantly, so that at night a prickle of lights extends across the view like tiny beacons.

Calès is a *causse* village – one of the prettiest – but dead now like so many *causse* villages, killed by a declining economy and the fashion for second homes. It boasts two hotels: Pagès for those who like home-grown duck, the Petit Relais and its owner Geneviève Xiberas for those who like a warm welcome and a pretty setting at the centre of an exquisite village. But the real commerce of Calès is long gone. The petrol pump is closed, the post office too, and M. Maury shut the shop years ago.

The shop was his front room, filled to the brim with tins of sardines, nutty-tasting Cantal, garlic sausage and wine, stamps, postcards, brushes and mops, everything you could possibly want except for bread and meat which came by van. M. Maury himself shopped there; a new pair of espadrilles every year. The right one, he joked, for everyday wear, the left he kept for Sundays. For M. Maury had had an accident as a young man. Born in the days when boys were 'sold' at the Souillac market to farmers who needed someone to guard the sheep at night, fend off the wolves and the wild boar, he had gone to Paris in search of a dream, fallen under a tram and lost his leg. Equipped with a new wooden one, he brought his Norman wife Rose back to Calès (only a kilometre or so from his birthplace, a precariously perched farm above the road on the way down to Lacave) and raised his family, his son-in-law later becoming mayor of Rocamadour as he himself had been mayor of Calès.

Although it was a Roman site and there was once a *bastide* at Les Vitarelles, Calès today has nothing much to look at beyond the picture-postcard setting of the actual village, with its banks of lavender, its church green and the beauty of its buildings. It is a place to retire to at the end of a day; at the end of a life, maybe. There are wonderful walks to be had by following any of the small

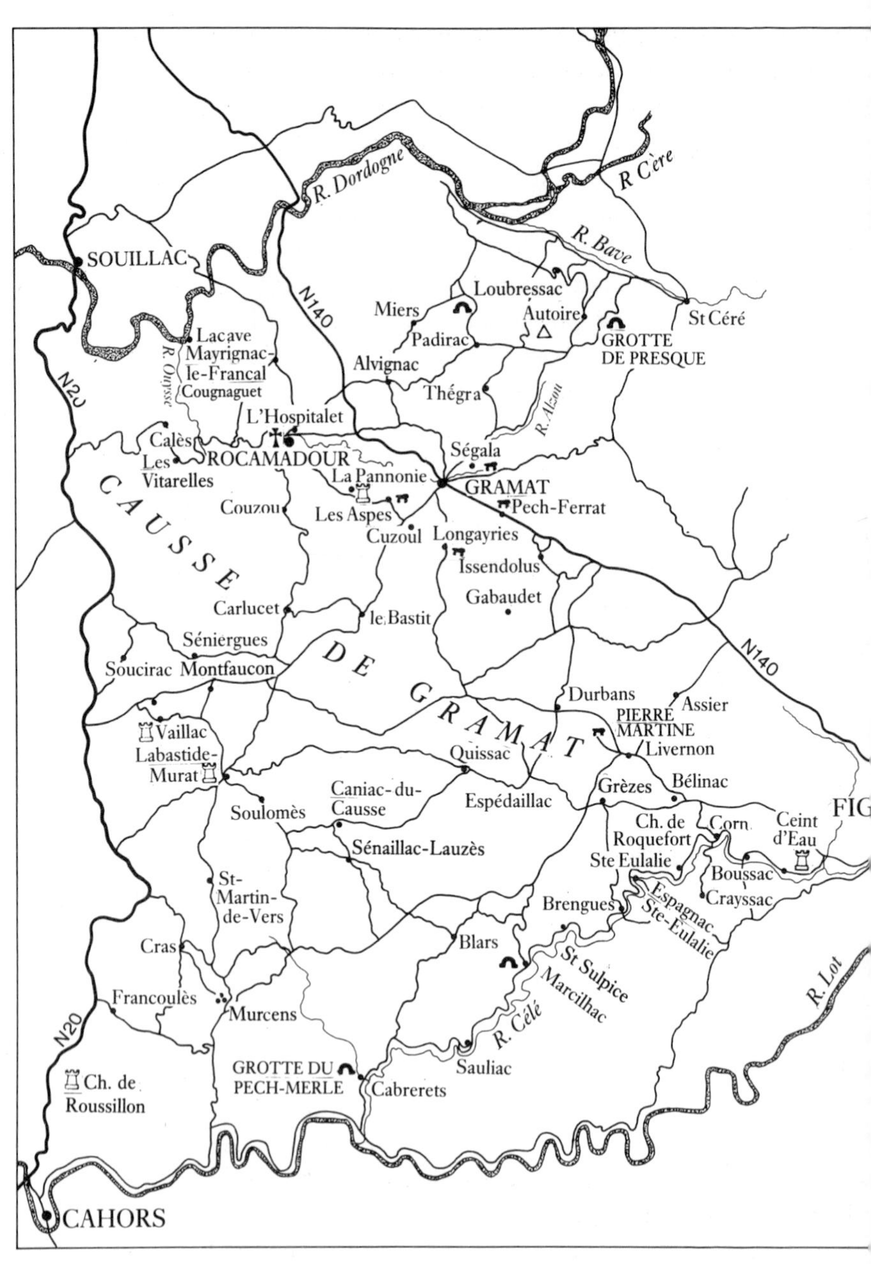
R. Dordogne
R Cère
R. Bave
SOUILLAC
N140
Loubressac
Miers
Autoire
St Céré
Padirac
GROTTE
DE PRESQUE
Lacave
Mayrignac-
le-Francal
Alvignac
N20
R. Ouysse
Cougnaguet
Thégra
R. Alzou
L'Hospitalet
Calès
Ségala
ROCAMADOUR
Les
Vitarelles
La Pannonie
GRAMAT
Pech-Ferrat
CAUSSE
Couzou
Les Aspes
Cuzoul
Longayries
Issendolus
Gabaudet
Carlucet
le Bastit
Séniergues
DE
N140
Soucirac
Montfaucon
GRAMAT
Durbans
Assier
PIERRE
MARTINE
Vaillac
Livernon
Labastide-
Murat
Quissac
Caniac-du-
Causse
Espédaillac
Grèzes
Bélinac
Soulomès
FIG
Ch. de
Roquefort
Corn
Ceint
d'Eau
Sénaillac-Lauzès
Ste Eulalie
Boussac
St-
Martin-
de-Vers
Brengues
Espagnac-
Ste-Eulalie
Crayssac
Cras
Blars
St Sulpice
Marcilhac
R. Lot
Francoulès
Murcens
R. Célé
N20
Sauliac
Ch. de
Roussillon
GROTTE DU
PECH-MERLE
Cabrerets
CAHORS

farm tracks, behind the church or alongside Pagès on the way to the eerily isolated hamlet of Terral, though watch out for guns on September Sundays when the shoot starts.

The tiny château of Calès and almost all of the houses have views that defy description. The village is decked with flowers and only springs to sudden life in the evenings with the return of the *troupeau*. Clanking bells herald its arrival, then the tiny street is a surging wave of wool; cartoon sheep, these, with their long arched noses, eyes ringed with black and ears that droop dejectedly, giving them a hangdog expression. They are shorn close because of the heat as much as the wool, and there are a couple of bearded goats to keep them in place.

The D673 leaves Calès to the south and winds through Les Vitarelles to Rocamadour. On the way a sign to the left indicates the fortified mill of Cougnaguet. **Cougnaguet** is a water-mill on the Ouysse, a limpid, green-weeded stream here, lined with tall poplars. The track down to the mill (which leads on to Lacave and the lovely church of Mayrignac-le-Francal) is also the GR6 for part of the way, for ramblers coming from Rocamadour to Lacave. It is a narrow road, newly tarmacked, with enormous hunks of limestone towering above and over you in smoothed-out river shapes. You can see quite clearly how and where the Ouysse has worn the rock away.

The mill is thirteenth-century and in working order – you can watch the flour being milled – but it is the setting of water and stone that never fails to delight. Fish slide amongst the weeds, eyeing the mayflies, and the spot can hardly have changed in centuries.

The jewel in the crown of the Gramat *causse* and, some might say, in all Quercy, is **Rocamadour**. Approaching it this way, along the D673, you would be well advised to stop the car at l'Hospitalet and look down on the site, but there is no doubt that the best view is from the road on the opposite side of the Alzou Gorge, on the D32 from Couzou. Rocamadour is classed as the second site of

France after Mont St Michel and, looking down on the village from l'Hospitalet, one is left in no doubt as to why. The tiny River Alzou has carved an enormous canyon in the rock; the sheer cliff face rises about 150 metres and clinging to that cliff face for dear life is Rocamadour.

It is easy to become ambivalent about Rocamadour over the years, torn as one is between its beauty and its commercialism. In summer the tiny roads are made more dangerous by coachloads of tourists bused in to see the sight. Often you have to queue to get into the town for the roads are so narrow that they can only cope with one-way traffic. Coaches inch their way through the town gates in danger of demolishing the whole arch and, although the town has long been used to tourists and their tacky ways, I find it hard to believe that the Middle Ages can ever have been quite as gaudy as this. The shops are full of over-priced rubbish: you fight your way down a street displaying giant chocolate walnuts, waxwork figures, named pottery bowls and stuffed sheep.

But you never get blasé and disillusioned about the setting. That thrills every time; indeed one feels that of all the miracles wrought at Rocamadour, the greatest is the one that keeps the houses from slipping into the ravine. There have been disasters in its history, of course. Rock falls have occurred, one demolishing the original shrine, and I doubt that any visitor gets through a visit without glancing up at that enormous overhang of limestone with some degree of awe.

As Venice is built on canals, so Rocamadour is built on steps. Defeatists can take the lift to the top and walk down, but true pilgrims climb the 216 steps to the Black Virgin on their knees. I remember one wet day, when the rain sat in puddles on indentations in the steps, coming across just such a person. Impeccably dressed in French classic style, she wore a silk dress whose skirt was permanently pleated. Nearly at the top, she had paused for a while to recite her rosary and recover her breath. She knelt there, head bowed under the grey sky, in a grey village, in her grey dress, the hem of which had become black with wet, streaks soaking up to her waist. Her pearls dangled in amongst the rosary, her good shoes were scuffed from the stone steps, and when she rose at the top a long time later, her stockings were laddered from knee to ankle. I wondered then about the commercialism of the place and at how much more at ease I felt with that than with this display of piety, which somehow shocked me in its sophistication.

You do not have to be a believer, however, to be moved by the **Black Virgin**. She has a mystical quality all her own. Naked now to preserve the wood (she used to be covered with tulle and before that silver), her medieval appearance tends to belie the claim that she is a ninth-century work, if not earlier. The chapel in which she sits is a dark, smoke-blackened cavern with sheer rock for walls, to which are pinned a million votive offerings and marble plaques with '*merci*' inscribed on them, including one from the mother of Fénelon. Toy ships hang from the ceiling, describing miraculous escapes, for sailors used to invoke the Virgin of Rocamadour in times of peril at sea, and the bell in the roof is supposed to ring of its own accord whenever a miracle has been wrought. The place is lit entirely by candles. Jesus sits on the Virgin's knee, both figures adopting a slightly rigid pose, and there is a definite family resemblance between the mother and the little old man who sits on her lap. Who knows where she came from, or how old she is, but kings and saints have worshipped at her feet and maybe because of that she has a magical power, something almost tangible, that to a believer may well be potent.

Although Rocamadour was a stopping point on the way to Santiago of Compostela, it was also a place of pilgrimage in its own right, in an era when pilgrimage was taken very seriously indeed. It was no mean undertaking in the Middle Ages to set out on foot to cross countries and sometimes continents, which was why pilgrimage was often imposed as a penance and in some cases replaced prison. Many Dutch and Belgian prisoners were forced to Rocamadour, and a Belgian law in Liège stated: 'Any person who strikes another without breaking a limb but leaving marks will be obliged to make the pilgrimage to Rocamadour on foot.' Wills were written before departure and what were often final goodbyes made to the family. The carrot was, at the very least, full remission of sins, but inevitably what began as a search for salvation very often ended up as a pragmatic search for benefits in the present. And there must have been genuine travellers among the pilgrims, people who thrilled at the sight of new places and different customs. Rocamadour, one of the most famous shrines of the Middle Ages, must have satisfied them on all counts.

Legend has it that Zaccheus, the publican who climbed a tree the better to see Christ as He passed, disciple, and husband of St Veronica, drifted into Aquitaine on a boat, made his way to Quercy and lived the life of a hermit in the rocks. Here he built two oratories, one to the Virgin and one to the Apostles, and the locals called him Amator, lover; lover of solitude, lover of Mary, lover of rock – Roc Amadour, as the little village which grew up round the oratories came to be known. Historians have failed to come up with anything that could legitimize this claim, but belief is more powerful than fact, and the discovery of a body under the Virgin's shrine in 1166 gave further credence to this particular belief. Rocamadour exploded into one of Europe's most important shrines. Heretics were forced there in chains but others came voluntarily and the shrine grew rich, so rich that the big abbey of Tulle in the Corrèze began squabbling with Marcilhac further south about possession. Up until then, Marcilhac had taken no interest in Rocamadour, allowing it to run down. Now it fought to keep it – and lost. The Rocamadour monks established hospices all along the Compostela road and so influential were they in Porto that natives of that town still talk of 'going to Rocamadour' when they mean hospital.

The shrine owes much of its popularity to the patronage of an English king, for Henry II was an early visitor. Wanting to press home his wife Eleanor's claim to Toulouse, and hearing of the discovery of the body which was immediately presumed to be that of Zaccheus or St Amadour, he sped to the shrine, prostrated himself before the body, covered it with silver and beseeched the Saint for help in besieging Toulouse – unsuccessfully. Henry was to return to Rocamadour, this time to make a rather more worthy promise. Kneeling before the Virgin this time, he vowed reconciliation with Becket. To this too, however, the Virgin turned an apparently deaf ear. But these failures did not deter other great men. Louis XI came, as did Philippe III, Philippe le Bel, Charles VII, St Dominic and Simon de Montfort, St Bernard, St Engelbert of Cologne, St Christopher, St Anthony of Padua and St Benoît. Bertrand de Born and Gauthier de Coincy sang of it.

> The Sweet Mother of the Creator
> Has Her Church in Rochemadour
> She makes so many miracles, so many beautiful deeds,
> That a very beautiful book was made on this subject
>
> from *Miracle of the Candle*, de Coincy

Anyone who was anyone came to Rocamadour. In more recent times the composer François Poulenc wrote of his experiences there: 'Alone, face to face with the Virgin who was without sin, I suddenly received an indisputable sign, a stab of grace in the heart.'

Six gates survive today, but in medieval times the town was much larger and very heavily defended. It needed to be, for the English, among others, were keen to capture its wealth. In 1369 John Chandos succeeded, but the most shocking of the crimes perpetrated against Rocamadour was carried out by an earlier Englishman. Henry Court Mantel, son of Henry II who so venerated the shrine and an evil, selfish, quarrelsome man, was caught up in one of the endless rows that dogged that family. Fiercely at war with his brother Richard the Lion-Heart, Henry found himself unable to pay his soldiers and turned to that unforgivable crime of the Middle Ages, sacrilege. Ill from a wound received at Limoges, tired and angry, he found himself at Martel along with his faithful friend Bertrand de Born, the troubadour. Henry had already announced his plan to be crowned king of Aquitaine at Rocamadour, so gathering together his retinue he rode across the *causse* to the shrine on the pretext of a pilgrimage. His intentions, however, were far from honourable. Once there he stole from the shrine every treasure and valuable he could lay hands on, even the silver that his father had placed on the body years before. He made it back to Martel and the house now known as the Maison Fabri, but once he was there the Virgin acted, his wound worsened and he developed a fever. And it was there he died, in 1183, aged only 28, lying on a bed of sackcloth and ashes, weighed down by the weight of an enormous cross, in an agony of guilt, with Bertrand at his side. Though his father's pardon arrived in time, the king had nevertheless been shocked by his son's death and ranted and raged at de Born, who was later to return to the shrine on his knees.

There are other chapels in Rocamadour, but none has the magic of the **Chapelle Miraculeuse**, although the twelfth-century frescos depicting the Annunciation and the Visitation in the Chapel of St Michael are well preserved and in a dramatic position under the precipice. The basilica of **St Sauveur** dates from the eleventh century and has a moving wood carving of Christ. Underneath St Sauveur lies the crypt of St Amadour, where the relics of the Saint are kept with modern paintings depicting the finding of the body and events in his life. Three further chapels, St John the Baptist, St Joachim, and St Anne and St Blaise, lead off the main square.

In the rock face above Chapelle Notre Dame is a sword said to be the famous Durandal, ancient sword of Roland and sent here after the Paladin's death in the Pass of Roncesvalles, although since Rocamadour was virtually unknown at that time this seems unlikely. At best it is a replica, but some say that the sword belonged to Henry Court Mantel, who left his own in exchange for the mighty Durandal during the pillaging of the shrine. Rocamadour, though, is just such a mixture of fact and fiction, and if it disappoints it is not because of the commercialism so much as the fact that the restoration, close up, has not been handled as sensitively as it might. Apart from a few buildings like the curious thirteenth-century *'lo poumeti'*, most have a slightly 'new' feel to them, although the old mill of Roquefrège and the accompanying houses down by the Alzou are charming in their medieval appearance, with their steep-pitched roofs and wobbly walls.

There is a Treasure at Rocamadour which you can see for a price and if you follow the steep path along the Stations of the Cross up to the château you get the sort of stupendous view from the ramparts – a sheer 150-metre drop to the Alzou – that makes people like me want to get down on all fours and crawl away!

From the château you can walk back to l'Hospitalet, past the towering Jerusalem cross brought by barefoot pilgrims. L'Hospitalet was, as its name suggests, a succouring place for pilgrims, and ruins of the old St John's hospice can still be seen. From l'Hospitalet there are some less erudite tourist activities to be enjoyed; namely the caves with a few engravings and paintings and what is called the Forêt des Singes. If, however, a nagging voice at the back of your mind asks what on earth monkeys have to do with a medieval pilgrimage site in the middle of France, then follow the signs to watch a more appropriate hawking display, where an Englishman flies hawks and eagles across the gorge.

A last look at Rocamadour as the sun sets, faults concealed at this distance. At the height of the town's prosperity, thirty thousand people might have gathered, making their way on foot across the stony *causse* in an inhospitable land of bears and wolves and robbers. One Easter, in 1403, the Dordogne boatman helped 3,918 people to cross the river between Creysse and Montvalent, one of the main pilgrimage routes. Images remain: the pulleys to haul suitcases up from the main street to hotel windows; Rocamadour lit up at night by its *son et lumière* display; soaring eagles over the shrine; but the secret of Rocamadour lies somewhere between the stiff, dark, walnut Virgin and the well-coiffured woman struggling towards her on bruised knees.

Leaving l'Hospitalet, take the D673 north-east to Alvignac. I have never much cared for Alvignac, it has always seemed something of an anachronism, stuck as it is right in the middle of the Gramat *causse* and looking like a very poor version of Vichy. It is too tidy, too clean, too spa-like. It is a spa, of course, and the waters of Miers, which is the little village to the north, were well known to the Romans and Frenchmen of the eighteenth century. The waters come from the source Salmière, a large, neat lake between the two villages. The high sodium sulphurate content of the waters is said to be good for liver complaints, so one might expect half France to be queuing round the town, but Alvignac is absolutely quiet.

Continue on down the road to Padirac, turning left up the D14 to Loubressac. On the way you will pass a monument on the right commemorating the enormous arms drop of 14 July 1944. Six hundred parachutes carried the weaponry down to the Maquis on the *causse* below. **Loubressac** itself is a delightful village in an elevated position above the river valleys of the Bave and the Dordogne. I first came across it *en fête*, with streamers hanging across the road and a noisy band playing. Whether or not it can be described as a *causse* village is a moot point, as we are now only about twelve kilometres from St Céré, but it seems to me to stand on the very edge, as the views from the château across wide, sweeping, green pastoral land confirmed in the days when it was open to the public. Probably because of this position a small English colony has put down roots here – but don't let that put you off.

The château used to be one of the few Lot castles open to the public. Restored by the playwright Henri Lavedan, it is far from being the medieval fortress the English besieged in 1352. The current building dates mostly from the seventeenth century and served as headquarters for the English mission to the area during World War Two. In recent years, however, it has been closed and (rumour has it) gutted and sold off in job lots, much to the consternation of the villagers, so visitors can no longer enjoy the marvellous view from its terraces across the river valley to the red, glowing castle of Castelnau.

From the village take the D135 and descend to **Autoire**, another astonishingly pretty village of manor houses and turrets, pepper-pot towers and *pigeonniers*, buried deep in a wild gorge; almost every building, from the Château of Lémargue to the Mairie has some architectural merit. Climbing back up to the D673, you can stop at the parking spot provided and make your way on foot round the *cirque*, for magnificent views around this amphitheatre of rock. If the weather has not been too dry, the path gives good views of a series of waterfalls, one of which drops about 30 metres, whilst above you a rocky stronghold, another *château des anglais*, affords a breathtaking view over Autoire and its *cirque*.

If you are a cave addict the Presque caves are nearby, but otherwise head back along the D677 towards the Gramat *causse* proper and the town of Gramat itself. Lavergne, through which the road runs, used to be the seat of a Benedictine priory and still has a good fifteenth-century church, but nowadays it is the beautiful *pigeonnier* porch there which merits a mention, although the setting leaves something to be desired. Thégra, to the north, has a fifteenth-century château, not open to the public, but worth a look if you are idling away the day, with its four pepper-pot towers presenting as delightful a roofscape as imaginable. This is the sort of manor house one dreams of acquiring through the sad death of a long-lost uncle.

Gramat does not figure much in guide books since, in spite of its history as the seat of an important baronry, it does not possess one notable historical building. But it is a pretty town for all that, reminiscent of the West Riding, with its wide central square, comfortable hotel and old houses. Gramat comes into its own as a market town – lambs, horses, truffles, cars, nuts; you name it. It is also the home of the French Police Training Centre for Handlers and Their Dogs, and in summer you can see the dogs being put through their paces, though one cannot imagine that there is much in the Lot to sniff out apart from truffles and the odd potholer.

The barony was a dependency of the viscount of Turenne and knew a stormy time in the Hundred Years War when it was captured by the English several times. During the Wars of Religion its Protestant lord, Gontaut d'Auriolle, helped Henry of Navarre across the *causse* to Cahors before the siege in which it was finally taken.

Prehistory addicts can spend a happy day visiting the tumulus marked on the Michelin map called Etron de Gargantua, and the area is positively littered with dolmens at Gabaudet, Bournerie, Plassous, Pech-Ferrat, Les Aspes, Segala, Terrou, Longayrie and Cavagnac, as well as the mesolithic earthworks at Cuzoul.

Issendolus, south-east of Gramat by about eight kilometres, was a hospice founded by the Knights of Malta in 1220, of which some remains, notably the chapterhouse, are still visible. The *causse* was full of these hospices, which catered for pilgrims *en route* to Rocamadour and beyond.

Livernon, with its tiny market hall half-way up the hill, its long tree-lined boulevard leading to Assier, its beautiful Romanesque belfry and its *routier* with the memorable name of Chez Lulu, is actually more famous as the centre of yet another area of megalithic monuments.

If you are only going to see one dolmen then it should, I suppose, be the Lot's largest and most famous. It lies to the north-west of Livernon, off the D2, and is well signposted. You park the car and walk across fields to the site, typical *causse* country, with the stony ground much in evidence, awash with thyme and yellow rock-roses. The table stone of **Pierre Martine** weighs a little over 20 tonnes. It is over three metres high and seven metres long – truly massive, though slightly spoiled by the concrete blocks put there to support it in 1966 after it had broken in 1948. Before that date you could oscillate the table stone with merely the pressure of a little finger, something which caught the imagination of Françoise Sagan when she visited.

Like many dolmens, Pierre Martine is built on a hill, though hedges, bushes and trees obscure the view somewhat. The name has existed for at least five centuries, it seems. There is a record of December 1489 detailing the sale of the place to a Figeac hotelier. An even older reference of 1397 to 'Martina' would appear to refer to the same place. The stone was quarried from a spot only yards away and the oscillation was unlikely to have been accidental; many table stones in France and England were deliberately balanced in such a way. Whatever the mysteries of the megalithic religion, this dolmen was held in no less esteem by the local seventeenth-century peasants, who believed that if you could cover it with flowers without being seen you would be protected from sickness for the rest of the year. Nearby at Bélinac, a tiny hamlet to the south-east, one of the Lot's few remaining menhirs, or standing stones, was subject to the same superstition.

Grèzes, with its pretty dew pond, at the junction of the D653 with the D13, was an old Templar *commanderie* as were Durbans, Soulomès and Espédaillac to the west, which also has some Roman remains at Champ-du-Sel. Quissac on the D146 has a place in one of the Lot's legends concerning St Namphaise, an officer of Charlemagne's army who left the soldiering life to become a hermit. It is supposed that he travelled through Quercy with Pépin le Bref and was drawn back to the area later on, establishing a monastery first of all before leaving the community for a life of solitude in the Braunhie, the rocky area around Gramat. Water was scarce in this limestone land and even today one comes across *sourciers* or water diviners. St Namphaise, then, apparently spent his days hollowing out depressions in the rock so that beasts and wild animals could drink. The whole Braunhie, winter, spring, summer and autumn, resounded to the echo of his hammer. The shepherds thought highly of this man – no longer did they have to lead their flocks for miles to water them – and even today any dew pond in the area is still called a St Namphaise lake. The saint had a sad end, however, torn to pieces by a mad bull at Quissac. He was interred in an oratory dedicated to St Martin, which later became the church at **Caniac-du-Causse**, south-west of Quissac on the D71. The present church is alarmingly modern, unlike the old hound chained up opposite who looked as though he might have been there since St Namphaise's days, but the old twelfth-century crypt remains and it is here that one can see the eleventh-century reliquary containing the relics of St Namphaise.

Quissac, however, has its own church, that of St Gilles, in which there is one of a number of Lot *pietàs* which formed the basis of an exhibition several years ago. This particular one dates from the beginning of the sixteenth century. It is a naïve study. Mary, hands clasped in prayer, looks down at her son, who lies outstretched on her knees. *Rigor mortis* has obviously set in, for His head, unsupported, lies level with His body. Only His thin arms, ending in enormous hands, fall free. Sénaillac-Lauzès, also down the D71 and south of Caniac, has another *pietà* in its church. This one, a seventeenth-century wood sculpture, is a much more sophisticated work. Christ's limp body is supported by a young woman with Mediterranean features.

Blars, south-east of Sénaillac Lauzès on the D17, is another of those typical Quercy villages which so delight the eye. The church, which used to be a priory of nearby Marcilhac Abbey, has a cupola and historiated pillars depicting apocalyptic animals and a curious sculpture of a bearded man, hands pulled in opposite directions, one by the Devil, the other by an angel. The Romanesque door has sculptures of grimacing men holding up the arch and of Christ before Pontius Pilate.

Back on to the D653, now, and turn left and west until you reach the Labastide Murat turn (D32), then watch out for the left-hand turn to Cras, another Templar village but a gateway, too, for the cul-de-sac that ends in the oppidum of **Mursens**. Here, high on a grassy, isolated hill, is another of the Uxellodonum candidates. In terms of gut reaction this is the one that speaks loudest to me.

I can well imagine being besieged on this lonely upland, waiting for Caesar's revenge. There are more Roman remains at Cours, three kilometres due south, including stones of the Roman aqueduct that took the waters of the Vers to Cahors.

Francoulès, to the north-west on the D49, through wild and deeply wooded countryside, has an old church with a sixteenth-century Entombment, but it is the nearby church of St Pierre de Liversou which has the frescos. The Romanesque apse is filled with a Christ in Majesty, Christ himself in flowing robes being ministered to by an angel and what is supposed to be a dove but looks more like a cross between a crow and a blackbird. The walls depict the Annunciation and the Three Wise Men. This tiny churchyard is situated above the road and miles from anywhere, but it has not managed to escape that universal scourge of France – a graveyard full of cheap, faded, plastic flowers.

The romantic ruins of the château of **Roussillon** can be seen from the N20 although you can make your way through the hills on the D22. The fortress was an important one, erected in the twelfth century, passing from one famous Quercy family to another. The original owner, Pons de Roussillon, was a knight in the Avignon court of Pope Jean XXII. Come the nineteenth century it was a total ruin, pillaged and ransacked by war and weather. Recently, though, it has been undergoing restoration, winning first prize in the 1966 Work of Art in Peril competition. The restoration has meant that the château can now open its doors to summer visitors, though the only taker on my last visit was a tortoiseshell cat perched in an arrow slit on one of the huge towers that protects the entrance. The walls here are three metres thick, and are themselves protected by a deep ditch or moat which you cross by a drawbridge, giving you a very good idea of the strength of the place. It its day this was one of the strongholds of Guyenne.

There is something very appealing about Labastide-Murat, which you reach by heading north up the N20 and then taking the D677 to the right. An alternative would be to take the slow road through the beautiful village of **St Martin-de-Vers**, which used to be the seat of the residence of the abbot of Marcilhac in the fifteenth century. Approaching from the south, you descend into the village over a sea of roofs dominated by the lovely church tower. **Labastide-Murat** has none of the picturesque appeal of St Martin and does not even have many of the typical *bastide* characteristics; but it is an honest, spacious, workaday sort of place with a marvellous hat shop. Originally it was called Labastide-Fortanière after its founder, a son of the Gourdon family, but many years later its name was changed in memory of a more famous local son. For it was from the old inn in a side street that the future king of Naples, Joachim Murat, set out for his life as a soldier in Napoleon's army. Later on he married Napoleon's sister Caroline, a step that did his career no harm at all, although he was acknowledged a brave, almost foolhardy, soldier.

Born in the village in 1767, Murat later built a superb château for his brother André. Approached by a magnificent avenue of plane trees, the château owes nothing to the medieval: this is pure Empire. The more humble *auberge* has been turned into a museum with letters and mementoes of Murat and his mother, on whom he doted.

Soulomès, to the south-east of Labastide-Murat, has a Gothic church with some interesting frescos. Soulomès used to be a Templar *commanderie* of some importance and although the frescos may have been painted after the dissolution of the Templars their subject matter is extremely interesting. Here at last are some contentious figures which may throw a chink of light on the mystical and esoteric practices of an order which was dissolved under the charge of heresy. Jesus is seen walking in the garden with Mary Magdalene and on the north wall is the enigmatic figure of St Thomas. It is thought by some that the Templars believed Christ to be married to the Magdalene, and the idea of St Thomas as Jesus's twin is an ancient and persistent heresy, Thomas in Hebrew meaning twin. One of the few stories concerning Thomas in the New Testament records his scepticism about the Resurrection – 'doubting Thomas' (John 21:25). Another of the paintings depicts Christ alongside a Knight of Malta after the Resurrection; in this area too there are doubts about the Templars' beliefs. The other painting is of the Entombment. All this is speculation, of course. The only real proof of the Templar period at Soulomès is the font, which is covered with their unmistakable crosses.

Retrace your steps to Labastide-Murat, take the D10 northwards and then the left turn to the D17 which will allow you to drive past the heavily fortified castle of **Vaillac**, which belonged to a branch of the Gourdon family. It is a marvellous ensemble of towers, turrets, keeps, machicolation and those immensely pleasing round towers which end in sliced-off sloping roofs and which to me always spell sun and heat. Rejoin the D10 and head for Montfaucon, another *bastide*, and easily spotted from a distance because of the massive PTT (post office) convalescent home which dominates the hill on which the village stands.

Montfaucon is one of the prettiest *bastides* in the Lot, with its little streets and market hall still intact. It was built by the English under Edward II, and then captured by the French in 1441. The church has a very sweet, naïve fifteenth-century sculpture of the Virgin and Child in a niche and invariably the door is decorated with juniper bushes, an old wedding custom in the Lot. The night before a marriage, friends of the groom cut juniper bushes from the *causse* and place them round the church door, along the processional route and by the bride's house. Friends of the bride decorate the bushes with white and pink paper roses. A heart of juniper with the initials of the couple intertwined is fixed above the church door. The reason for the choice of juniper appears to have been lost in the mists of time.

Séniergues on the D10 to the north is a well situated village dominated by its Romanesque church and *gentilhommière*. The views all around here are spectacular, but to reach the highest point of the *causse* you have to make for Soucirac to the west. **Le**

Bastit, on the Gramat road (D677) eastwards, is a deserted little village lying just off the main road, so deserted that I have never been able to track down the vestiges of the Roman villa purported to be in the village. Blank stares of incredulity were all I could get from the two villagers I could raise, though people are universally helpful. Le Bastit was a *commanderie*, as the château and farm can still testify. There is also a Roman fountain, a Virgin's grotto and a very pretty tower, Tour de la Dîme, with a dovecot – not bad going for a village with just over 100 inhabitants.

Carlucet, on the D50 east of Le Bastit, is a strange village built on two levels on the side of a hill. Turn right here to one of my favourite *causse* villages and names: **Couzou**. Couzou is long and straggly, with some beautiful houses ripe for restoration or ruin and a couple of very beautiful barns. The village was wiped out in the Hundred Years War but the place is more ancient than that. There are vestiges of human habitation here which go back to 500 BC.

From Couzou you can make your way easily to the Moulin du Saut for a pleasant stroll by the Alzou or you can follow the tiny roads west to the extraordinary hamlet of **La Pannonie**. To call this village off the beaten track would be an understatement, but once there you come across what is really a village green. The church is an architectural hotchpotch of the seventeenth century, and although the roof rises at the east end, the tower is at the west, as if added on as an afterthought. Almost certainly this chapel belonged to the truly enormous château which dominates the green with its arched gate, which must be at least seven metres high.

It is difficult to tell which is the front of the château and which the back, but what appears to be the back is a graceful curved edifice with two delapidated wings. The front is eighteenth-century, set in English-style parkland with enormous and graceful trees, where magnificent-looking cattle graze on luscious grass. Cattle are rarely seen on the *causse*. So is grass. Their home is a huge and beautiful barn to the right of the small road, and La Pannonie had its origins in the barn, a Cistercian one belonging to the abbey of Aubazine in the Corrèze. It was in the late fifteenth century that Pierre de la Grange, a Rocamadour merchant, started work on his château.

At La Pannonie, with the château behind you, the green and the church to your left, a slight Englishness in the air, you look out across the *causse*, and if the architecture here does not exactly typify the Gramat *causse*, then the silence, the sheep-dotted view and the hot sun on your head do. Not for the first time today one thinks of Saint-Pol-Roux: '. . . . *Si pur le troupeau! que ce soir estival, il semble neiger vers la plaine enfantine*. . . '

11

Souillac: 1

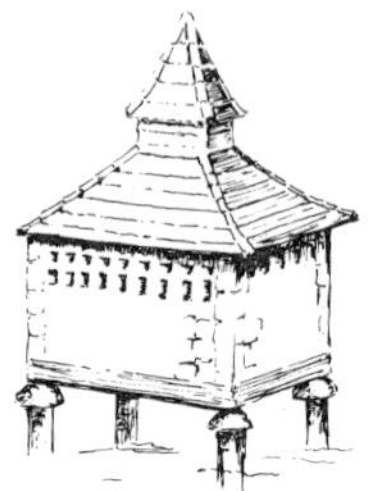

Souillac, gateway to the Lot, stands, confusingly, on the River Dordogne and belongs in spirit to the Périgord. The name comes from *souilh*, meaning a muddy place where wild boar wallow, and indeed the coat of arms of Souillac depicts a wild boar.

The Dordogne is a long and graceful river. Swallows and housemartins dip into its waters in the summer and there are kingfishers too. It is wide and swift-flowing here, especially after heavy rain in the Monts Dore, and the Souillagais make the most of it with riverside walks shaded by huge poplars. There are several bathing points, though one should beware of the current, and even a diving board opposite the campsite. It is all within an easy walk from the town: past the laundry and through fields of maize alongside the allotments, where old men still have time to stop and talk and offer you a handful of strawberries. 'Scratch a Frenchman and you will find a peasant', wrote Walter Schwarz in *The Guardian*, with some justification.

Souillac, like Cahors, is divided by the N20, but it is not quite big enough to overcome this disadvantage and tends to prostitute itself to the tourists who stop *en route* to or from Spain, attracted by the string bags of pâté by the Codec goose and the sight of English papers outside the Maison de la Presse.

They sit in the cafés and *pâtisseries* that line the main road, bronzed and competitive, telling travellers' tales to each other with that I've-been-further-than-you air, whilst the British 'locals' walk by quickly, pretending to be French and feeling superior. Who wants crowded beaches anyway? they think, with a furious look at the sun disappearing behind a black cloud.

Stray off the road, though, down the hill, and Souillac becomes itself again. The **market** is on Fridays, spilling out from under the old market hall and even back up the hill and across The Road. A better vegetable market, this one, than at Gourdon, and there are lots of flowers and herbs, honey and cheese. There are fish stalls too, though, unlike Gourdon, Souillac boasts an excellent fish shop of its own, whose iced white slab is alive with *langoustines* and other delights.

There is a jumble of old streets and squares. In the Place de la Nau, you can see an old pilgrims' hospice with the Compostela cockleshell carved above the doorway. In the Place de Rancon there is a fifteenth-century tower. And there are some good hotels and restaurants. The Nouvel Hôtel has just reopened. I generally go by car these days, but it was the stuff that dreams are made of to fall off the train after the long journey from London and into a meal of thrush pâté, a dozen *escargots* stuffed with *causse* herbs, a rich, thick, black *coq au Vieux Cahors* served with stuffed artichoke hearts, then cheese and half a melon filled with Monbazillac. And just as well, for the juggernauts seemed to thunder not so much past the bedroom as through it.

Even if you do not like Souillac, if the N20 is too much and the villas on the hill too modern, give it time. Wander the old town and do not, whatever you do, leave without seeing the church.

The church is one of those magnificent ones built in the Périgord Romanesque style with cupolas, and inside there is a Romanesque sculpture of such magnificence that it assures this little town a place on the map for as long as it survives. It is in fact an abbatial church, and tradition has it that St Eloy founded the community. There are no records of the existence of a monastery until after the tenth century, although there are the vestiges of an early Carolingian church under the choir. However, as St Eloy was born at Chaptelat near Limoges in about 590 BC, it seems quite a likely story.

Eloy was a goldsmith's apprentice who showed such aptitude that he was soon on his way to Paris to work for Clotaire II who had a yen for a golden throne. Clearly an opportunist, Eloy made two thrones and immediately became court favourite, exalted in Dagobert's reign to be Master of the Mint. Noted for his eloquence, he turned his attention to evangelizing Flanders and was made bishop of Noyon and Tournai before returning to the Limousin to found the abbey of Solignac, which slightly resembles Souillac.

The Souillac abbey was a dependency of the big abbey church at Aurillac, and Géraud of St Céré was the first Benedictine prior. Soon the marshy land had been reclaimed and cultivated and the town grew up outside the fortified abbey walls. The abbey finally gained its independence in 1473, but then, as with all old buildings in this part of the world, history ran its course; and anything which managed to survive the Hundred Years War, as the abbey did, usually managed to get knocked for six in the Wars of Religion. So, having been rebuilt in 1351 and 1356 (thanks to English excesses), the abbey succumbed to Protestant pillaging and finally to fire in 1572, which destroyed everything except the church.

The church dates from the twelfth century and is very solid and massive, whilst at the same time remaining very pleasing to the eye, with its ranks of circular and semicircular buildings, cupolas and polygonal apse. This is pure and nearly unadulterated Romanesque, much better than Cahors and more than enough to uplift the soul of any lover of the style. The cupolas are roofed in *lauze*, the rest in canal tiles. Inside there is a single nave, which gives a feeling of spaciousness, ending in a semicircular choir with Romanesque windows under the vaulting and polygonal chapels which open from the apse. The three cupolas (the third is across the transept) are 33 metres high.

All this will at first be mere impression, though, for you will undoubtedly have been halted by the west door. This door would seem to belong to the Toulouse School. Some say it is the work of a Burgundian who came to work with the craftsmen of Moissac and Toulouse. It dates from around 1130 and one can only regret that so much of it was damaged by the Protestants during the Wars of Religion. It was turned inwards during seventeenth-century restoration work.

Your eye is drawn straight away to the figure of Isaiah on the right, his cloak swirling around his body, every fold sculptured in. His beard, too, is flowing and he has a smiling, compassionate face, albeit mutilated. The figure seems to move. Next you are caught by the extraordinary pillars of intertwined animals – lions, birds, half-devoured men depicting, so it is said, the seven deadly sins, but seeming much more pagan. They resemble those at Moissac (Tarn-et-Garonne) and Beaulieu (Corrèze). Opposite Isaiah is another figure, generally said to be Joseph but thought by some to be the prophet Osee. You will pick out other figures: St Peter and an abbot holding a cross, thought to be St Benoît. Also depicted are the semi-naked Cain and Abel, and Abraham, clutching Isaac to his breast, knife raised.

Above the door in bas-relief is the story of Théophile the Monk, who signed a pact with the Devil as an act of revenge, having been moved from his post as treasurer of the monastery of Adana. Repenting, Théophile prayed to the Virgin, who appeared to him in a dream clutching the agreement which she had snatched from the Devil. As Freda White points out in *Three Rivers of France*, the only person who ever emerges from these legends with any credit is the Devil, tricked out of every pact he ever makes.

Apart from the door there are some Romanesque capital heads in the choir, depicting Daniel and the Lion and plenty of doves and foliage. Of the paintings, the one showing Christ in the Garden of Olives is by Théodore Chasseriau, a disciple of Ingres.

Across the Place de l'Abbaye in the Place St Martin are the

ruins of what used to be the old parochial church. Only the sixteenth-century belfry is extant, as it too suffered at the hands of the Calvinists. It has a bas-relief belonging to the twelfth century, showing Christ in Judgment between the Virgin and St John.

Souillac, however, has lost its other sculpture, the Junoesque lady who used to stand outside an antique shop on the south side of town. A large breast had escaped from the folds of her robes and dangled amongst the basket of fruit she clutched to her body in such a way that fruit and breast were barely distinguishable and one was left with the titillating fear that some unsuspecting consumer might accidentally gather up the wrong item.

12

Souillac: 2

The Dordogne Valley

After Souillac the majestic Dordogne continues its rocky way eastwards before taking a ninety-degree turn at Bretenoux and heading off into the Massif Central.

Lovers of that fashionable stretch of river in the *département* of the same name will like this Lotois piece of the Dordogne almost as much, although the edges are a bit rougher. All those 'British' Dordogne ingredients are here: roads that wind along river banks caught between the water on one side and tall cliffs on the other; villages that climb up cliff-faces or develop, ribbon-fashion, along the water's edge. With this similarity comes, unfortunately, a similarity of prices and you will pay more for drinks and meals and see more tourists along this stretch than you will in practically any other part of the Lot.

That said, it is an interesting stretch of water with a variety of sights, including the picturesque quaintness of Carennac and one of the most famous military castles in France – Castelnau. But if it is purely scenery you want, then this Dordogne valley, for all its magnificent grandeur, does not to my mind compare with the less well known, less sophisticated charms of the Célé.

You will be reminded frequently on this trip of the Dordogne's former navigability by signs all along the route which read Port de Souillac; Port de Pinsac; Port de Creysse; Port de Carennac; Port de Gluges – from these the plentiful juniper berries of the *causse* began their journey to Dutch gin distilleries.

Make your way through Pinsac, having turned off the N20 on the outskirts of Souillac to follow the D43, and across the river you will come to the beautifully sited **Château de la Treyne** which stands on a cliff above the river. In autumn the creeper and the shrubs on the cliff turn bright red. The water rushes past at the foot of the rock, flowing quite fast and deep on that side. The château, rebuilt in Louis XIII's reign, has a round tower on its east wing and used to be open to the public. It still is, in a way, for it has now been turned into a château hotel and a far prettier one in my view than the famous château hotel of the Lot, Mercuès. It stands in attractive parkland running alongside the road, but first you must cross the narrow suspension bridge to the south side of the river.

The earliest château at La Treyne was built under the orders of the viscount of Turenne in 1342, probably to protect the river crossing, and there is still a keep dating from this time. The Wars of Religion saw the castle set on fire so it had to be rebuilt in the early seventeenth century before passing to that other powerful family, the Cardaillac, in 1711. The classical park which was planned around the reconstruction is rather unusual for these parts, although the Romanesque chapel in the grounds is not. Inside, the château is beautifully furnished and has a good art collection, all enhanced by the views from the windows – particularly on the river side where the drop is sheer to the water.

But if sheer drops to water attract you, never mind castles perched on cliffs, then the next stop has to be one of the most dazzling in the Lot. The château of **Belcastel** occupies a position so utterly stunning, on a cliff jutting out into the confluence of the Lot and the Ouysse, that every other consideration such as the intrinsic interest of the château for example, becomes secondary. In fact the château is rather disappointingly modern; even the

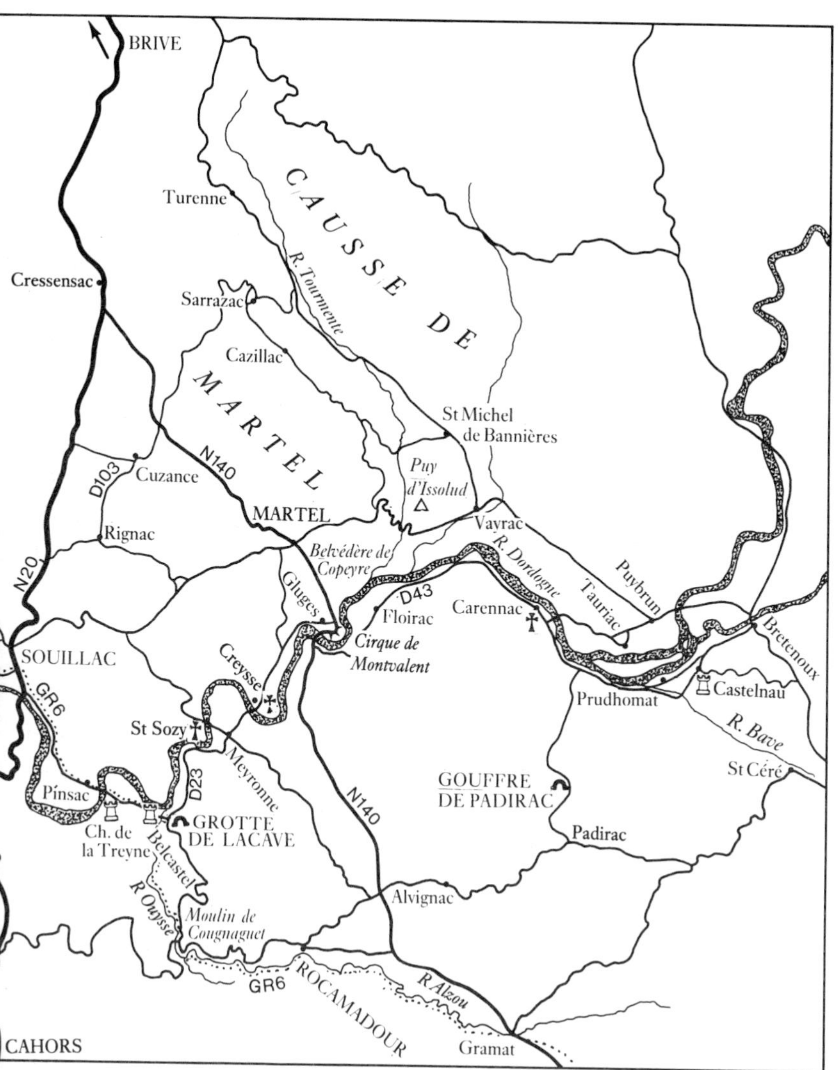

fourteenth-century chapel on the very edge of the cliff was much restored in the eighteenth century. Only the gardens are open to the public, by appointment, but it is only the setting that could ever hold your attention at Belcastel.

Continue following the river road and very shortly you arrive at **Lacave**, from where you can follow the GR6 from the Moulin de la Peyre to the Moulin of Cougnaguet and beyond, a lovely walk which follows the path of one of the Lot's prettiest rivers, the Ouysse. The caves of Lacave were discovered in 1905 by Armand Viré – a name which crops up time and again in the Lot – who was exploring a cave system in 1902 at the bottom of the *igue* or rift (where a watercourse disappears underground) of St Sol. Searching for an alternative way out, he came across the caves of Joucla, as they had been known for thousands of years.

The high spots of these cave visits tend not to be the formations, which although beautiful are sometimes much of a muchness, but the means employed to get you to the viewing galleries. At Padirac it is a punt. Here at Lacave a little train shunts its way through underground tunnels before depositing you at a lift. After that it is all on foot. Much fun is had by the French in naming the concretions in a slightly quaint and Victorian way after the shapes they seem to resemble. Thus you have the Palm Tree and the Elephant, and so on. The Salle du Lac is probably the most impressive, simply because water in these underground settings reflects the ceilings and the colours and enhances their beauty. Here, as at Cougnac, the most magical display of all comes as the lights are turned down, leaving the natural phosphorescence of the living stalactites and stalagmites glowing eerily in the dark of the other concretions that are dead.

The D23 becomes more dramatic as it makes for the pretty village of **Meyronne**, one-time home of the bishops of Tulle and perched above the still-wide Dordogne, which was declared navigable to this point in 1862. The village presents its best view of towers and turrets from the suspension bridge. From Meyronne you have a choice: either to cut off the loop of the river and aim for Creysse along the D23 or to follow the river road. If, like me, you have begun to fall in love with the Lot *pietàs*, then cross the bridge and make for **St Sozy** where the church of St Barthélémy has a wooden panelled *pietà* belonging to the early eighteenth century. A rather hefty Christ, albeit with a sweet face, lies limply in the folds of His mother's robes, a peculiarly effete right arm held aloft by Mary's enormous hand; the artist presumably trying to bring some form of perspective to the bas-relief.

Creysse is lovely. It used to be more lovely in the days when the little riverside hotel did not have a car park packed with British cars and when the prices were more commensurate with little riverside hotels. Perhaps one should not be so churlish. There are a million undiscovered restaurants and hotels in the Lot, and Creysse is an obvious place for tourists to flock to. Approaching from the other side, you drive past a goose farm, something which still instils in me a childish delight, and the tiny cobbled streets up to the church and castle are picturesque in the extreme.

The church is Romanesque with the very rare feature of twin round apses, giving it a slightly Greek look. Seen from below it is a strange sight. Inside there are several relics, including one of the many thorns said to have come from Christ's crown, given to the church by St Louis and venerated on the first Sunday in May. The church used to belong to the castle, a fifteenth-century structure with a pepper-pot roof, and from up on the terrace there are views of other, smaller fortified houses. The Turenne had a knack for picking good sites, it seems.

The road from Creysse to Gluges is magnificent, the cliff face rising straight up from the road on one side and a drop into the river on the other. Passing places have been built into the route, but logical fears about overtaking on blind bends do not seem to apply here, so caution is advisable.

Gluges is a typical Dordogne-style village, even down to the railway, climbing up the cliff which overhangs the village. You should park the car at the bottom and walk up. For myself, I find the towering cliff-face rather oppressive on anything other than a sparkling blue day; otherwise it has a tendency to darken and drip. Once you have climbed up a little way, perhaps to the semi-troglodyte church founded by Gérard de Mirandol on his return from the Crusades in 1108, the view is undeniably pleasing as you scan over the roofs to the river. There are even better views to be had in every direction. A climb up to the N140 and then the

D32 leads you to the **Copeyre Belvédère** from where you can see the river, the Cirque of Montvalent and the Puy d'Issolud, or you can make your way to the other side of the river and take the corniche round the *cirque.* **Montvalent** itself, another Turenne stronghold, has an enviable position, with its fortified church tower and fifteenth-century castle overlooking the river.

Floirac on the south side, too, is an impossible little place built on two narrow terraces. Its fifteenth-century church with the belfry stuck on to its front huddles under the rock-face next to a keep. The altar in the church and the apparently damaged *pietà* are strangers to me, I must admit, since whenever I have visited Floirac I have seen absolutely no one who could tell me where the key was kept. The only two inhabitants I met last time were a pair of delightful puppies gambolling across a quiet but lethal road. It would be helpful, though, if the French could start leaving notes on their churches indicating who holds the key, so that *bona fide* visitors could gain access more easily. Hunt-the-key is a time-consuming game to play on holiday and few would think it worth the effort. From Floirac the D43 leads you round to one of the Lot's high spots, the village of Carennac.

Try not to visit **Carennac** in high season if you can help it. Choose instead a bright day at the beginning or end of summer. I still remember the shock of driving there one hot Sunday late in July only to find there was no room to park the car.

The place was thronged with people, of whom I was one, of course, pushing their way into the church, crowding round the Entombment, laughing around the cloisters. It was unacceptable in the way that crowds at Rocamadour are not. 'Crowded' of course is a relative term, for the Lot rarely has the look or feel of the worst bits of the Spanish Costas. But tourists do funny things wherever they are. *'C'est magnifique!'* said the man ahead of us seriously as he rounded the corner into what was apparently a cul-de-sac, for back he came almost immediately with a look on his face of having been impressed. We hurried on, eager for some architectural detail or vista. Behind us the pace had quickened too but, rounding the corner into what was indeed a cul-de-sac, all we could see was a man relieving himself in that peculiarly public way that is the hallmark of all Frenchmen. Stifling childish giggles, we too turned with serious faces, so as not to spoil the fun for the next group who were now approaching in the lemming-like way of all tourists *en masse*.

Alone with the town you eschew these habits and Carennac has much that is moving and beautiful to offer. It is built of golden-white stone, quarried nearby. In the heat the town glows warm and dazzling and lends a sparkle to the old buildings that huddle together in a lop-sided way. It is unsurprising that Carennac's most famous son wished to be buried here, for it is a tranquil, timeless place but his wish, unfortunately, was not to be realized.

François de Salignac de la Mothe Fénelon, prior of the abbey of Carennac, archbishop of Cambrai, Quietist philosopher and theologian, a gentle man who believed in the art of persuasion at a time when it was unfashionable and the Huguenots were being severely persecuted, lived in Carennac for a good many years and it held a special place in his heart. The deanship had passed to the family as an hereditary title in 1605 and in 1681 Fénelon himself sailed along the Dordogne to take possession of it. He was warmly welcomed and much loved by the people of Carennac, holding the position for a further fifteen years.

He already knew the town, for this after all was Quercy and although the family château was just over the Dordogne border, they had long held land in the Lot, and before he inherited the title he used to stay at Carennac with his uncle, senior prior at the old abbey.

It is said that Fénelon wrote his famous work *Télémaque* at Carennac, an allegorical tale about statesmanship which follows the adventures of Telemachus, son of Ulysses. But although you can see what is known as Télémaque's tower, it is doubtful whether the prelate actually wrote the book here, as he had already taken up his post as tutor to the duke of Burgundy. Certainly, though, Carennac seems to have served as his inspiration and the small island in the Dordogne, the Île Barrade, has been renamed Calypso's Island after its description in the book, watched over by a bust of the prior.

The church with which Fénelon was associated is approached from an odd angle, under an arch to which the church stands sideways on, only a glimpse of the remarkable tympanum giving a hint of anything special. And special it is – another tympanum of the Toulouse School. Christ sits in a *mandorla*, blessing the apostles ranged beneath Him. Above hover two angels, and below, the lintel is covered with animals: lions, bears and peacocks. At the right time of day the door is picked out in the sunlight, while the rest of the street and the arch remain in shade. Of the four capitals on the inner door, two bear an inscription: 'Gerbert the Mason made this porch, blessed be his soul.' It is possible that Gerbert was also responsible for the fantastic door of Beaulieu further upstream, as the two doors share similarities.

Inside the church and removed now to the cloisters is another sculpture of a very different style and period, a remarkable Entombment belonging to the sixteenth century. The figures are carved with an astonishing attention to detail; every curl of the beard, every lock of hair depicted, the faces expressing the resignation one feels all people of that century would be familiar with when death came so quickly and frequently. They are dressed in the style of the period, so that one has the impression that it is not so much Nicodemus who holds the shroud as a good burgher of Carennac. The cloisters, which were used as stables at the time of the Revolution, have been restored now and are a peaceful, shady place to contemplate the perennial beauty of Carennac. One Romanesque gallery adjoins the church; the other three are in Flamboyant style. A climb to the top of the tower in the corner affords a pretty roofscape. Back inside the church, the main aisle is supported by a row of pillars which would have made St Bernard turn in his grave, decorated as they are with monsters.

Tear yourself away from Carennac as there is another treat in store further upriver, just where the Dordogne turns north around the ordinary *bastide* of Puybrun and the frescos of Tauriac. Cross the River Bave on the D14 and make for **Prudhomat**. The church there has another sculptured group, not entirely dissimilar to Carennac in its quaintness, although it belongs to an earlier century. Christ kneels in the water, looking a trifle anxious. Behind loiters an equally worried-looking angel trying hard to seem invisible, and beside them both is John the Baptist in the act of baptism, with water pouring from his cup.

The massive proportions of the castle of **Castelnau** dominate the surrounding countryside and glow red in the setting sun. The well-known French author Pierre Loti spent much of his childhood in the shadow of Castelnau, a fact he wrote about at length in *Roman d'un Enfant*, and from him comes the famous but accurate description: 'This cock's comb of blood-red stone rising from a tangle of trees'.

The castle strides out confidently across its hill, a perfect example of feudal military architecture; angry red ironstone, proud and impregnable, for the lords of Castelnau feared no one. The pennant they designed for the Crusades was a silver lion on a golden château, and from this period of the eleventh century they owed allegiance to none but the counts of Toulouse. But their pride was badly hurt in 1184, when Raymond of Toulouse gave the suzerainty of Castelnau to the viscount of Turenne. This was more than the powerful family could endure. Turenne was practically a neighbour; they regarded it as an equal and there was much jealousy at its power. Skirmishes broke out, during which the people of Quercy suffered greatly as the argument wore on, paying in lives, disruption and money. The baron of Castelnau could not stand the humiliation and declared himself a vassal of the king rather than endure this blow. The abbots of Tulle and Souillac conferred and decided in Turenne's favour. The baron was forced to accept the decision but refused to supply men-at-arms to Turenne. In a feudal system this was, of course, unacceptable. Finally under great pressure, the Baron did agree to render service but several years later, still smarting, he announced that all his other lands would pay allegiance to none but Toulouse. When the English arrived in Quercy, he placed himself under the French king's protection against the English. Any and every loophole was sought. But here again the king found for Turenne, ordering that Castelnau should pay a derisory egg to Turenne as a symbolic gesture to their overlords. Oxen bore this ironic cargo annually northwards.

But the key to the family's arrogance, the reason they had felt confident enough to challenge the Church and kings and viscounts, was the castle. People feared the war-like Castelnau and their gigantic fortress. In fact, though, the castle was not impregnable, as history proved. Henry II of England occupied it for a while, as did the guerrilla fighters of the Grandes Compagnies after the Hundred Years War, and it was only later in the fourteenth century that the castle took on the form that we see today, an irregular triangle with a round tower at each corner. The angle was a common device when artillery started to put in an appearance, the hope being that by presenting an angle to the enemy rather than a flat wall, cannon-balls would be deflected. The round keep had existed since the eleventh century, erected in 1000 by Hugues de Castelnau, but there had been a castle on this hill for as long as anyone could remember and certainly since the tenth century.

As the family, always fiercely loyal to the French king, grew more rich and powerful, so the fortress grew. Three parallel walls were erected. As well as the keep there was the Saracen's Tower, which rises over 62 metres. At the height of its power this magnificent castle could hold 1500 men and 100 horses at any one time; enough to fend off Edward the Black Prince when he arrived at its gates in the fourteenth century. Not long afterwards the peace treaty did award Castelnau to the English. Feudalism was a strong force here in the south and the baron submitted to this more readily than he had to Turenne, as he awaited an opportunity to rise against the occupying force. Nationalism would not appear in his lifetime, but it was nationalism that finally spelt the demise of feudal castles like this one.

After the Hundred Years War, luxurious living prevailed at Castelnau. Windows and galleries were added and the castle became more of a château in the accepted sense. During the eighteenth century, however, it fell on hard times; perhaps its military lines were felt to be unfashionable and the fire that gutted it in 1851 was said by some to be an act of arson designed to collect the insurance money.

Enter, happily, Jean Mouliérat of the Opéra Comique in the early twentieth century, who spent a lifetime restoring a wing of the castle in a quite remarkable way. Aubusson tapestries hang on the walls, there is an impressive art collection and a lapidary museum, and two of the rooms have had their original sixteenth-century painted ceilings restored. The provincial Parliament Room with its Romanesque windows has been restored to its former glory. The restoration is continued by the State now, and Castelnau is open to the public, classed after Pierrefonds (Oise) as the second most important military castle in France.

A walk around the extensive ramparts shows the different architectural styles and gives you an idea of why the barons felt so powerful perched on top of this commanding hill. Views extend in every direction. Away to the north-east is Bretenoux, a *bastide* founded by one of the barons in 1277 under the name Villafranca d'Orlienda; two sides of the arcading in this old town have been preserved, as has the sixteenth-century *pietà* in the church of St Catherine. But north-westwards, away on the horizon, less well preserved than anything here, rise the towers of Turenne, dominant still.

The Martel Causse

You feel the presence of the Limousin in the *causse* of Martel, green and bosky and distinctly less arid, with a feel of the north about it, and indeed we border on the Corrèze here. Just over the border are the towering turrets of Turenne, which ruled over the Martel *causse* and beyond with a rod of iron.

The only town of any importance on the Martel *causse* is the ancient town of **Martel** itself, about fifteen kilometres north-east of Souillac, and a Turenne stronghold. It is pretty well unspoilt and quite, quite beautiful but I always have the urge to pick it up lock, stock, and barrel and dump it in the middle of the Gramat *causse*, where it seems to me to belong. It is a typical Quercy town, displaced and isolated.

Long years ago I used to pass weeks here. In the heat of the day we would walk out of the town a little way to picnic and doze in one of the flowery meadows that surrounded it. The towers of Martel would lie on the field's edge, through a veil of swaying grasses, swifts swooping between the buildings, with nothing at all to indicate the century.

Martel is said to be named after Charles Martel, grandfather to Charlemagne who, having defeated the Saracens, built a church to commemorate the fact and give thanks. There is, however, not a shred of evidence to support this. Indeed the reason for Martel's existence is more obscure than most, since there was neither château nor abbey here. There is probably more truth in the other legend which says that it was founded by Rodulphe, first viscount of Turenne, but as no records exist for the town before the eleventh century this too is unverifiable. So the origin of the town of seven towers, with three hammers emblazoned upon its coat of arms, remains puzzling. *'Martel'*, of course, comes from the French word for 'hammer'. Charles was supposed to favour this weapon.

From the beginning of the twelfth century Martel belonged to the French king, but it was familiar with the English royal family too. It was here that Henry Court Mantel, son of Henry II, fled after the family row which ended with his sacking Rocamadour, and where he died, a victim of his parents' squabbles and his own jealousy.

In 1219 Martel was granted its first charter, setting it on its commercial way, and even today it is a market centre for truffles, nuts and the canning of the rich and exotic food for which Quercy is famous.

The Hundred Years War left Martel if not exactly untouched, then at least unbowed, for it was never taken and it was only the Treaty of Brétigny that finally allowed the English access to this proud little town. They were sent on their way again when du Guesclin liberated the region. But where they had stood firm against the English armies, the folk of Martel were not so successful in the face of the Grandes Compagnies, the marauding bands of soldiers left out of work and idle by the lack of war. Like so many towns in the Lot, Martel paid dues to these bands of brigands who bled the town dry with their greedy demands until exasperation made bold, and they were hounded to their lair in the Cirque of Montvalent and vanquished. The familiar cycle of the Lot was played out here, too, and the next trouble came with the Wars of Religion, when Protestant bands pillaged the church; Martel had remained largely Catholic.

The church, dedicated to St Maur, is one of the highlights of Martel, a Gothic fortified structure with a massive flat front, buttresses and battlements and a huge belfry. Under the twelfth-century porch, where swallows nest in spring, the Romanesque tympanum has been preserved. Christ sits in glory, His arms and hands outstretched and angels attending on either side. The outstretched hands show the nail wounds and the body shows the mark of the lance; there is no need for a cross. The lintel is adorned with palms, foliage and animals and if Martel is smaller and less spectacular than some tympanums, it is very much in the same tradition and equally moving.

Inside, you forget the fortifications of the exterior. The glass in the choir is thought to belong to the celebrated School of Arnaud de Moles. There are also four paintings attributed to Van Loo, as well as an eighteenth-century bas-relief *pietà* and a very life-like Christ, pain etched all over his face, an early fourteenth-century work.

For an idea of the size and layout of Martel, you would be well advised to follow the circular **Fossé des Cordeliers** (which later becomes the Fossé du Capitain) around the town, marking the line of the ancient ramparts. There used to be double perimeter walls but today only the gateways mark the route. You can also see the famous towers: the church tower of St Maur, the Belfry of the Raymondie, Tournemire, the Prison Tower, the Tour des Cordeliers, the Tour d'Henri Court-Mantel, the Tour Vergnes de Ferron and the Tour de Mirandol. The **Hôtel de la Raymondie** is a quaint fourteenth-century building built by one of the viscounts of Turenne, which today serves as the town hall; you can go into the delightful courtyard to admire the fourteenth-century windows. The attractive **market hall** is eighteenth-century. It rests on stone pillars and looks older; the old weights are still visible. On the south side of the **Place des Consuls** is the site of the Maison Fabri, with its round turret, although the house that stands there now postdates Henry's death. There is much to admire in a walk round the town; Martel has preserved a picturesque quality and it is easier to spend longer than you had intended. There are plenty of Renaissance houses and old *hôtels*, the house of Vergnes de Ferron, the old prison, Mirepoises cloisters, a museum and a hundred delightful courtyards that it is difficult to resist peeping into. Note, too, the gargoyles on the **Maison Delanis** depicting an English leopard and the king of England, each holding a *fleur de lys*, signifying the English claim to France.

After Martel you can wander its *causse* which, although it is pretty enough and will give a flavour of the countryside, will not reward you with anything spectacular, though it is rich in small country hotels. The tiny hamlet of Rignac, due east of Martel and close to the N20, has a church with decorated pilasters at the door but there are no animals here, only Celtic scrawls belonging to the twelfth century; it has an octagonal tower. Cuzances, on the D103 northwards out of Rignac, is a flowery village where every house seems to be a restaurant or café. L'Hôpital St Jean has a long, long street with overhanging houses and the pleasant, untouched feel that all this tourist-deserted corner has, but there are few remains of the Templars whose town it originally was. You descend into Sarrazac, ancient seat of the Turenne parliament, down a steep road to the village, lost in a deep valley full of cuckoos. You wake in the night to nightingales. Sarrazac too had a hospice, which passed to the Knights of Malta. The church by the school has a welcoming, disjointed hand at the door, blessing all who enter. As long ago as the year 8, iron was mined in these parts, but today there is little that is profitable left – even the truffles are nearly finished.

The nicest church is the one above the no-place of **Cazillac**, westwards off the D20, with its free-standing belfry – not so much for any architectural detail but because of its position. It stands high on a hill, with horses grazing the fields outside. You simply would not see grass like this further south. The view is fantastic, pastoral and undulating. What spoils it is the graveyard. If there is one thing worse than plastic flowers, rain-washed and faded, it is china flowers attached to marble books. Why are the French so utterly tasteless in death? Are there no real flowers to be had? Or are they too much effort? All around, the purple spires of the pyramid orchid push their way through the soil. In spring the fields are full of narcissi. Let the graveyards run wild: they will be a hundred times more beautiful.

Don't take the D20 southwards to **St Michel de Bannières**; wind your way through the little roads. St Michel lies in a quiet valley watered by the exceedingly calm waters of the Tourmente. Dozens of tiny streams criss-cross the valleys here and the area abounds with water mills. The towers of fifteenth-century Blanat are easily visible but nothing moves in St Michel. The twelfth-century church, fortified and with historiated pilasters outside, decays as you watch it.

Above St Michel stands still another Uxellodonum claimant, the Puy d'Issolud. Approaching from Vayrac, a town of little charm, the road is steep and narrow and the view remarkable. Once at the top, however, the view is less remarkable, obliterated by hedges and houses. Puy d'Issolud is the site favoured by historians and archaeologists, but there is little there to fire the imagination, although excavations were made in the 1920s by M. Laurent-Bruzy of Brive. Evidence of a battle was found and it seems that the watercourse could have been dammed in the way that history claims the Romans used to starve out the Cadourques. There are signs of excavations on the St Michel road, some Roman walls and bones in an ossuary. But Puy d'Issolud, like most of the Lot, is disappointing where Roman remains are concerned, and of all the claimants I find it hardest of all to imagine life here in Roman times, as one looks down on the houses of Vayrac and the tamed beauty of the sophisticated Dordogne.

13

St Céré: 1

Heureux qui vit obscurément
Dans quelque coin de terre
Et qui s'approche rarement
De ceux qui portent le tonnerre.

So wrote François Maynard, poet and member of the Académie Française, who spent the last years of his life in St Céré.

But Maynard was wrong in one respect, for St Céré, lying in the north-east of the Lot, is not as cut off as he implied. It stands huddled at the foot of the protective towers of St Laurent, the southern *causses* to one side, the Limousin to the other. St Céré was always a natural crossroads between the Auvergne and Aquitaine, the North and the Midi.

The **fort** at St Céré had existed for centuries, first held by the Romans as a buffer to the High Auvergne, into which they never dared penetrate to any great degree. Then the counts of the Auvergne moved in, and after them the ubiquitous Turenne. The fief of Turenne in the Corrèze was an independent one, recognized by the kings of England and France. So while most of the Lot looked south to Toulouse, St Céré looked north.

The name of St Céré (and the place has changed name no fewer than five times) came from the fourth-century St Serène, a saint who had a great following in the Auvergne and to whom the early castle chapel was dedicated. Indeed the lords of St Céré took their name Sérénus, and later St Séré, from this chapel.

The actual town, however, was a later, eighth-century development and was founded by a daughter of the St Séré family, herself a saint, Ste Spérie. Legend has it that Spérie, or Espérie, virginal and pure, had secretly vowed herself to God. Her plans were seriously upset by her brother, Clarus, who promised her hand as a means of reconciliation with his pagan neighbour at Loubressac, with whom he was continually fighting. The idea was anathema to Spérie and, rebelling against this atrocious example of male manipulation, she stuck fast to her vow and refused to have anything to do with her brother's plan.

Angered and humiliated, for he had made a deal and given his word, Clarus plotted with Elidius of Loubressac to kill his sister instead. It was to Elidius that the actual act of murder fell. Stalking Spérie through the woods, he pounced suddenly and decapitated her with his sword. Not a bit put out by this development, Spérie picked up her head, carried it to a nearby stream and carefully washed it. At this spot a miraculous spring appeared and, as the troubadour wrote, '*En tel endroit, oncques depuis, ne cesse de murmurer la source, toujours plaintive …*' A chapel was erected in the venerated spot and around it grew up the town. The year of Spérie's martyrdom was 794. Pilgrims started to come almost straight away, fired by the story of a young virgin who refused a pagan; besides, it was relatively easy to get to St Céré, placed as it was on a T-junction between the Auvergne, the Limousin and Quercy, although it was not until 1600 that St Céré was really thought of as belonging to Quercy. Until that time, its roots were firmly Auvergnat, in spite of the Turenne.

St Céré escaped the ravages of the Hundred Years War, falling to the English only via the Treaty of Paris in 1259. Up until that time and well ahead of the official dates of the war, the English advances had been resisted, since Turenne was very firmly allied to the French Crown, having sworn an oath of loyalty to St Louis at Rocamadour, or so it was claimed. Historians now say that St Louis never visited Rocamadour!

Following the treaty, however, officers of Henry III arrived at the gates of the château of St Séré (the château was spelled with an 's', the town with a 'c'). After some time the viscount and the English appeared on the terrace in front of the assembled crowd. The English, carrying the banner of St George, shouted '*Angleterre*' three times. By this old custom did the people know to whom they were expected to pay homage, and that their franchises would be protected. In fact, the English seemed to take to St Céré, granting it the privilege of minting money, a privilege quite frequently granted in Quercy, however.

The Black Death made enormous inroads into the population of the town twice, resulting in the consuls issuing some excellent rules of appropriate behaviour for the townsfolk, which included their washing the streets three times a week and walking in the countryside as much as possible.

The Wars of Religion led to a number of Protestant occupations of the town, which suffered now in a way it had not in the Hundred Years War. These sufferings were relieved for a time in 1569, when Henry of Navarre stopped off at St Céré for a breather after his defeat at Montoncour. But in 1574 trouble came again when the Protestant Cardaillac scaled the walls and slit the throats of everyone who got in their way. The town was liberated by Gilles de Montal, but by 1575 the Protestants were back in force in both the château and the town, establishing themselves in the Chapelle Notre-Dame. They stayed until 1617. By now the château was in ruins and the town had changed names again from Ste Spérie to St Céré, while the château ruins were named after the neighbouring church, Tours de St Laurent.

St Céré might not be one of the more typical Lot towns, but it is well placed for visiting much of the *département* and pleasant enough, with the waters of the Bave flowing through the centre. There used to be lots of branches of this small river, giving the place a slight Venetian air, but today most of these have been filled in. Some very charming waterside parts do remain, however; most notably the **Quai des Recollets**, where gardens and houses crowd in on the water. The chapel of the convent of the Recollets still stands, its pretty tower reflected in the river.

A wander round the town reveals several notable buildings. The **Hôtel de Puymule** in the Place de l'Eglise is one of those lovely chunky round towers roofed in *lauze*, to which has been added some elegant Renaissance detail. The **Place de Mercadial** has some well preserved half-timbered buildings behind which the St Laurent towers rise up. Then, on the corner of Rue St Cyr, there is the house of General Ambert, a native son of St Céré noted for his part in the Empire wars and for being the father of the military writer Joachim Ambert.

Indeed, St Céré has had several modestly famous sons, who were either born here or chose it as their home. There is a monument to Charles Bourseul, whom the French claim as inventor of the telephone. Pierre Benoit the author lived here, as did Marshal Canrobet, soldier and veteran of the Crimean and Franco-Prussian wars; and Antoine Lauricesque de Lagarouste, who died a pauper in the eighteenth century in spite of having invented the astronomical mirror. Even the Gluck brothers stayed here for a while. 'We're tiring of everything', they wrote after a visit to Assier, 'even admiration.' And of course there is Maynard, who lies beneath the chancel of Ste Spérie.

Ste Spérie was rebuilt in the thirteenth century, but little remains of this period. Far and away the most interesting thing in the church is the crypt, thought to be Carolingian, with its Celtic-looking altar stone in front of the niche where Ste Spérie's relics are supposed to be; and there is also of course the miraculous spring. Every October around the Saint's fête day, the crypt is open to the public for twelve days.

But St Céré has a more modern son, too. In the **Casino**, in the north-east of town, is a permanent exhibition of the works of the man who did so much to revive the art of tapestry-making, Jean Lurçat. The exhibition contains paintings, prints and tapestries, including his famous cockerels. They are dramatic works, if not my favourite, by a man who became master of his art and who for a time lived and worked above the town in the ruins of St Laurent, attracted by the size of the rooms. More of his work can be seen in the main hotel of the town, which has renamed itself **Le Coq Arlequin** in his honour.

You can drive up to the towers through the modern and wealthy-looking suburbs of St Céré and enjoy the view from the top. Little remains of the medieval buildings, but the two towers are there; the oldest one twelfth century and 26 metres high, the other fifteenth-century and eight metres taller.

Lurçat apparently loved to sit here working on his cartoons and, from this gentle hill, not unlike the *mamelon* of Turenne further north to which St Laurent used to belong, he could look down on the little town. 'These ruined towers which chip the sun', wrote Pierre Benoit of this eyrie, but Lurçat, painting away before views stretching out across the *causse*, would probably have been more likely to recall Maynard:

> Adieu Paris, adieu, pour la dernière fois
> Je suis las d'encenser de la Fortune
> Et brûle de revoir mes rochers et mes bois
> Où tout me satisfait et rien ne m'importune.

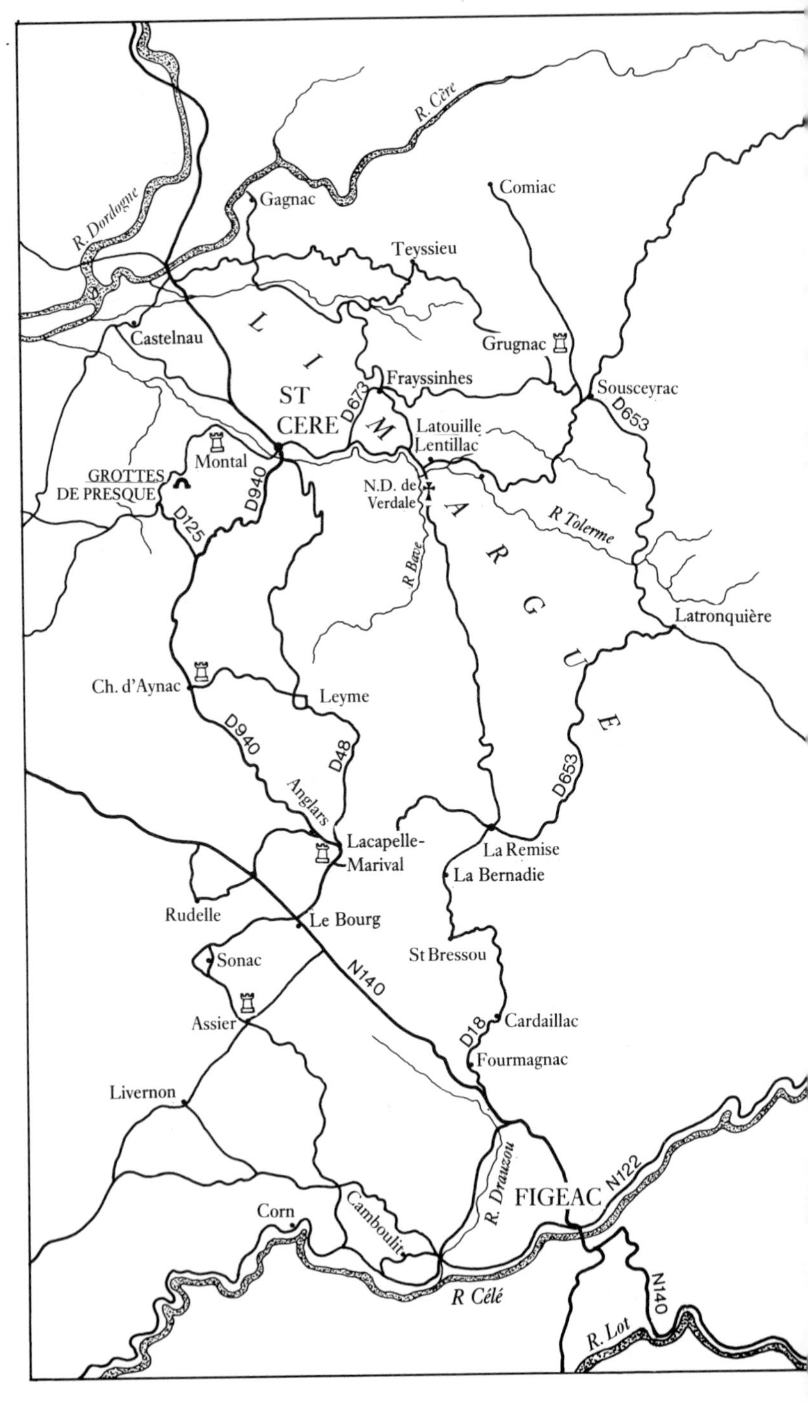

R. Dordogne
R. Cère
Gagnac
Comiac
Teyssieu
Castelnau
Grugnac
L I M A R G U E
Frayssinhes
Sousceyrac
D653
ST
CERE
D673
Latouille
Lentillac
Montal
GROTTES
DE PRESQUE
D940
N.D. de
Verdale
R Tolerme
D125
R Bave
Latronquière
Ch. d'Aynac
Leyme
D940
D48
D653
Anglars
Lacapelle-
Marival
La Remise
La Bernadie
Rudelle
Le Bourg
Sonac
St Bressou
N140
Assier
D18
Cardaillac
Fourmagnac
Livernon
R. Drauzou
FIGEAC
N122
Corn
Camboulit
R Célé
N140
R. Lot

14

St Céré: 2

The Ségala and the Limargue

The easterly regions of the department mark the boundary between the limestone *causses* and the foothills of the Auvergne. The Ségala, with its high pasture-land and views away over the Cantal, is a hard landscape with a chill in the air, harsher by far than the Limargue, the fertile plain dividing Quercy from the Auvergne. You will notice the change in landscape and architecture straight away. The Ségala is certainly atypical of the area and only mountain-lovers will feel uplifted as they leave the golden stone behind and head for the bleaker landscape of the Auvergne. Nonetheless, landscapes like this do have their charm. The area is totally free of tourists, for one thing, and the views across to the Cantal mountains, much nearer now, are spectacular. And once you have descended back into the gentler, greener Limargue, the richness of Renaissance Lot awaits you.

Notre-Dame-de-Verdale is a pilgrimage chapel in the middle of nowhere. Leaving St Céré and travelling east on the D673 and the D30 to Latouille-Lentillac, you notice the road rising almost immediately as you travel through a wooded ravine alongside the River Bave. After Latouille-Lentillac you will see a sign to Notre-Dame-de-Verdale which leads you up a narrow, precipitous road, leaving the river far behind. The scenery is curiously different. Gone is the limestone, replaced by granite. As so often in the Lot, it is the houses that indicate a locality, with a surreptitious change of style as well as the scenery, which takes on an almost mountainous look. There are cows, rarely seen on the *causse*, and the vegetation belongs to high places too – harebells, foxgloves and ferns.

Although Michelin advises walking up to the church, it is a far easier thing to walk down to it from above, for the road there rises to a dead end with space to park the car. From here you walk down a stony path edged thickly with wild strawberries. The church, not a pretty one, clings to the rock face on an extremely steep ledge, with only a narrow path round to the back protected by a wall. The ground drops away to the thickly wooded gorge of the River Tolerme about 60 metres below. Although the visit is made to the accompaniment of the sound of rushing water and cascading waterfalls, pounding away below, you cannot actually see anything unless you continue on down the path where the noise of the fierce little torrent becomes deafening.

The legend attached to the site concerns a young shepherdess, Elizabeth, employed by a farmer, Viscontin, at Corn, during the Hundred Years War. As she was guarding her sheep one day on the slopes of Verdale, the Virgin appeared to Elizabeth and asked that a chapel should be built in the valley. By a curious coincidence, which the peasants regarded as miraculous, it transpired that, at the very moment the Virgin had been talking to Elizabeth, a woodcutter felling trees nearby had discovered a statue of the Virgin.

Easily persuaded by the Virgin's wish, the more so as Quercy was then in the grip of an outbreak of plague, the peasants set to work with a will; but every morning, arriving at the spot they had chosen to erect the chapel, they discovered their work of the previous day demolished. In exasperation one of them threw his hammer in the air, crying out as he did so that he wished to God the Virgin would indicate where She wished the chapel to be built by directing its fall. The hammer fell on a granite outcrop high above the Tolerme. Work began on the spot and the chapel was erected without further problem. Beyond its spectacular site the chapel has little to offer, or so at least a peep through the keyhole indicated. The doors were firmly locked on the day I visited and the torrential rain that fed the Tolerme that day dampened my enthusiasm for a key search. It does open on at least a few days each year, 12-19 August, the dates of the pilgrimage. The legend does seem to be borne out by the fact that a stone taken from the door was dated 1315 and the statue of the Virgin dates from the fourteenth century also. The way down to the river is labelled with threatening signs reading '*Chemin très dangereux*' – a fact not hard to believe the day I was there, since the *chemin* had actually disappeared beneath the river, though presumably this was the route taken by the pilgrims.

Rejoining the D673 at Frayssinhes, you might feel tempted to explore the Cère gorges only a few kilometres to the north but, apart from a few viewpoints you will be disappointed, for only the railway runs through them. There are few villages in this north-eastern part of the department.

Gagnac, with its *pigeonniers* and *pietà*; Comiac, the first place in Quercy to be taken by the Holy Leaguers; and Teyssieu with another *pietà*, a sixteenth-century interpretation: none of them worth a detour.

Approaching Sousceyrac on the D673, you will have to leave the road and head north for a glimpse of the pretty fourteenth-century towers of Grugnac, built by the Turenne family. It is a nice squat affair, with machicolation all round.

Sousceyrac, gateway between the Auvergne and Haut-Quercy, was also a Protestant stronghold in the sixteenth century, and another fief of the viscounts of Turenne. Some of the ramparts still exist, most notably the Notre-Dame Gate with a curious aerial chapel above the arch. The road under the arch leads into an old part of town containing a fourteenth-century coaching house, the Ostal des Presté, which now houses antiques. But although the road signs describe Sousceyrac as *'pittoresque'*, I find it an unappealing sort of place, with its large, untidy square. Even the famous Hôtel, scene of Pierre Benoit's *Le Déjeuner de Sousceyrac*, looks seedy and run-down, although it has to be said that it sports a Michelin star. There are, of course, many wonderful restaurants in France which you would not give twopence for from their appearance. The transition from the familiar and pretty Quercy style is now very marked and, although the high-pitched slate roofs with their dormer windows are very typical of the Ségala and reminiscent of Scotland, the grey stone and slate have a slightly depressing effect and you feel drawn westwards back to the limestone.

Leaving Sousceyrac and heading for the Templar town of Latronquière on the D653, the *causse* has been left far behind: away in the distance the Monts du Cantal tower in a sea of clouds. Houses now have mansard roofs, cattle graze everywhere on what seems like lush pasture-land, but the villages tell a different tale. Life here is without visible luxuries. As with so much of the Auvergne, one sees a lot but there is nothing much to see. It is a relief to turn westwards at Latronquière and head for the ancient town of Cardaillac.

Turn off the D653 at the wayside church of La Remise and head for La Bernadie and St Bressou, which is what the French call a *'village perché'*. Here you can pick up the D5 but the best approach to **Cardaillac**, another 'perched village', is probably up the D18 from Fourmagnac; then the town on its rocky cliff presents its fortified face to the world – a series of towers and defences. The family of Cardaillac was one of the most important in Quercy and among the most powerful. The barony dates back to the eleventh century, perhaps its most famous baron being Hugues de Cardaillac who did a great deal of work on cannons and artillery and established rules of combat for these weapons in 1346.

The village itself is rather neglected, although one feels it is only a matter of time before it is all done up for the tourists and looking a bit like St Cirq-Lapopie. There is already, in the western end of the village called The Fort, an excellent tour marked by arrows round the rather overgrown ramparts, with framed notes hanging at strategic points. The route takes you past lots of large but friendly dogs, and pots of geraniums spill from the little houses caught up between the towers – two square and one round. You can climb the **Tour de Sagnes** for an excellent view of the Drauzou valley. The Edict of Nantes decreed Cardaillac a safe place for Protestants, for the ruling family had converted to the faith in the sixteenth century. That they were a powerful bunch with pretensions way beyond Cardaillac is demonstrated by the rather charming arrogance of the family motto: *'Toto noscuntur in orbe'* – 'They were known in all the world'. And indeed their progeny spread far and wide; even the mother of Mme de Maintenon, the morganatic wife of Louis XIV, was born Jeanne de Cardaillac.

The town is full of old, old houses and there is a good little hotel. Rich farmyard smells emanate from barns up side-streets and there is an interesting museum containing old farm instruments, children's school exercise books and local accounts of the drastic effect of the phylloxera outbreak at the end of the last century. Whilst the American vines were known to be far more resistant to the disease they were also expensive, and the farmers could not afford to replace their European vines with the new strain. The population in the town (and all around too, of course) fell drastically. In 1784 there were 1,650 inhabitants in Cardaillac; in 1986 a mere 434.

Leave Cardaillac by the D18 and follow it across the N140 until you reach the D13. Turn right here and almost immediately left to **Camboulit**, even more forgotten and almost more charming. Strictly speaking, Camboulit is not in the Limargue but it would be a pity to miss one of the most picturesque villages in the Lot. You enter through a narrow fortified gate into a medieval world of as pretty a conglomeration of houses, châteaux and churches as you could wish for.

Assier lies north-west of Camboulit, once again on the edges of the Limargue; the roughness of the Ségala has been left behind. In a land of medieval castles and Romanesque churches, the ruined château of Assier is a Renaissance anachronism. The village is neat and tidy, well laid out. You will be amazed, if not shocked, on first sight of its church, for encircling it is a frieze, a strip cartoon, of armaments. Cannon take aim at castles, cannon-balls roll across the bas-relief like croquet balls, bags of gunpowder and goodness knows what other horrors lie propped up against cannon wheels, alongside coils of rope. Inside, the creator of all this death and destruction lies apparently at peace in a marble tomb. Above the tomb the statue of a man leans back in relaxed fashion against the barrel of a cannon, his foot idly resting on a cannon-ball. This is Galiot de Genouillac (1465-1546), armourer, in case you could not have guessed, to François I. The star vaulting in this chapel is said to be of Spanish origin and is very beautiful, if you can drag your eyes away from this extraordinary piece of theatre. For in truth the whole church is Galiot's tomb and memorial. Outside, the Renaissance door – a tympanum resting on columns – is just another vehicle for Galiot's insignia, which are being offered to the Virgin in the owner's confident knowledge, one feels, of acceptance. It is all in tremendously bad taste. The church, Gothic in style albeit the decoration is Renaissance, everywhere reflects Galiot's love of himself. The keystones bear his coat of arms, the frieze depicts his famous battles; even the angels on the door carry messages saying 'Long Live Galiot', just as the frieze and the château proclaim his motto.

That Galiot was well appreciated by François I we are left in no doubt, for François wrote to his mother saying Galiot was responsible for the victory at Marignan (1515) and that never had man served better. Like most people dealing in arms, Galiot soon amassed a great fortune and possessed property not only in Quercy and the Charente but as far north as Montrichard on the Loire, and Paris. He began work on the new château of Assier in

1525, a task which would occupy him for the next ten years. The old medieval thing inherited from his mother was demolished; too poor, uncomfortable and old-fashioned for his taste. Galiot mixed with kings and he wanted something more fitting.

Preserving only the south-west wing of the old castle, he erected an enormous quadrilateral flanked with domed, round towers at each angle. Brantôme, who seems to have studied the fortunes of Galiot at some length, said that he wanted to build the most superb mansion one could imagine. Today only the west wing still stands. After Galiot's death his daughter's husband, Charles de Crussol d'Uzes, was responsible for its upkeep. He lived there until the end of the sixteenth century and then abandoned it. By 1766 the château had fallen into such a state of disrepair that, unbelievably, it was dismantled and plundered by the buyers, local carpenters and a mason for the most part, in a deal which allowed them all that they could take within twelve years. All that was left belonged to the Uzes family.

It was a sad end to the pretensions of Galiot but, even though so little remains today, we can still get an idea of those pretensions. This was no château; this was a palace. The outer façade is still defensive-looking, but the inner façade is pure Renaissance, with windows similar to those at Blois, and friezes depicting the labours of Hercules and Galiot himself. You can go inside for a few francs, entering the loggia above the main gate by a Gothic-Renaissance staircase; but although we can have a taste of the grandeur of former days the true magnificence has gone and Galiot's palace has the sad air of all ruined buildings.

Galiot had served under four kings but his real fame and fortune came with François. He built his palace to last, one feels, as a sort of memorial to his life and in a desperate search for eternity. It is a sad reflection on that ambition that the only thing standing intact is the château's *pigeonnier*, one of the biggest in Quercy and indeed the south-west. The pigeons were valued for their manure, of course. Was this God's revenge, I wonder?

Leave Assier by the D11 and head for Sonac, and from there by the D25 to the main N140 at **Le Bourg**. The church here, with its round apse and squarish front, dates from the twelfth century and used to be fortified. Inside, the capitals are all decorated in Romanesque style and support some blind arcading. The work is of a high quality, but if it is defensive churches that interest you then head north to **Rudelle**, where, by the side of the road, you will come across what is little more than an ecclesiastical keep founded in the thirteenth century by Bertrand de Cardaillac. Be careful where you park and how you walk along the road, for the cars speed by very fast making access a bit nerve-racking. It really is an extraordinary building, quite unrecognizable as a church at all, a great hefty bulk of a place with crenellations, arrow slits, enormous buttresses and tiny windows.

You step down into the church-cum-hall, with ogive vaulting, but you can also climb up to the gallery, as did the villagers in times of trouble, and thence by ladder, trapdoor and staircase to the top, from where you can look westwards towards Lacapelle-Marival.

The town of Lacapelle-Marival, built of red sandstone quarried locally, is a pretty if slightly vapid place completely dominated by the enormous château built slap-bang in the middle of town, a huge square keep with round towers at each corner today housing the Syndicat d'Initiative. This is Cardaillac country and the family established themselves in the town from the thirteenth to the eighteenth century. To the basic keep were added a mass of turrets and towers, houses and windows. This hotchpotch of a château is a powerful symbol of Cardaillac might and by the time the last Cardaillac had sold the land in 1736, he was able to sell the title of marquis along with it.

A plaque on the château wall commemorates the deportation of 86 people from Lacapelle-Marival on 11 May 1944, but this is virtually the only reminder of the twentieth century. The market hall lies crushed up in a tiny square, looking rather as if it has been lowered in place by helicopter, so tight is the fit. In fact it was built in the fifteenth century, so this has to be an unlikely theory. You approach it under an arched gateway fortified with a round tower. The fifteenth-century church is unremarkable, although it does have a painting by Gamelin, the Carcassonne painter.

Anglars, a small hamlet just off the D940, is an extremely old village and home of an ancient Lot song. At least, there is some dispute about this, with some authors attributing it to Anglars-Juillac. All the evidence, though, points to the place nearby called Le Touron or Le Cros, where a rock not unlike a dolmen can still be seen. The legend is that the king of Navarre tried to seduce a young girl he met at an Anglars fountain, and it is sung today by harvesters as they gather in the hay. It was written by a troubadour in the thirteenth century after the Albigensian Crusade and the conquest of the Languedoc by the combined forces of the Church and the 'French', and is apparently rich in veiled hints about the Cathars. For an explanation you would have to turn to a populist French writer steeped in the mysteries of the Templars, the Cathars and the priory of Sion, Gérard De Sède, whose many books include one entitled *Le Trésor Cathare*. At face value, however, the song is merely a neat sidestepping by a pretty girl, subjected to advances she has no intention of accepting:

Al roc d'Anglars	Au roc d'Anglars
I a 'na clara fontana	Il y a une claire fontaine
Joana d'Aimet	Jeanne d'Aymet
I va querre son aiga	Y va chercher son eau
Lo filh de rèi	Le fils du roi
Sola l'a rencontrada	Seule l'a rencontrée
–Joana d'Aimet...	–Jeanne d'Aymet...

Leyme, to the north along the D48, is not worth the journey although it was the one-time home of the Cistercian Abbaye des Filles, built, so tradition has it, on the spot where Ste Spérie was martyred, which rather puts paid to St Céré's claims. This, too, was Cardaillac country and it was that family which founded the abbey in 1221. Today the remains of the abbey are in land occupied by a psychiatric hospital.

The château of **Aynac** stands in the village of the same name, a sixteenth-century edifice erected by the powerful Turenne, whose tentacles stretched ever further afield. The building, with its central keep some six storeys high, is nicely symmetrical and surrounded by four towers, each with the onion-shaped dome more common to the Rouergue. Renaissance work is rare in the Lot, though in this particular area it is well represented, as with Aynac's chimneys; the central keep, however, is thirteenth-century. The property is private but you can easily see the château, set in parkland, from the road. The Romanesque church has an octagonal belfry, some beautifully carved wooden choir stalls and magnificent capitals.

But the true Renaissance jewel of the Lot is still to come. Take the left turn off the main St Céré road, the D125, and turn right down the D673 which also leads to St Céré. **Montal** lies off this road and is signposted. Approaching Montal from the west, one is presented with the big round towers of yet another feudal castle; climbing the grassy bank to the château is like walking into a painting from the *Très Riches Heures du Duc de Berry*.

Great plans had been made for Montal, but in the end only two wings were built. It was enough. Once you are standing in Montal's courtyard, its full Renaissance beauty becomes apparent, for what was rustic and medieval on the outside is simple sophistication in the inner courtyard. Here is a building that can rival anything on the Loire, unashamedly romantic, decorated in that delicate bas-relief style so beloved of Renaissance architects. It takes the form here of a thirty-two-metre frieze between the first and second storeys depicting those subjects so typical of the style. A fantasy of lovers, birds, curlicues, cupids and unicorns waltzes round the courtyard, interspersed with the initials of the baronness of Montal, Jeanne de Balzac d'Entraygues, daughter of the *sénéchal* of the Agenais and widow of Almeric, governor of the Haut-Auvergne; and those of her two sons, Robert and Dordé.

Jeanne began the massive alterations to the manor house in

1523, whilst her elder son Robert was away fighting for François I in the Italian Wars. Legend has it that it was the Marot family, including the poet himself, servants of the king at Fontainebleau, who told Jeanne of the beauty of the Loire castles and inspired her dreams to turn into reality. The new building grew gradually, light and delicate, with only the strong outer towers preserved. Above the frieze and between the beautifully proportioned mullioned windows are carved busts of members of Jeanne's family: her husband Almeric, Jeanne herself, Robert and Dordé, Jeanne's father, Robert de Balzac, and Dordé de Beduer, her cousin and abbot of Vézélay. They are famous, these busts, set in special niches and, we are told, closely resembling the people concerned. The face of Jeanne is strong and tragic-looking. The gabled windows are sculptured in commemoration of son Robert's death, with a skeleton representing death and carrying a scythe. A knight with a scroll bears the legend *'Plus d'espoir'*. 'No more hope' – these words have caused endless speculation and add considerably to the romantic image of Montal. No one knows what they mean or why they were carved. There is a local legend about Rose de Montal, wildly in love with her neighbour across the valley in the blood-red magnificence of Castelnau. For hours on end she sat by the window watching for his visits. One day, looking through the window as usual, she saw not the noble lord but the wedding procession of the woman he was to marry. *'Plus d'espoir,'* cried Rose before hurling herself to the ground through the open window. History tells us, though, that even if Rose was in love with the sire of Castelnau, she later married elsewhere, so we must cast around for another meaning to those woe-begotten words. Nowadays another theory is presented: Jeanne, rich and powerful, was building the château as a homecoming surprise for her adored elder son. But Robert, fighting at Pavia, did not come home and the window from which Jeanne watched for his return took on a painful poignancy for her; hence the inscription. Dordé was released from his churchly vows to take over the role as head of family and he lived out the earlier legend, in part, by marrying

Catherine of Castelnau. But the marriage produced no sons and that was to be Montal's downfall.

Inside, the château is just as beautiful in its delicate simplicity. The main staircase in the white, white stone of Carennac is a spiral delight of birds, shells and curlicues, all carved on the underside. The glass in the windows is beautiful, too; very old and set into modern frames of such simple excellence, locking as they do into the protective clear glass, that one rejoices to see such craftsmanship still alive and well. If you notice it at all, that is, for the eye is drawn out to the views, across the Bave or up to the cliffs of Cayla where the Gauls established camp. Caesar knew the spot were Montal would be built.

Other famous people knew Montal, too, as an interesting piece of grafitti at the top of the staircase confirms:

Que ces murs coquets
S'ils n'étaient discrets
Diraient de secrets

It is signed Léon Gambetta.

All the rooms of Montal are of inspired proportions, the ceilings beamed and vaulted, the chimneypieces enormous and the rooms exquisitely furnished. Montal, preserved in all its splendour, belongs now to the State and one cannot help wondering if the story of its restoration will itself one day belong to the stuff of legend. It is a remarkable tale, the only visible record of which is a plaque on a wall of the château which declares: 'Maurice Fénaille 1853-1937 Hanc Donum Dilexit et Resituit'.

After the marriage of Dordé and Catherine failed to produce sons, the castle passed from one family to another. It did not suffer overmuch during the Revolution. The real vandalism came at the end of the nineteenth century, when a M. Macaire bought the place. Always short of money, he divided the château into lots and sold them off one by one. Thus were all the masterpieces of Montal dispersed around the world, all the chimneypieces and the doors, the windows and the art work, the furniture; everything, until only the shell with its beautiful staircase remained.

Enter M. Maurice Fénaille, oil millionaire, who bought the place to restore it to its former glory. M. Fénaille did not undertake this task lightly. It was not enough for him to buy things of the period and install them in his château. He wanted the originals back. And little by little back they came, until by 1908 the restoration was nearly complete. Nearly, but not quite, for some of the treasures in the Louvre belonged to the State and could not be returned to a private house. But Montal had become Maurice Fénaille's obsession and rather than be defeated by bureaucracy he gave his castle to the State, so that the Louvre could 'lend' the pieces back. Still there are some pieces that have never been returned. The Vanderbilts and the Metropolitan Museum in New York hung on to their loot, while allowing casts of the originals to be made.

When I was there last, attention was being turned to the little chapel in the château grounds. M. Fénaille reserved his right to stay at the château, a well-deserved right, surely, and one still enjoyed by his family today.

So this chapter ends with the Renaissance charm of Montal, built at a time when people thought war seemed distant. If they had known of the horrors of the Wars of Religion that were soon to follow, Montal, ill equipped for battle, would never have been built. Only eight kilometres away across the valley the mighty defensive proportions of Castelnau rise up on their hill and finally it is these which prevail and are the more typical. The flowering of Montal was brief indeed, and all the sweeter for it.

15

Figeac: 1

It was Pépin le Bref, so the legend goes, who was responsible for the founding of Figeac. He had just fought a battle with the duke of Aquitaine and was feeling good, if weary. The company had halted at a fast-flowing river when all at once a cloud of white doves rose from the ground and flew off in the shape of a cross. The year was 753 and the world was young yet for scepticism. Coincidence was not a word to conjure with and it was not long before Pépin had decided that he would build a church here in gratitude for all his victories.

By 838 there certainly was an abbey by the side of the river that the monks had christened Celer and in 1035 the abbey was affiliated with Cluny.

The church became something of a rival to Conques (Aveyron), not least because of its position on a Compostela route, and today Figeac's position still remains strategic. At the very edge of the Lot, indeed at the very edge of Quercy, it straddles the divide between the high Auvergne country and the *causses* and borders on the edge of the ancient country of the Rouergue, which is today Aveyron. Only a few kilometres east of Figeac the transition becomes obvious. The stone changes to the dour, dark grey-brown of the Auvergne, the houses change shape and the land seems to brace itself against the mountain cold.

Figeac was a Roman site and although the story about Pépin as patron cannot be authenticated the abbey did well for itself and the town grew up around it. Although legend is rich in Figeac – another claims that Pope Etienne II was beaten to the consecration ceremony in 755 by Christ himself, who descended to do the job with an escort of angels – documentation is slight before the eleventh century. It seems though that the abbey began to grow under the Benedictines, occupying in those early days a site on the left bank of the Célé. But the feud with Conques grew too, ending only with the intervention of the Concile de Nîmes in 1090. By 1092 all was forgotten as another pope was awaited to consecrate the big church. The buildings of the abbey now occupied most of the south-east part of Figeac and from within the monastery walls the abbot ruled the town with the help of seven consuls.

It was not long before the abbot and the consuls began to disagree and the town was ceded to King Philippe le Bel, destroyer of the Templars, who had constantly found himself at odds with Rome. Under royal authority the town became rich. The consuls were now elected by the townsfolk themselves and Philippe installed a *viguier* or royal justice administrator, and even a mint. Thirteenth-century Figeac had seven consuls, seven gates and seven *quartiers* – Montferrer, Montviguier, Aujou, Orthabadial, Benagut, Tomfort and du Pin – and it prospered.

But then came the Hundred Years War and things were not quite so rosy. Figeac, fortified by walls and the river Célé to the south, resisted the English attacks successfully. But the Treaty of Brétigny dictated that the town be handed over to the English and on 6 February 1361 a delegate of the Prince of Wales arrived at the town gates to take possession. In spite of this, local opposition was so great that it took until 1372 for the English to get their hands on the town, and when they did they occupied it for one year.

The Protestants stayed much longer. It was Jean Chevery who introduced Calvinism to Figeac and many people who heard the message were greatly impressed. By 1562 the heresy had taken hold to such an extent that the Protestants thought it worth an attempt to take the town. They were beaten off in this and subsequent attempts, however, until a curious turn of events finally led to a Protestant victory.

It appears that Duras, the Protestant chief, had been continually trying to persuade First Consul Rouzet to hand over the keys to one of the gates, but Rouzet had refused all bribes and offers. Not so his wife; she waited until her husband slept, then quietly stole away clutching the keys, to the Montferrier Gate on the north side of town. In return for money she handed them over to Duras. One wonders at the story behind these events. Had Mme Rouzet long planned this expedition? Was it an act of revenge? Was hers an unhappy marriage? Was she attracted to Duras? Was she a sympathizer who wanted the Protestants to control the town? Whatever the truth, Figeac had a fine Christmas present thanks to her efforts. On 23 December 1568 the town was burned and pillaged. A chapel in the gate commemorates the dreadful events.

Meause, another Calvinist chief, moved into the old church of Le Puy and there he stayed until 1622, in spite of a Catholic uprising in 1577. In 1598, after the Edict of Nantes granting freedom of worship to the Protestants, Figeac was recognized as a place of safety for the Huguenots, along with its neighbours Cardaillac and Cajarc and, further south, Montauban, a fact which was to cause problems for Louis XIV, whose famous armourer Cisteron was accorded the right to asylum there. The Protestant rule was being challenged, the Revocation of the Nantes Treaty was not far away and Louis needed Cisteron, whose exquisite work now graces many a museum round the world. A safeguard was nailed to his house instructing the Figeaçois to accord him all the ordinary privileges and rights of a royal armourer.

Another famous Frenchman sought asylum in Figeac in the early seventeenth century; the famous duke of Sully was governor there for a while. The relationship between Figeac and Sully was a long one. The duke had originally sought asylum in the town after the assassination of Henry IV, for Sully, a dour Protestant, had a son who was governor at nearby Capdenac le Haut. Sully had a house in each town, the one at Figeac large and notable enough to have the whole square named after it. Alas, it fell into such a state of disrepair that it exists no longer, although the very beautiful door can still be seen in the museum, giving an indication of just how grand the whole mansion must have been.

The years leading up to the Revolution were prosperous ones for Figeac, but the Revolution itself engendered mixed feelings in the town, where loyalties swayed from king to republic and back again. But Figeac had still another occupation to endure. On Friday, 12 May 1944, with the SS division of the infamous 'Das Reich' stationed all around the town, the men of Figeac were invited to present themselves at the police station for an identity check. Those who turned up were divided into three groups – Jews, Resistance leaders and accomplices of the Resistance: everyone who did not fit the first two categories was accorded the third. All day they were held, the Germans moving them to the school yard. The rumour spread that the liberation was to be announced and the release of some men towards three o'clock did nothing to dispel this, even though they were to a man gas and electricity workers, railwaymen and workers at the Ratier factory which produced German aircraft.

At five o'clock, when the lorries arrived, some were still labouring under the same misapprehension. Five hundred and forty Figeaçois and an English officer, Richard Pinder, who had been hiding in the area, clambered aboard and began the long journey, not to Cahors for an announcement, but to the German labour camps and Dachau. One hundred and forty-five people did not return. A simple plaque in the Place du 12 Mai 1944 commemorates the event.

Avril – Mai 1944
540 deportés
145 morts
Leur sacrifice appartient à la patrie, leur souvenir à Figeac

By 7 June there was increased activity on all sides, the Germans heading as fast as possible towards Normandy and the Allied landings, the Resistance doing everything in their power to slow them down. Aimé Noël in a book on Figeac tells how at four o'clock that morning the Nazis paid a visit to the mayor and the *sous-prefet*. They none of them spoke the other's language but it was clear that something was being planned. Note was made by the Germans of strategic points in the town – the police station, the railway station, the post office. Later on the two Frenchmen were taken up to the heights of Le Cingle, from where they could clearly see the German artillery focused on the town.

Whilst they had been away, the secretary-general had succeeded in telephoning Cahors from the independent phone at the station and had also enlisted the help of a fluent German-speaker, Mme Besse. The two men were returned home at ten o'clock and summoned again at lunch time. This time Mme Besse went with them. They were asked where the Resistance was hiding, but the mayor said he did not know of any terrorists. Dr Schmidt, the SS officer, was angry but the presence of Mme Besse proved invaluable. Introductions were exchanged and through her the mayor was able to tell the officer of the events of 12 May. Dr Schmidt seemed genuinely concerned, reported the observers, claiming that many innocent people had to suffer to catch the culpable. In the rather more traditional manner of the SS, however, he continued that he had orders to hang 120 Figeaçois and bombard the town. For whatever reason neither deed took place. It seems unlikely that an SS officer would risk disobeying orders for reasons of sentimentality, as some later claimed, and it is an undeniable fact that the SS left Figeac and headed for the Gramat *causse* and Gabaudet, where 35 members of the Maquis were soon to die in combat. All over the Lot there were vicious reprisals, and if Figeac escaped this time many others did not. At Tulle (Corrèze) only two days later, 99 people were hanged from the town's balconies and lamp-posts.

The other monument in Figeac stands above the town on the

same spot from where a despairing mayor and his *sous-préfet* looked down on Figeac and the artillery ranged upon it. The Monument du Cingle is a vow from the people of Figeac that such happenings will not be repeated, as well as a monument of remembrance. The names of the martyrs are engraved along the stone with a tall cement cross standing guard, and it is nice to record that it was a German priest working in Figeac who collected the funds which enabled it to be lit.

But war is not so neat. In its aftermath came recriminations. People had been betrayed and some found this hard to forgive. In Figeac a new mayor was primed with the task of dealing with these sensitivities. They were lucky. In Cahors collaborators were executed.

Augustus Hare described Figeac as 'more of a town of the past than of the present'. In some ways that holds true today, but Figeac is also a lively place, with a lived-in feel to it. The oldest street in town is the **rue Emile Zola**, formerly Rue Droite, which still retains a wealth of old doors and windows. A route has been worked out by the Syndicat d'Initiative which takes in the best examples; you simply follow a series of old key signs, rather like the red line that runs round parts of old Boston. The streets all carry their alternative Occitan names. The Rue Clermont, for example, is also called the Carriera de la Bonas-Manas because the residents here came in frequent contact with Figeac's high society. Even a casual stroll among the streets, though, gives glimpses of a richness in architecture which can be compared to somewhere like Cordes (Tarn). Ordinary places such as Prixunis and the Crédit Agricole are often housed in quite extraordinary buildings.

There used to be a canal, giving the name Poor Man's Venice to the area it passed through, but sadly it has been filled in and no longer exists; neither does the old and rather spectacular market hall still stand. You should certainly try to see the **Orthabadial**, where the person in charge of agricultural matters at the monastery lived. In the rue Balène you can see the extant wall of the old château, built originally by the Templars but, after their dissolution, passing to the Balène family. It did not stay in their hands, however, following a row of dramatic proportions between the two brothers, which ended with one brother and one monkey dead. Edward III dealt with this by confiscating the building and selling it to the town consuls.

The Templars had another residence in the old Place Haute, now **Place Champollion**, with a powerful-looking façade, next to a tall thin building with a *soleilho*, although you do not have to travel far in Figeac to find that particular architectural feature. A *soleilho* is an open gallery at the very top of a house, generally with a flat roof supported by columns. The reason for them seems to have been, quite simply, that in tall houses in crowded towns a spot of fresh air was welcome. They closely resemble spinning galleries and many of the town's tradesmen put them to good use. It is tempting to speculate on Figeac's Huguenot tradition, however, and compare the *soleilhos* to the galleries found in Huguenot homes in London's Spitalfields.

There is a significance, too, in the name Place Champollion, but you have to move on to the **Place de la Raison** to find it. Here you will find what looks like a small version of Cleopatra's Needle, and that is exactly what it is, for Jean-François Champollion, the man who deciphered the Rosetta stone, was born at Figeac in 1790.

Near the Place de la Raison is the old abbatial church of Figeac, **St Sauveur**, much destroyed in the Wars of Religion. The oldest part is on the south side which dates from the eleventh century. The north entrance door is thirteenth-century and replaced a very beautiful Romanesque work of zodiac signs and allegorical animals. The Notre-Dame chapel has some interesting seventeenth-century wooden panels depicting naïve scenes from the Passion.

The other church, that of **Notre-Dame-du-Puy**, stands on a hill overlooking the town and has also been greatly restored. Only a few Romanesque capitals survive. The nave is Gothic. This is the oldest parish of the town and a church has existed here since records began. It is the site of yet another legend: that the Virgin, wishing to see an oratory built, made a rose tree bloom here one Christmas, amidst the snow, and indeed the popular name for Notre-Dame-du-Puy still exists – Notre Dame à Fleurie. By and large, though, the churches of Figeac are a disappointment for a town which has conserved its past in other ways so well. There is some good Gothic glass in the Eglise des Carmes, and on the outskirts of town is Notre-Dame-de-la-Capelette where they used to hold processions for rain. Well, times have changed!

Although there are vestiges of the ramparts still extant, the only remains of the once great abbey are curious needle-like obelisks, which look like something a medieval Champollion might have erected. Twelfth-century and fifteen metres high, two of the original four survive and are thought to be boundary markers delineating the land over which the abbey had jurisdiction. In the days of real pilgrimage beacons were lit on top of the needles to guide the pilgrims in.

But if Figeac's ecclesiastical remains are something of a disappointment its civil ones are not. The **rue Gambetta**, formerly du Griffoul, and the principal street of the old town, has half-timbered houses. In the **rue Tomfort** stands the elegant house – and how could it be otherwise? – of the flamboyant lord of Assier, Galiot de Genouillac, with its corner turret. The Hôtel Dumont de Sournac is to be found in the rue Clermont, and Cisteron's house, occupied by the Crédit Agricole, in the Place Carnot. The *viguierie*, a shadow of its former self, is in the **rue Delzhens** climbing up to Notre-Dame-du-Puy, as medieval a street as you could wish for. Every step in Figeac reveals an arch, a window, a turret, a *soleilho* or something to catch the eye, although it is not a pretty town in the conventional sense.

The tour already mentioned begins and ends at the **Oustal de lo Mounédo**, the Hôtel de la Monnaie or Mint. It was an honour for any town to mint money and the building now reflects this, following an unfortunate decision to demolish all the buildings around it. It now stands in splendid isolation on the edge of a car park, a handsome Gothic building dating from the thirteenth century, with tiers-pointed windows and the ubiquitous *soleilho*. It houses the town's museum, containing a cast of the Rosetta stone and information about Champollion, some old coins and seals, the door of the Sully mansion and odds and ends of local interest.

Figeac was also the home of the Quercy poet Jules Malrieu, born in 1854 and dying tragically young at 34. He wrote of his town and its magnificent Mint:

> ...les siècles ont jeté
> Sur cet atelier mort les cendres du silence...
> ...ses vieux murs face de reliquaire
> Où repose et survit le coeur de la cité.

16

Figeac: 2

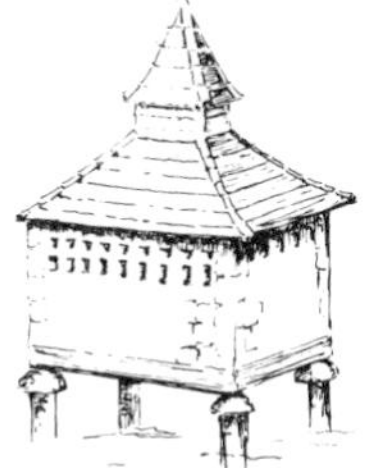

The Célé

The Célé is to the Lot what the Vézère is to the Dordogne. This dramatic valley, where the river turns a tortuous route through the huge cliffs, is the prehistory centre of the Lot. Stone Age man prowled amongst its caves, fished in its river and engraved its rock walls.

Much later on, the powerful Hébrard family ruled the valley, giving their name to the area they controlled – the Hébrardie. The English knew the Célé too, and there is evidence of their stay – from place-names to the fortified caves that dot the valley, still known today as *'châteaux des anglais'*.

For today's walker or motorist it is a dramatic route. The cliffs rise sheer above the road, sometimes in enormous overhangs, sometimes the road plunging right through the middle of them. Yet this is not a wide, Dordogne-style valley, and the river that flows through it is not elegant or mature; it is a happy-go-lucky, gurgling river, swirling around rocks, tickling fish, babbling round bends, secret and sinuous, shielded by trees and shrubs and creepers. No railway line runs along the Célé as it does the Dordogne or the Lot. Explore it out of season and you will share it only with the kingfishers and the orioles. And although the railway does put in an appearance above Figeac, we shall explore the valley downstream, where the river flows to join the Lot.

Leave Figeac on its westerly side, following the D13, and turn left where the D41 joins it near the fifteenth-century castle of Ceint-d'Eau. Drop down to Boussac, where the *pietà* in the church of St Jean Baptiste is worth a visit. Mary has the hard, weathered look of a Lot countrywoman and, although tears course down her cheeks at the sight of her son lying in an advanced state of *rigor mortis* across her knees, one feels sure that her grief is silent.

Corn, less than a mile further on, is where you descend to the Célé if you have approached it over the *causse*. The road drops steeply on to a wonderful roofscape with the tower of Corn's ruined fifteenth-century château towering over the village. The *gentilhommière* is the one-time Château de Roquefort, bought in 1810 by Count Murat, brother of the King of Naples; and across the river on the cliffs of Goudou are the ruins of the château of the same name. The English stayed here during the Hundred Years War and beyond, fortifying two caves for safety.

Continue downstream through **Ste Eulalie**, where the intrepid Abbé Lemozi discovered some prehistoric engravings in a cave suspended in the cliff face above a garden opposite the mill. Magdalenian reindeer and some horses prance across the left-hand wall. Only a few yards further on you will be tantalized by the sight of an extraordinary half-timbered belfry peeping through the trees across the river. Give in and cross over, for this is the priory of Val Paradis at **Espagnac-Ste-Eulalie** and one of the sights of the Célé. It is a beautiful village, one of the prettiest in the whole *département*. You can park by the fortified thirteenth-century gateway that leads into the ruined priory. The main gates to the church are usually locked. But by now you may well have been approached by the small woman who perches on the wall alongside where the cars park. 'Do you want to see the church?' she asks in a low, almost unintelligible mumble, and then beckons. It is done for love, for she directs any offers of money into the coffers of the priory. The tour is a depressing one despite the appeal of the decrepit thirteenth-century church, for she talks so quietly and with such unvaried intonation that unless you bend down beside the monotone to listen you cannot hear a thing. Questions, it seems, are out of the question. The priory was founded in the twelfth century by an Augustinian monk from the abbey of La Couronne near Angoulême, but in 1211 it became a convent in which Aymeric d'Hébrard St Sulpice took a great interest and under his protective wing it greatly prospered. The tall church in Flamboyant Gothic is unusual in that it has tombs: one of Aymeric d'Hébrard St Sulpice, member of the Célé family and bishop of Coimbra in Portugal, who died in 1295; one of Hugues de Cardaillac Brengues who died in 1342; and one of his wife, niece of Pope Jean XXII.

Damp and mould streak down the walls of the church, which is peculiar in that the chevet is higher than the nave. There is a faded elegance about it, though, and about the massive painting of the Assumption after Vouet but overall there is a light, airy feel, probably owing to the height of the roof.

Outside on those neat lawns that tend to surround abbeys and priories today, visitors are allowed to stroll for a few minutes before the gates are locked again. The lawn stretches down to the river banks, swallows and house martins swoop around and up under the eaves, and it is easy to see why this was called Paradise Valley. Every turn of the head frames a view more exquisite than the last.

Walk under the fortified gate and you find yourself among the ruins of the priory and its land, giving a good idea of its former size. The path leads down to the banks of the Célé and from here you get a very good view of that eccentric belfry, half-timbered with an open gallery, surmounted by an octagonal roof and *lauze* tiles. Viewed from here, all the buildings are of exceptional beauty, especially with the evening sun shining on the walls and the cliff face beyond. The cliffs in the Célé have a beauty all their own in terms of colour. Normally a soft peach, at times of the setting sun they develop violet and pink streaks. One is struck, probably for the umpteenth time that day, by the happy marriage of architecture and landscape that exists in the Lot.

Downriver again is **Brengues**, one of the few places in the Lot where you can find not only one, but two shops open on a Sunday afternoon; one attached to the hotel, the other up the steep hill to the right. Ring the bell and wait. Here again, as all down the river, there are *châteaux des anglais*, fortified caves, above your head. Incredible that they should have preserved their bizarre name down the centuries, but the English presence in this valley was formidable and even after the war marauding soldiers stayed behind to eke out a living by terrorizing the local population. It is said that the name Brengues derives from an English name, although it is hard to see what it might have been.

St Sulpice lies under the cliff face, guarded by the castle belonging to the family who gave their name to this river region; the Hébrard family still own it today. During the Middle Ages this old and powerful family ruled the Célé, fiercely protecting its inhabitants and pouring money into its two abbeys – Marcilhac and Espagnac. There is a feudal air still about the Célé, with its ancient buildings, its pretty villages and poplar-lined river.

Next stop is **Marcilhac**, another Célé 'must'. Marcilhac has caves too – though none with paintings – which were the victims of some royal vandalism when their stalactites were ripped out to make *objets d'art* for the castles of Catherine of Medici. The caves are sometimes called the caves of Robinet, but the newer ones of Bellevue were only discovered in 1964.

The real point of Marcilhac is its Benedictine abbey, a very old one indeed with one of the most charmingly naïve Christs in Glory that you will see on your whole journey round the Lot. The abbey, set in a *cirque* round the widening valley, was in its early days attached either to Moissac or St Amans de Cahors (no one is sure which) but became independent in the tenth century. It was one of the two protagonists in the argument over who owned Rocamadour. In the event, Marcilhac lost. It had never been interested in Rocamadour until it became a potential money-spinner with the discovery of 'the body'.

The abbey suffered at the hands of the English (who seem to have regarded the entire Célé valley as some sort of guerrilla hide-out) and later at the hands of the Protestants, but after the Reformation it was the Hébrard family who gained control. The Revolution finally killed it, although it had never recovered its fourteenth-century prosperity.

Most of the Romanesque part of the church is in total ruin, although the whole abbey is currently undergoing extensive restoration. Luckily the door has been saved, though it is badly worn. It is a very, very early work, a Last Judgment of the tenth or early eleventh century. A doll-like old man of a God is flanked by two angels looking, it has to be said, more like messengers from the Devil, and beneath them are St Paul and St Peter, the latter clutching his keys as if they were a baby's rattle. The sun and moon are also depicted, the sun looking more like a Lot sunflower. Each figure is neatly enclosed in something resembling a mandorla, but much has been lost with the passage of time. The only other remnants of the Romanesque are the capitals in the chapterhouse, which depicts monsters, devils and biblical scenes.

The Gothic part of the church is better preserved and boasts some excellent wood panels showing scenes from the lives of Christ and the Virgin. The *pietà* is a sixteenth-century wooden sculpture, nicely proportioned, with Mary supporting Jesus's head in the cup of her hand. The two towers are both fortified.

Two Black Virgins grace the river at this point, one the **Notre-Dame-du-Bon-Rencontre**, the pilgrimage to which takes place on Ascension Day, and the other at **Sauliac**, housed in the troglodyte chapel – one of six in the Lot – of the Notre-Dame-de-Roc-Traoucat. This chapel was built in 1889 to house the ugly Virgin who until then had lived in the natural tunnel through which the mule path passed before the D41 was built. The Virgin would be invoked by travellers before they entered the dark reaches of the tunnel:

> Sur les bords du Célé, Marie
> Dans le creux d'un rocher sourit:
> Le Pélerin s'arrête et prie;
> Et la Madone le bénit.

Sauliac is another pretty village with an abundance of old houses, which makes it an attractive spot for holiday homes, always a killer to rural life. In 1870 its population was seven hundred; today there are only about one hundred making a life for themselves in this rocky valley.

Sauliac is the turn-off point for Cuzals and the Open-Air Museum of Quercy. I have spoken of the museum elsewhere in this book and I strongly recommend a visit to anyone who wants to make any sense at all of the Lot and the way in which life was and is lived here. After Sauliac, the road hugs the river and the scenery becomes more and more spectacular. At La Pescalerie, better known today as the home of a luxury hotel run by two Cahors doctors, water cascades from the cliff face beside an old mill and only yards further on is **Cabrerets**.

The village occupies a commanding position at the confluence of two rivers, the Sagne and the Célé and is guarded by two formidable castles. The Gontaut-Biron castle is still intact, but the aptly named Château de Diable is in ruins; as well it might be, for records show that it was well in place in 1259. It was from this castle, captured by the Hébrard in 1390, that the English conducted their guerrilla war up and down the Célé – hence the name, no doubt.

But Cabrerets has more to it than castles. It is a name that will leap to the lips of any prehistorian or palaeontologist in the land, for Cabrerets, home of the Abbé Lemozi, was also the home of a museum of prehistory. The museum has moved now, up the road that climbs out of Cabrerets towards the famous painted cave on which the village depends for a living, the cave of Pech-Merle.

Pech-Merle has always been the largest cave in the area, and since the closure of Lascaux it has become one of the most important as well. The paintings are thought to be somewhere between 20,000 and 40,000 years old. The cave of course is a lot older, but it was rediscovered in 1922, in the proper tradition of French caves everywhere, by a child, André David. André knew exactly who to tell about his discovery and why not: it was Lemozi's work and discoveries in the area which had fired him in the first place, and it was to Lemozi that he went. In due course the priest, too, crawled through the rock fissure to discover what he was later to call the *'grotte-temple'*.

A temple it almost certainly is, but it is the proportions of Pech-Merle which impress, for unlike most other caves in the area this one is enormous; the paintings are almost dwarfed by the dimensions in which they find themselves. Pech-Merle offers plenty of interest to the prehistorian. To the amateur, though, it is the revelation of the dappled horses that will linger in the mind. You see them first from above, from a rock gallery rather like a theatre box. They are life size, these horses, they dominate the cave not so much because of any skill in artistry, but from sheer position. Later on you can get closer, but this is the best view. They are fat, healthy, glowing horses with round, plump rumps and black manes. They stand together, facing in opposite directions, the hindquarters of one superimposed on the other's, their bodies covered with the blue-grey spots of manganese which gives the dappled effect. Dappled mares, I like to imagine. They seem very feminine horses to me.

The rock on which they are painted might have been deliberately faced for their creation, a smooth, flat surface, stained with ochre, and you can see quite clearly where the artist got his idea from, for the slab ends in a curious formation exactly the shape of a horse's head. The right-hand horse, therefore, has a sculptured head, naturally sculptured. In the dim light of his lamp or fire the artist saw this. Did he look for it? Was he lolling back watching the shadows with half-closed eyes when the shape took form? We shall never know.

As with all cave art, these animals are enigmatic and full of mystique, but they are decidedly pleasurable too and eminently recognizable. These great grey mares are circus horses with broad backs; acrobats should be standing tiptoe on their rumps as they circle the ring. Even if prehistory leaves you cold, the Pech-Merle horses will stay alive in your mind's eye for many years to come.

The entrance to Pech-Merle is near the original entrance and in summer you will have to queue, although your ticket does also entitle you to slide shows and the excellent prehistory museum as well. The queue results in an infuriating situation as the anarchic French jostle for position while the resigned English seethe and moralize in low voices; their own cultural inadequacies and inhibitions prevent similar behaviour in deed if not in thought.

You enter down a staircase. There are formations, stalactites and stalagmites. The roots of a tree trail down from the roof of the cave, hanging free, like old Christmas decorations. The perspective is upsetting, like being in a coffin and looking up. There are frozen limestone waterfalls, and tiny cave 'pearls' lit with a delicate light to show their translucence; and footprints, the footprints of an Aurignacian man and his child. It is hardly credible.

There are over three kilometres of these sights and if they do not appear to crowd in on you at the time it is only because the cave is so vast. And beyond all the bones of cave bears and the petrified footprints are the paintings. What a range there is here, from the macaroni scrawls of earliest Aurignacian man, who trailed his fingers across soft clay walls, to the mammoths and bison, so much better depicted than the human figures who appear here, too, as at Cougnac – women with dangling breasts, crudely drawn outlines.

On the frieze that includes the dappled Gravettian horses you can see one of the rare fish depicted in cave art, a pike, superimposed on the back of the right-hand horse. Sometimes cave-art viewing can be a bit like painting by numbers: the subjects are not immediately obvious. Usually the guides will outline the drawing with the light of a pen torch. All around the horses are hands; tiny outlines, smaller than ours, of the artist's hands. But in such a cave there would have been several artists over the long years. The hands are known as negative imprints.

When you surface the air seems hot and everything just a bit too normal. Cave viewing always gives you a new perspective on life, somehow. Below you the dappled horses graze on.

17

Excursions

The Lot is lucky enough to be relatively central, surrounded on all sides by countryside as disparate as the flat wastes of Les Landes and the high volcanic peaks of the Auvergne. Visitors wishing to explore beyond the boundaries of the Lot will have little difficulty in selecting some place or area of interest; even the Spanish border is only a few hours away.

The routes I have outlined here, however, do not stray that far, requiring at most a one-night stop-over. The best of France, it seems to me, is found in its small villages and market towns, but the Lot is full of villages like these and there seems little point in directing the traveller a hundred kilometres further on to a community of a few hundred souls. By and large, then, these routes have some focus to them: either a large town or grouping of towns, or a landscape of particular interest. They are not meant to be followed to the letter – treat them merely as suggestions and guidelines. If Romanesque tympanums leave you cold, then so will Moissac. Leave it out. If bleak mountain countryside bores you, don't go near the Aubrac.

To the west and north of the Lot lies the much frequented Dordogne. People unfamiliar with the *département* will find much to interest them there; the delights of Domme and Sarlat are minutes away from the Lot, Beynac and La Roque-Gageac only a bit further on. But the Dordogne is well documented and for that reason alone I have not included it here. Likewise, the northerly reaches of Lot-et-Garonne which border on the Dordogne are well covered, but you could organize a very pleasant day from Gourdon, drifting in and out of the *bastides* which lie in both those *départements* – Monpazier, Beaumont, Issigeac, Villeréal, Montflanquin – taking in the magnificent castle of Bonaguil and Villefranche-du-Périgord on the way home. There is an immutable quality about these *bastides* and not all have fallen prey to the tourist. A restaurant sign I recently saw in Issigeac advertised a five-course meal, with coffee and wine thrown in, for under 50 francs.

For the same reasons, I have not covered the big centres of Montauban and Toulouse. Both places are best reached by train. There are frequent and fast services from Souillac, Gourdon and Cahors, which save hours of parking frustrations by depositing you right in the middle of town. Toulouse, of course, has all the attractions of a large city and a historical pedigree of some note. Like its much smaller neighbour, Montauban, it is a town built of brick. Montauban, ancient capital of Bas-Quercy, is built on the Tarn; an old Protestant stronghold whose marvellous collection of Ingres paintings is housed in the episcopal palace above the river. It houses, too, the work of that other son of Montauban, the sculptor Bourdelle.

Those areas I do include in this section will give a taste of D'Artagnan's Gascony in the Gers; a feel of the south in the Impressionist landscape of the Tarn; a glimpse at the versatile countryside of the Aveyron, from the thick wooded gorges of Najac, to the juniper-covered wastes of the *causse* outside Rodez, to the high pasture-land around Laguiole; a view over the peaks of the Auvergne; and a stroll through the chestnut woods of the Corrèze.

From south-west Lot to Lot-et-Garonne and the Gers: Agen, Condom, Moissac

The *département* of Lot-et-Garonne borders on the western part of the Lot, and offers a gentle rolling landscape that is becoming increasingly popular with the *gîte*-loving British. I cannot say it is a *département* that greatly appeals to me, however, except in its northernmost reaches where it borders on the Dordogne, and there is a rich feel to the undulating countryside.

Further west, towards Marmande, there is a hint, the merest suggestion as the land flattens, of encroaching industry, and south-west towards the Garonne and Agen this becomes more than a suggestion. From Fumel onwards, through the bustling market *bastide* of Villeneuve-sur-Lot and on to Agen, there is a scraggy feel to the place; ribbon development along the roads on the lead-in to towns, for example. Intensive fruit and vegetable farming means that great acres of fields are covered in ugly plastic and interspersed with supermarkets.

All this is unsurprising, for the area is well served by communications. Agen to Bordeaux, Bordeaux to Paris, Agen to Toulouse and on into Spain; these are all linked by motorway and parallel to that great river, the Garonne, lies the massive **Canal Latéral de la Garonne**, up which the working barges still plough their way. The Canal Latéral was part of Pierre-Paul Riquet's dream to link the Atlantic with the Mediterranean. He had to wait until he was 63 to see the first stone laid on the Canal du Midi (which the Canal Latéral joins at Toulouse) and died penniless in 1680, without ever seeing boats sail on his masterpiece of engineering.

Visitors, too, can rent barges on this stretch, although many would prefer to stick to the Canal du Midi. The local Syndicats d'Initiative have several books outlining routes on both canals, some meandering through the Bordeaux vineyards, one of which started with the sound advice: 'You are the only ones to judge your dayly rythm of navigation [sic]'. The French Government Tourist Office has plenty of information on fly-cruise holidays. These three, the Autoroute des Deux Mers, the river and the canal, run alongside each other, cutting a curved swathe through the countryside; lorries overtaking barges, complicated concrete under- and over-passes, and one must not forget the railway, which overtakes the lot.

There are exceptions to the industrialized rule. **Pujols** on the D118 above Villeneuve is one: a white-walled village set on a hill overlooking its younger but larger neighbour to the north-east. Pujols had three lines of defences in the old days. Today only the second still exists. The castle has gone too, destroyed for the part it played in the Albigensian Crusade.

You can leave the car outside the ramparts and walk in under the town gate, through the little streets to the church of Ste Foy and its frescos, visiting the museum and admiring the view over the valley, catching your breath before you face Agen.

There is only one real reason for going to **Agen** and that is the **museum**, so the first thing to check is that you are not planning to go on a Tuesday. All over France museums shut on a Tuesday. Most of them will also shut for a long lunch, so aim to arrive well before midday.

You may wonder what is so special about Agen's museum that it merits a visit to this bustling city of Must-Burgers and busy shops. The reason is the art collection, which surprisingly enough includes five Goyas. Not as complete or impressive a show as that at Castres (Tarn), but worth a detour. There is a revealing self-portrait of Goya, one of the Caprichos series of etchings, the ascent of a balloon from the Buen Retiro garden in Madrid (with the people on the ground rushing to follow its progress), a portrait of Ferdinand VIII of Spain, and 'La Misada Parida', painted apparently on top of another painting which threatens to overwhelm the Goya. Other exhibits will not disappoint either. Courbet, Corot, Sisley and Boudin are all represented, along with a collection which belonged to the count of Chaudordy and the ceramics of Boudon de St Amens, an Agenais who brought English methods of earthenware-making to France. The other treasure is a statue known as the Venus du Mas d'Agenais, discovered by a surprised farmer in 1876. This is one of the best and most beautiful Venuses ever discovered in France, dating from the first century BC. She is an elegant, beautifully proportioned figure, even without her head and arms.

The museum is housed in Renaissance mansions between the Place de la Mairie and the Rue'des Juifs, Agen does indeed have some very lovely buildings and corners, even though the sum of its parts is not too inspiring. You might think you would like to see the cathedral of St Caprais whilst you are here, with its twelfth-century apse and apsidal chapels. Unfortunately you cannot, for Agen locks its cathedral, except in the summer months or by appointment with a guide. A sign of the times, perhaps, but while one may expect country churches these days to follow this line, one hardly expects it of cathedrals. So, you are left with the aqueduct which carries the canal across the river, and the *pruneaux*. Agen prunes are definitely superior to most other prunes – it just depends on how much you like prunes. If you do, then you can apparently taste them at the Syndicat d'Initiative, which will also provide you with a list of prune factories to visit. But the Syndicat was the other cause of my irritation with Agen. I found its staff decidedly unhelpful – an unusual occurrence in my experience – added to which all the really useful pamphlets and papers were charged for.

I was glad to leave Agen, felt untempted even by its *Circuit des Eglises Romanes*, its wide *boulevards*, its Le Chicken-stop, Rotonde Fast Food and Windsor Pub. At **Layrac** things started to look up again. The square was triangular and arcaded, the church looked more Russian than French with its onion-shaped cupola, and the friendly native we asked for directions was so friendly that he had to be dissuaded from actually climbing into the car.

Pretty well the minute you cross into the Gers things get better.

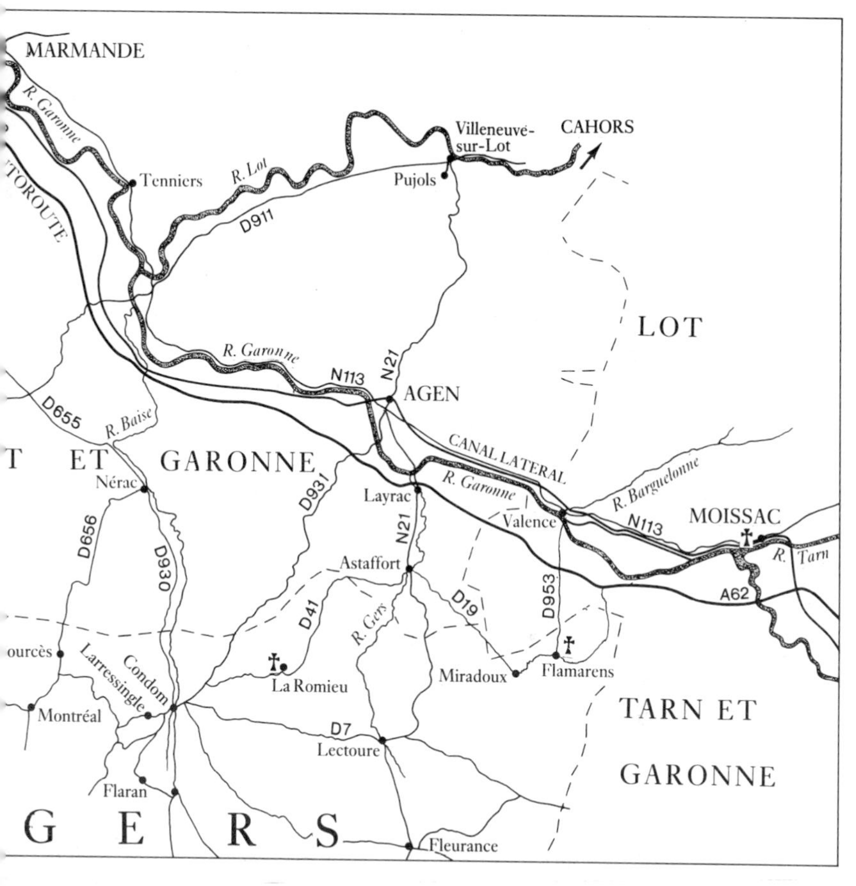

The countryside is still gentle and pastoral, yellow soil patchworking with the deeper coloured rape, but the dirtiness has gone. Here, too, the fruit is grown under plastic cloches, or else the strawberries push their way through plastic strips that lie on the ground to keep their undersides clean. There are vines as well for this is Armagnac country and we are heading for Condom, about 40 kilometres south-west of Agen, capital of Armagnac, and a good place to send postcards from in the middle of a government Aids campaign.

You round a corner on the D41 Astaffort-Condom road and there is **La Romieu**, its two Gascon towers overshadowing the tiny *cité* and peeping up between the hills – and two giant rubbish bins at its entrance. The French have never really got to grips with the problem of what to do with rubbish. Invariably they choose the most picturesque spot they can find and hurl bottles, bags, beds and chairs into it. If there is a cliff or a depression so much the better: that way you can never get it out. Occasionally they set fire to it, leaving ugly black scars surrounded by boxes of Kleenex, old tyres and plastic Evian bottles. The other, worse aspect of this failing is the way in which whole woods are turned into gigantic public lavatories, with streamers of tissue paper waving from every branch and bush. A new drive has placed enormous plastic dustbins and bottle banks in most *communes*, in the Lot at least, but often they lie empty. Well, La Romieu was trying, the bins were there, and once you get past the rubbish it is exquisitely beautiful.

The houses all face inwards in two rows, making a double 'wall'. You can drive into the centre but it is best to leave the car in the outer street, a wide one with the war memorial in the middle and a small garden with 'topiaried' bushes. Over the drawbridge and under the gate and you find yourself in a dilapidated and deserted semi-ruin. Tall buildings dominate the tiny square, grey and silent. There did not seem to be any people actually in La Romieu apart from *madame* in the *alimentation*; they clustered on the outside road too, their backs to the town, maybe afraid that too long a visit and they would all turn into ghosts and vanish into the depths of the cloisters. Rounding the corner on a group of ghosts would not be particularly surprising in La Romieu. The place is lost in and totally dominated by its history.

The town's name comes from the Gascon word *roumiou* meaning pilgrim. It is said that a German pilgrim, Albert, returning from Compostela, put down roots here and founded a Benedictine priory, which in 1002 was acquired by the abbey of St Victor de Marseille. Enter, nearly two centuries later, Arnaud d'Aux, son of a local lord, a man with a dream. Arnaud was well connected, particularly for someone embarking on a career in the Church. His friend and cousin was the archbishop of Bordeaux, shortly to become the first Avignon pope, Clément V. Arnaud's career blossomed. Soon he was bishop of Poitiers, then elevated to be the pope's Minister of Finance.

He was sent to England on several occasions, striking up a friendship there with King Edward II who, coincidentally, owned La Romieu thanks to the 1279 Treaty of Abbeville. Arnaud told Edward of his plan to found a collegiate at La Romieu. Edward was helpful and by 1318 negotiations had taken place with St Victor de Marseille, and the Benedictine priory was already a collegiate and something of a palace too. Sadly, Arnaud did not live to see his dream completed; he died in Avignon in 1321. But the venture was a successful one and the town knew some prosperity. Trouble came with the Wars of Religion and later with the Revolution, when the archives were burned and some more of the buildings damaged. The priory church was so badly mutilated that it was finally demolished completely in 1804.

Today the collegiate church still stands, along with bits of the palace and the cloisters, but the cloisters in particular are badly damaged, with much of the detail crumbling away before your very eyes. You can still make out some faces, though, along with lions, griffins, dogs and lots of floriated design. These are Gothic cloisters, more reminiscent of some of the cathedrals in the Ile de France than of the local southern variety. The galleries are all complete and restoration work has started, but restoration on this scale inevitably means that some of the essence of the place will be lost.

The collegiate church with its ogive vaulting has only one historiated capital left, depicting some pigs. The church in its original state would have been painted, and to get an idea of what it would have looked like, step into the real gem of La Romieu, the **octagonal tower** which houses the sacristy. Here an amazing sight greets you, for the wall is covered with paintings; not frescos but tempera. The design is one of linking octagons arranged in groups of five: the central rose blank, the four surrounding and irregular octagons depicting scenes from the Bible, saints, prophets and an interesting trio of Christ and two women, the Virgin Mother and the Virgin Queen, a familiar bit of twelfth-century iconography but one wonders all the same at its origins. We are quite near the Cathar stronghold of the Pyrenees here, and it is interesting to note that Clément V's mother was a Blanchefort whose ancestor Bertrand had been Grand Master of the Templars in the twelfth century. Equally, of course, it was Clément V who along with the French king was responsible for suppressing the Templars. These paintings, in any case, belong to the early fourteenth century.

The vaulted ceiling is another wonder, for the octagonal design continues upwards into a star of painted angels, laced with the blue of the thin lancet windows. It is very lovely.

Arnaud, whom legend has a poor boy adopted by a rich family, was returned to his collegiate after his death. In the legend, too, he returned dressed anonymously in pilgrim's robe and cowl. Knocking on his mother's door, he received the customary greeting of having his feet washed. But he was forced to admit who he was when she noticed his sixth toe; a small detail, which you can't help feeling he might have anticipated. One wonders what he would make of La Romieu now, its wistaria-draped walls, its chestnut candles in full flower, its pruned plane trees and the silent arcades in the *place*. There would have been noise and bustle in the fourteenth century; the mason's hammer singing out on the soft fossilized limestone which was to have such difficulty surviving the centuries, some plainsong drifting from the church, perhaps; clergy and builders busying themselves around the town; very different from now.

Two kilometres east of La Romieu the caves of Nautéry threw

up a palaeontological first with the discovery of the bones of Ursus Romeviensis, the Romieu bear, a species hitherto unknown. Press on, though, to the warm and welcoming town of **Condom**, which optimistically advertises *'son climat'* on the outskirts. It is a calm, relaxed sort of place, but the odd thing is that you hardly see a sign, any sign, of the brandy trade that is Condom's *raison d'être*.

Armagnac is a brandy, the only one which can bear comparison with Cognac, although techniques in the making of the two differ enormously.

The best Armagnac probably comes from the country to the west of Condom. The land in the Gers is, in any case, marginally hotter than the Charente, where Cognac is made, but the real difference between the two lies in the type of still used. For Armagnac, a type of pot still is used which distils the alcohol at a much lower strength than Cognac, which allows for more flavour. Sugar is rarely added, so Armagnac tends to be drier than Cognac and particularly smooth. The brandy is then matured in black oak rather than white Limousin oak used in the Charente, which further distinguishes the taste and means that the wine matures much faster. Because of the methods used to make it you can drink a dark, rich matured Armagnac which is only eight years old. Real *aficionados* would probably say that the very best of Armagnacs could not match the quality of the very best of Cognacs, but for anything less it is a matter of taste, and many might choose Armagnac.

If you are hungry then Condom has plenty of places to eat, including the famous but expensive Table des Cordeliers off the Avenue de Gaulle, where you can relax with a coffee and Armagnac after the meal. After lunch you can go off to see the Armagnac Museum (which *is* open on a Tuesday), housed in the early eighteenth-century stables of a building which used to be the Bishops' Palace. The museum displays some of the old equipment which used to be used for brandy making, and the process is shown, together with a bit of folklore. Hail and storms are the enemy of all vineyards and there is a description of what was called the *carillon de tonnerre* next to an old bell. This refers to a local custom, which persisted until relatively recently, of ringing all the church bells when it looked as if a storm might be approaching. Believers attached a religious significance to this, while others thought that the vibrations somehow kept the storm away, but it made such an appalling din that the authorities sought to prevent it. A worse danger that had to be dealt with was the phylloxera outbreak of the late nineteenth century. American vines were substituted.

The cathedral of St Pierre is south-west Gothic, with a commemorative inscription above the sacristy door relating to its consecration in 1531. It started life as a Benedictine abbey, becoming the seat of a bishopric in 1317. The church suffered greatly under Montgomery, leader of the Protestants, and was even ransomed from him by the townsfolk for 30,000 livres. It is unusually light, with great emphasis placed on the windows, uncommon in the south. The south door is Flamboyant Gothic, and if you look at the keystones in the roof of the nave you will find St Peter holding a gigantic key.

There is nothing special about Condom; it is just a thoroughly pleasant place, and if you are enjoying the Gers and its gentle green countryside then there is much to keep you. The abbey of **Flaran** (again shut on Tuesdays) is a beautifully preserved Cistercian abbey, set in lovely grounds and only eight kilometres south of Condom. **Larressingle** is a fortified village, with bridge and moat still intact, which used to belong to Condom's bishops, and the tiny round *bastide* of **Fourcès** is another medieval gem. There are other *bastides*: Fleurance, Montréal and many, many more.

Rich gastronomes might be further tempted by the fact that they find themselves only 60 kilometres or so from Eugénie-les-Bains and Michel Guérard's famous hotel Les Prés et les Sources d'Eugénie. If you are lured by all this you will certainly have to stay overnight, but be careful: the Gers is not a tourist area and those unable or unwilling to afford Guérard may find that hotels are rather thinner on the ground here than they are in some parts of France. So many villages are deserted or near-abandoned that you will by no means have an extensive choice of village inns.

Well, the traveller is free in a way that the author is not and we are a long way from base, so we shall start heading back across the rolling green hills and yellow soil to Moissac. The patchwork stretches from one gentle summit to the next; the houses are low, massed affairs with lots of roof. It is worth noting again how well the architecture complements the landscape in these country areas. Past the vines, the strawberries and the plum trees, **Lectoure** looms distant on its hill, flourishing Roman town, hideaway of the counts of Armagnac, its Gothic tower standing sentinel; the sort of place it is an agony to rush through. Most of the churches in the Gers are Gothic; the Romanesque has all but vanished.

The **museum** has an interesting collection for a small town: Roman mosaics, altar stones dedicated to Cybele and dating from the second and third centuries and a collection of taurobilia. Initiates were washed in the blood of a slaughtered bull and thus cleaned of their sins. A stone was then set up to commemorate the fact.

Lectoure lies west of Condom at the junction of the N21 and the D7. Head north-west now, on through Miradoux with its ruined church tower, and the crumbling deserted Flamarens, the Virgin in the niche by the graveyard draped in lilac and flowering currant, and all too soon you are back at the main road again and depression sets in. If you are in a hurry you can zoom down the motorway to Moissac, but it would be better by far to climb to the pleasant hills on the far north side and descend into it from above.

The straggly *bastide* of Puymirol has a good and notable restaurant, L'Aubergade, but no hotel. There is no hotel either in any of the surrounding villages, which restricts one's alcohol consumption, for the roads are narrow and twisty, requiring good concentration at night. Indeed, there is a dearth of hotels in this whole area, and unless you head northwards you are almost forced to seek shelter in either Agen or Moissac; but the hotels in Moissac, while they exist, are nothing to write home about.

Moissac is trying hard. A restoration programme is going on around the church and some of the houses have that lovely mellowed brick that one always associates with the Tarn, which joins the Garonne just below the town, but most of it is frankly awful. The **Church of St Pierre** makes up for it. It makes up for this whole rotten corner, for the motorway and the railways and the tacky river and the straight, unappealing canal on whose banks Moissac sits.

I find it hard to imagine that anyone could fail to be moved by the south doorway of Moissac, for here – leaving aside perhaps Beaulieu (Corrèze), which it greatly resembles – is the tympanum to end all tympanums, the door to end all doors and, as at Cahors, it is the composition as much as the subject matter which calls for admiration. For it is the composition that lifts these doors above craftsmanship into the realms of art and makes them truly inspirational.

The theme is the Vision of the Apocalypse. Christ, an austere God, this, with His right arm raised in benediction and His left hand holding the Book of Life, sits on His throne above the sea of Paradise, surrounded by the symbolic figures of the Evangelists: Matthew as the winged man, Mark as the lion, Luke as the bull and John as the eagle. Apart from two seraphim squeezed in beside the Evangelists, the rest of the tympanum is filled with the 24 Elders of the Apocalypse. Each sculpture, each face, has a different expression. But what makes the door so commanding is the way every single subject of the tympanum is looking, with some fear, at the central figure of Christ. Every eye in the sculpture, whether of the old men or the twisted bodies of the Evangelist animals or the angels, all are looking at Christ. I say 'looking', but that is maybe the wrong word here; this is compulsion.

Beneath the last row of Elders is the lintel, on which are carved eight roses enclosed in a cable emanating from the mouth of a gruesome monster at one end and disappearing down the throat of a second at the other end. The central column supporting the lintel is composed of twisted lions, their bodies forming an X, very reminiscent of Souillac and Beaulieu. On the sides of this central column are two further sculptures, one of Isaiah and the other of Peter, to whom the church is dedicated. The edges of the engaged columns are scalloped, and even the central column appears to have wavy, uneven edges by virtue of the carving, so that the whole of the bottom of the door has an appealing lack of straight lines. This work is clearly Moorish in influence, probably explained by the fact that Moissac was well positioned on a Compostela route. The engaged columns have sculptures as well: scenes from well known Bible stories such as the Annunciation and the Adoration of the Magi on the right and less well known ones, including scenes of damnation, on the left. Even the sculptors themselves are to be seen if you look carefully between the capitals of the first and second vaults. Look and look, for this door is unique and powerful in its magnificence.

The abbey church of Moissac was founded in the seventh century but its importance in the eleventh rose from its attachment to Cluny in 1047. It suffered greatly under the English, who occupied the town twice, and during the Wars of Religion and the Revolution, and nearly suffered the indignity of being knocked down altogether to make way for the railway line. When you enter the church your first impression is that a Laura Ashley freak must have just moved out, for the walls appear to be covered with wallpaper – a large pattern of sand, red and greyish-brown – but in fact this is a restoration of the original decoration. It is the 'furniture' that sticks in the mind rather than the architectural details. There is a fifteenth-century coloured sculpture of the Flight into Egypt, showing Mary sitting sideways on a sweet-faced donkey; a fifteenth-century Entombment, and a *pietà* of the same century showing an elderly Mary with Jesus on her knees, flanked by St John and Gaussen de la Garrigue (he of the huge head), consul of Moissac. There is also a Merovingian tomb and a twelfth-century Christ. Nothing to match the door, though.

Moissac does have another marvel, however, and that is the **cloisters**. If cloisters are for contemplation and should have harmonious lines and fine craftsmanship, then these qualify. The round, marble-faced columns in different hues of pink, white and green, single and double alternately, are flanked by square stone columns at each corner, adorned with sculptures of various saints and men connected with the abbey. They date from the eleventh century. Once again there is a delicate Moorish feel to the place, and once again it is the sculpture that takes pride of place, for the capitals of the pillars are all intricately carved, either in geometric designs or with foliage, animals or Biblical stories. There is a hint, the merest suggestion, of the Alhambra in those slim and delicate columns.

Nothing could impress you after this. Cahors is about 60 kilometres away, north-eastwards.

From Figeac to Aveyron, Tarn and Tarn-et-Garonne: Villefranche, Cordes, Albi

The goal of this excursion is Albi, some hundred kilometres from Figeac, so it is certainly possible to leave early and return the same night. But the route takes us through such a delightful area – Aveyron, the northern reaches of the Tarn and a corner of Tarn-et-Garonne – that you may well regret rushing it.

You pass through another *bastide* on the way to Villefranche-de-Rouergne: Villeneuve-d'Aveyron, on the D992, stands on the *causse* on the borders of Quercy and the Aveyron, its arcading and part of its ramparts still intact and making an interesting contrast with its larger neighbour a few miles further on.

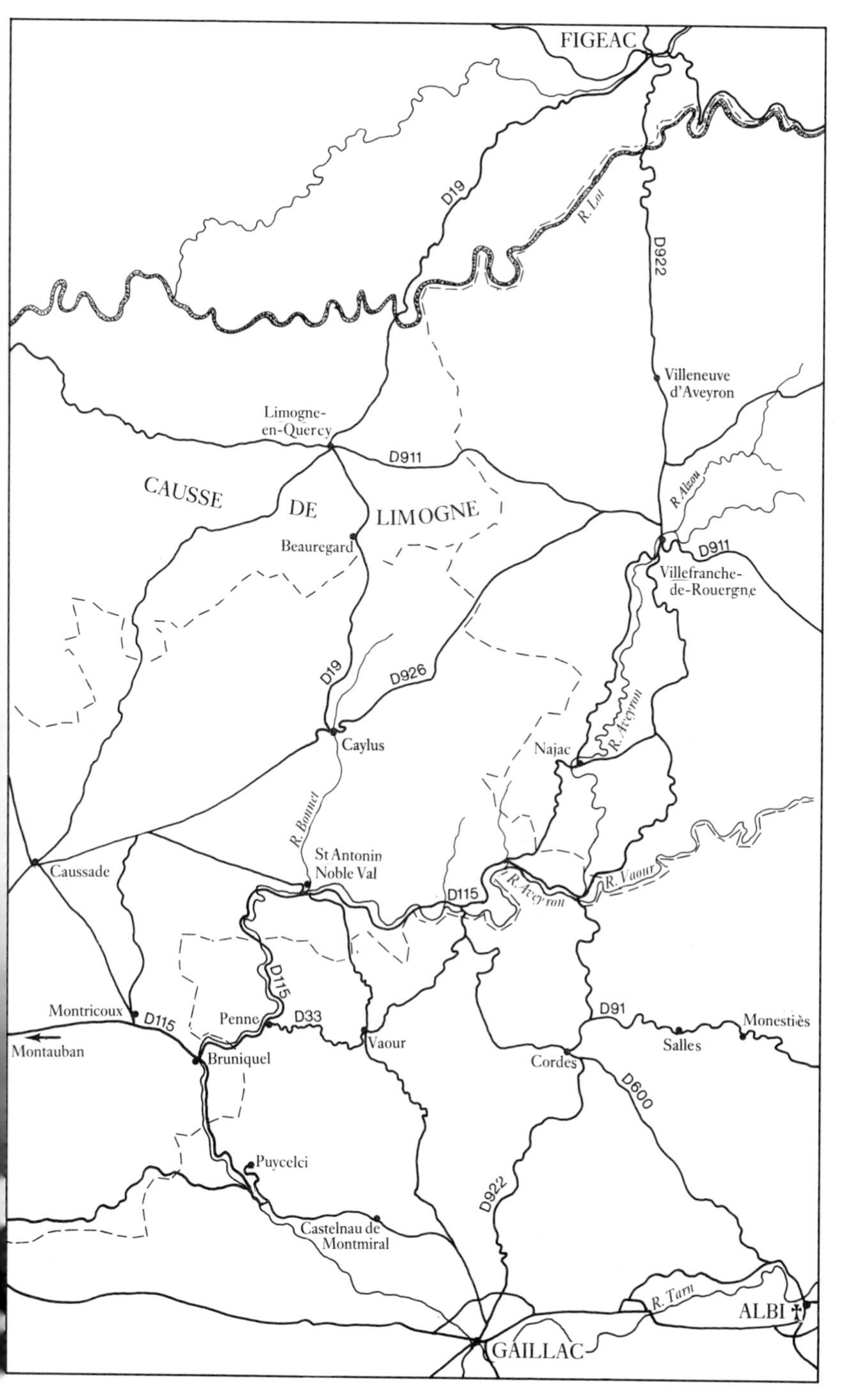
FIGEAC
D19
R. Lot
D922
Villeneuve
d'Aveyron
Limogne-
en-Quercy
D911
CAUSSE
DE
LIMOGNE
R. Alzou
Beauregard
D911
Villefranche-
de-Rouergne
D19
D926
R. Aveyron
Caylus
Najac
R. Bonnet
St Antonin
Noble Val
Caussade
D115
R. Aveyron
R. Vaour
D115
Montricoux
D115
Penne
D33
Vaour
D91
Monestiès
Montauban
Bruniquel
Cordes
Salles
D600
Puycelci
D922
Castelnau de
Montmiral
R. Tarn
ALBI
GAILLAC

Villefranche-de-Rouergue sits on the confluence of the Alzou and the Aveyron just before the latter plunges into a series of gorges. Its position on this natural crossroads has always made it a wealthy town, trading on the wool from the *causse* sheep and the silver and copper mines nearby. The town started life thanks to the counts of Toulouse, but the *bastide* as it is today was built by that indefatigable builder, Alphonse of Poitiers. Further prosperity came from its position on a Compostela route, and even the constant and bitter rows with its rival across the *causse*, Rodez, could not dent the town's success.

Hemmed in by the Aveyron on the south side, which is crossed by a fine fourteenth-century bridge, the **Pont des Consuls**, the town has lost most of its defences, but it has preserved its central arcaded square, watched over by an iron crucifix and the massively defensive church, whose intimidating tower is nearly 60 metres high.

The square is on a fairly severe slope, surrounded by the homes of rich merchants, but the whole town is wrecked by one thing – cars. Villefranche takes twice as long to get round as most other places because you spend half your time with your back against a wall. Walking along the pavements, you are obliged to step into the road in order to negotiate the cars parked in your way. Once in the road, you are hooted back on to the pavement again. Even under the *cornières*, where you would think you might be safe, cars are allowed. The only thing for it is to adopt the same sort of anarchic attitude as French pedestrians (who are also, of course, French drivers): make them wait – if you dare.

In spite of this problem, Villefranche is an appealing higgledy-piggledy place with good shops and a friendly, bustling atmosphere. The **church**, which fairly dominates everything around it, has a porch tower which forms part of the arcading. Inside, the masterpiece is the carving on the **oak choir stalls** by André Sulpice from Marvejols (Lozère). They are late fifteenth-century and display a marvellously rich conglomeration of misericord monsters and biblical panels, carved with the skill and attention to detail that is typical of his work, which has an earthy naturalism about it. His faces are the faces of real people – peasant faces – and he is equally at ease with nature, leaves and foliage being effortlessly carved. The stalls are lit by the diffused light of some fifteenth-century glass.

You will see signs in the square directing you to the **Chapelle des Pénitents Noirs**. Formed after the Wars of Religion, the Black Penitents were founded as a preaching order to induce people away from the Reformed Church. Their fervour was reflected in their habit, reminiscent of a black Ku Klux Klan outfit. The way to the chapel takes you through side-streets rich in splendid houses; many with wrought-iron balconies, the work of a school of metal workers which existed in Villefranche. The chapel itself is a curious structure in the shape of a Greek cross. Although you cannot see this from the front, it is crowned in the middle by a cupola and lantern tower. Inside, it is octagonal and heavily Baroque.

On the outskirts of the town, to the south, is the old **Chartreuse de St Sauveur**, erected in 1461 by a rich merchant of the town. Because it was built quickly, within the space of eight years, it managed to retain a great purity of style. It consists of two churches. The outer one, the Chapelle des Etrangers, was used to welcome Compostela pilgrims. The inner one, with more stalls by André Sulpice, was for the Order only. There are two cloisters, too, one of which is said to be the largest in France, with the rooms of the monks opening off it. The smaller one is prettier; pure Flamboyant, linked to its neighbour by the refectory. The entire building escaped the worst excesses of the Revolution, being turned into almshouses and a hospital in the eighteenth century.

After Villefranche head south into the deep, wooded hills that enclose Najac. You plunge up and down these furry hills, emerging occasionally, as we did for a picnic, into high clearings where the view is extensive but boring. The meadow in which we picnicked was thick and deep with cowslips, speedwell, buttercups and deep purple orchids. Cuckoos called from the depths of the woods, answered by the drumming of a woodpecker.

Najac can claim some notoriety in Britain, where it was the subject of a long television series some years ago, examining life in a small French town. It is a peculiar place in that you catch glimpses of the castle from the hill tops, losing it again as you dip into the ravines, but once you arrive it becomes apparent that Najac is actually peculiar in being built on twin hills, the town straddling the central ridge. Because of this there is no cohesive centre to Najac. It is a long, straggly village serving decidedly military rather than economic ends. The market square, for example, is not a square at all, but a long steep slope surrounded by houses supported on pillars. It was Alphonse de Poitiers again who noticed the defensive properties of the situation and erected a new castle there in 1253, which was always used as a strictly military stronghold, never as a feudal home. Much of it today is a romantic ruin, but as to its strength you are left in no doubt; your eyes are constantly drawn to the castle which is protected by a double row of houses along the ridge.

Today Najac is classed as a '*village fleurie*', and indeed flowers do spill out from tubs and window-boxes, reflecting its new role as a tourist centre of some importance, with two holiday villages nearby. Today the British paddle in the Aveyron and puff up and down Najac's ancient streets; in 1369 it was John Chandos, among others, who stood at the bottom of the hill looking up at the fearsome round keep and wondering how on earth he would capture it. (He did.) But the English had been here much earlier. In 1185 they took the older castle and signed there an alliance with the king of Aragon against the powerful counts of Toulouse. To no avail – the counts were reinstalled by 1196, and because of that the Cathar heresy was allowed to flourish in Najac until Simon de Montfort arrived and put a brutal stop to it all. As a punishment for their wicked ways, the townsfolk were ordered to build the Catholic church, the first Gothic church of the

Rouergue. It is unembellished and simple, as if they felt that they had done their bit in building it at all. After that the castle was used to imprison Knights Templar.

Plunge on down through the hills following the Aveyron, although only the railway gets very close to the river here, and turn westwards to **St Antonin-Noble-Val**, just before the river enters another series of gorges. St Antonin is an ancient town built on the confluence of the Aveyron and its tributary the Bonnet. Legend has it that St Antonin was decapitated here and that the town grew up around an abbey founded in his honour, but the abbey was burned down long ago during the Wars of Religion.

It is a fortified town spread out along the river banks, hemmed in by hills all around, and it has some lovely and noteworthy buildings; in particular the **Hôtel de Ville** which now houses the museum. An extraordinary building, this, it dates from the twelfth century and is said to be the oldest civic building in France. It ends in an enormous and rather eccentric belfry. Though the shops are dull as ditchwater there is plenty to see if you wander along the streets: the Maison de Sonnets, the Maison Bibal with its thirteenth-century windows, and even the Maison de L'Amour – brothel to you and me, but how much nicer and more fun it sounds in French – with its plump-faced kissing couple above the doorway.

Moving on down the valley on the D115 towards **Penne**, you have a choice of two roads: either the high corniche with views over the gorge, or the gorge itself, where the road fights its way through tunnels. It is not that dramatic and there are better gorges to be had, but it does add a bit of interest to the road.

This, however, is the wrong way to approach Penne.

If you come from the *causse* side along the D33 from the east, you get a stunning view across the fields of this bizarre village stuck on top of what must have been an old volcano core. From a distance it seems impossible that anyone can reach the castle without the aid of ropes but, once you are in the pretty streets, you see that the path winds up to the top quite easily.

Penne heralds your arrival in that beautiful department of the Tarn where the true south is within touching distance. Penne is a delight: exquisite houses complete with wooden balconies and exposed beams, gates and fortifications, and a castle at least a thousand years old which was besieged by just about everyone, including the active and redoubtable Simon de Montfort in the Albigensian Crusade.

Somewhere nearby are the caves of La Madeleine with prehistoric rock engravings. I have to own up: much as I would have liked to see these, we just could not find them. We stood in the middle of the main road in Penne (which does after all lead to Montauban, a town of some 55,000 people) for the best part of twenty minutes, discussing the merits of Penne with a woman doing her garden, and saw absolutely no one else to ask. A walk through the village discovered an 'incomer' reading a book, but he knew nothing of the caves either. In vain did we search Michelin for the little humpback-bridge sign that denotes a cave, but La Madeleine is really a rock shelter, I believe. We pored over all the maps we had, but finally time pressed and we left Penne with the secret of La Madeleine still intact. More persistent visitors might like to pursue this expedition.

Vaour, on the D33 which cuts across the *causse* to Cordes, was a Templar *commanderie*. Ruins of the refectory, barns, kitchens, chapterhouse and keep are still visible and worth a halt if you are a Templar fan. Otherwise, head on for **Cordes**, which might be a good place to stop for lunch if you have taken a direct route from Figeac, only about 80 kilometres distant; alternatively it is a good place to stay the night. Cordes has a number of excellent hotels, but I can recommend the Hostellerie du Parc in the hamlet of Les Cabannes, at the foot of the hill on which Cordes stands. This nineteenth-century manor house has a nice lived-in feel to it, emphasized by the resident poodle in nappies who curls up on any available chair. There is an elegant dining-room with an interesting menu and a nice, scruffy, overgrown French garden full of large trees, and orange blossom and an air of faded elegance.

Cordes is worth a long visit, but I cannot help wondering what it is like in summer. I was there on a late April day, temperature well in the seventies with not a coach or a tourist in sight. All the late afternoon and long, light evening we strolled its streets, wandered in and out of its shops, with time to chat to the owners, several of whom were very kind. The woman in the bookshop gave me a book on Monestiés; the woman who draws cats took time to tell us about the town and about the cat legend she had been trying to track down. The old people would know, she said, but we stopped to talk to several of them, too, and they didn't. It is not hard to believe there is such a legend, though; the town is full of cats. They sidle up to nuzzle your ankles; they sit prettily posed in windows beside old lace curtains; they drape round, over and inside flowerpots; they skulk under cars, miaowing and hissing as you walk by. Tiny kittens squeeze through minuscule holes in large wooden gates protecting secret courtyards. The older ones lie sprawled out in the road, sunbathing. This might be enough to put some people off, I suppose, but no doubt the cats vanish with the arrival of the tourists.

Cordes *sur ciel*, as it is sometimes called, gets its name from the fact that the town is built on a hill with a commanding view of the countryside, supposedly reaching up into the heavens. Take your camera, because it is almost unbearably pretty. They were getting ready for summer when we were there. All the pots had been planted and stood at the ready by doors and on the balconies, but the geraniums were not at their peak, not spilling over into that mass of tightly packed flowers in the way of all French geraniums. The roses were still in bud, ready to cascade down golden walls. But the wistaria was out. Long purple streamers hung from branches which had wound their way along balconies and window-sills, above doors, wafting their scent around the town as the tendrils swung gently in the breeze. There is not much in Cordes which is misplaced;

even the telephone boxes are hidden discreetly out of the way.

Cordes was a *bastide* founded hurriedly by Raymond VII of Toulouse to defend his lands against the advance of the French and Simon de Montfort, who was already making mincemeat of the Trencavel lands. The idea was that Cordes should gather up the people displaced by the Albigensian Crusade and put them in a look-out post on a hill to keep an eye on de Montfort's progress. But it was all useless. The Treaty of Paris meant the defeat of Raymond, the lands of Oc were committed for ever to French rule; and Cordes, which started life as a Cathar town resisting the French, became a French town resisting the English and finished up a Catholic town resisting the Protestants.

The name Cordes comes, it is said, from the leather and hemp workers who used to live and work in the town, which by the end of the thirteenth century had become very prosperous. The Toulousain court had their hunting lodges there and merchants moved in to service them, growing rich in their turn. As well as the leather workers there were linen merchants; hemp was woven here and dyed with saffron collected from the fields. In the fourteenth century 6,000 people lived in Cordes, some in very rich and elegant houses; today there are fewer than 1,000. Plague and Protestants and the quarrels of the bishops of Albi lead to the town's decline, which was more or less total apart from a slight surge in the 1920s when two Cordais, exiled in Switzerland, returned with machinery that allowed mechanical embroidery. For a while more than 300 people worked away at the embroidery, but by the time of the Second World War the town was deserted and falling down. The last hope for Cordes is tourism, attracted there by the artists who have moved in and restored the houses.

If you are energetic you can leave the car at the bottom of the hill and walk up to the top. This way you can get an idea of the three defensive walls which used to surround the town; several of the gates remain. It is hard going, up steep streets and flights of steps, of which the Paternoster flight is so named because there is a step for each word in the prayer. The steps climb up past old houses with exposed beams, under the Porte d'Horloge with its clock. Lizards dart away as you approach, only to scuttle back into the sunshine once you have passed.

There is too much to see in Cordes to mention everything here, but of the large mansions you should not miss the **Maison du Grand Fauconnier** (today the town hall) decorated with carved falcons. The **Maison du Grand Veneur** has marvellous hunting friezes carved on its wall, where hounds chase after plump *sangliers* – wild boar – almost as big as the huntsman's horse. The **Maison du Grand Ecuyer** has stone dogs and birds of prey. Wonderful Gothic mansions, these, but there is one Renaissance house too: **Gorsse**. The **market hall** is still standing, fourteenth-century, and with a well said to be nearly 113 metres deep. Wells in these hilltop fortress towns were of supreme importance, especially in times of siege. Legend has it that two inquisitors were thrown down this one. Then there is the **Maison Portal** with its paintings, and the Gothic church of St Michel, and the views from the Rue du Planol or the Terrasse de la Bride over the peaceful Tarn countryside: green fields, red roofs and blue sky, like a child's painting. I liked Cordes. I liked sipping a glass of Gaillac under a wistaria, strolling down the streets in the cool of the evening with the sun setting and a nice meal waiting.

Those not fed up with churches might like to make the short detour to the little medieval *cité* of **Monestiès**, north-eastwards along the D91 and past Salles, which has an interesting church too. The church at Monestiès has three incredible pieces of sculpture; most notably a *mise au tombeau* but also a Christ and *pietà* of great quality, all found in the **Chapelle St Jacques**. The Entombment at Monestiès is famous, indeed some say incomparable, for the quality of its feminine sculptures; but all the sculptures have a wealth of expression carved into their faces. The face of Christ on the Cross is one of resignation and peace; the outstretched arms seem all-embracing. But it is the face of St John in the *pietà* which is, for me, the most moving. Holding Christ's head in his hands, he looks down in a sad effort at comprehension, his mouth downturned and twisted in an agony of love. Young and handsome, this innocent St John seems to encapsulate the whole Christian message. In the Entombment it is the women whose faces draw you. Mary, composed, resigned and strong. Mary Cleophas, almost neglecting her supporting role in her curiosity to see the body. The Magdalene alone with her thoughts; the thick, rich, wavy hair that spills out on the *pietà* sculpture tucked this time under her veil. And on this end, Salome, eyes swollen with grief, whilst at the other, Mary, mother of James, wipes away her own tears with a corner of her veil. These are no ordinary sculptures. All of them fifteenth-century, they were made for Bishop Louis I of Amboise for the chapel of his country seat at the Château of Combefa, of which only the ruins remain today.

But head south now for the Languedoc town of **Albi**. The real treats are still in store. Albi stands on the Tarn, a red brick city that positively glows with warmth and colour, and if you do not like the sound of brick, don't worry; these are not the bright red, evenly cut blocks of Britain. The brick of Albi, and indeed of many of the towns hereabouts, is an old, mellowed brick, cut into small blocks with uneven edges and set into thick mortar. The colour varies. In the heat of the afternoon it seems terracotta hot, but in the dying rays of the sun it can glow rose red against a darkening sky.

There is much to see in Albi, but the two most important things are placed conveniently side by side and the road from Cordes is by far the best way to approach the town. From the Pont du 22 Août (from where you get a good view of the old bridge), your eyes are drawn to the cathedral and to the palace of La Berbie, which contains the largest collection of Toulouse-Lautrec's work.

The history of Albi is irrevocably tied up with the Cathar heresy of the thirteenth century, for the town had traditionally sheltered Cathars, as indeed had the entire Languedoc. There are several explanations as to why the name Albigensian stuck – the term Cathar was not used in the thirteenth century. It could have come from an incident when the townsfolk saved some Cathars from being butchered, or conversely it might have been that the famous

Concile de Lombers took place in a field only about eight kilometres from Albi. The gathering of local noblemen and bishops met to condemn Catharism, and from it arose the Crusade and the subsequent persecution of the heretics.

Albi was not lucky in its bishops. They were a quarrelsome, tiresome lot with a great deal of power and Albi owes its curious cathedral of Ste Cécile to one of them, Bernard de Castanet – a powerful statement from Rome to the people of Albi that heresy would not be tolerated, certainly, but also a place to which Bernard could flee and be safe. At the back of his mind must have been the incident when the Albi people had hounded their previous bishop into the old cathedral, from where he had been forced to excommunicate them *en masse*.

The townsfolk were not impressed. For years they had been at the mercy of their bishops and particularly of Bernard de Castanet, who had been inquisitor of the diocese, torturing heretic and Catholic alike provided he could be sure of getting some money out of it. In the end, appalled, the people of Albi appealed to their new and distant king in the north. After an inquiry by a group of bishops de Castanet was removed – promoted to cardinal. But not before the great cathedral of Ste Cécile, born of every tawdry motive imaginable – fear, greed, cruelty, the imposition of will, hatred and the desire for power – had been started. It was a church built against the people, and it is no wonder the people turned to heresy as something pure and fundamental. Begun in 1282, it was a century before even the main body of the building had taken shape.

But there were happier times. Albi was well placed geographically near the big centres of Toulouse and Rodez, perched above a river that flowed via the Garonne to Bordeaux. For a long time it had been a market town of importance. Gaillac wine, grown all around this region, is one of the oldest wines in France, and Albi had another export as well – blue pastel. Later on, in the nineteenth century, came the steelworks, which even today are a blot on the nearby landscape.

Albi has several famous sons. Strolling round the town you come across the houses of Galaup de Laperouse, the navigator, who died at sea exploring the East Indies in 1788, and Henri de Rochegude, another sailor. One wonders why it is that Albi, miles from the sea, should have produced such good sailors.

But the best known person to come out of Albi was Toulouse-Lautrec, whose family had long been noblemen of the area, descended from the influential counts of Toulouse. Henri was born at the family home in Albi, l'Hôtel du Bosc, in 1879. His early life was blighted by two accidents. The first one was a fall from a chair in his home, which resulted in his breaking his left leg, and the second occurred, ironically enough, whilst he was being taken for a cure to his leg at Barèges. This time it was his right femur which broke. Both accidents probably contributed to some loss of height, although at one metre and a half Lautrec could not be described as a dwarf. His real problem was the congenital bone dysplasia with which he had been born and which left him vulnerable to accidents of this kind. All his life he walked with the aid of a cane, which in later life he filled with alcohol.

He came from a family of talented artists, and it was his mother who collected his works together after his death and gave them to his native town. It is sad but not unusual that his genius went largely unrecognized during his lifetime. Albi has been the beneficiary of a marvellous collection simply because no one in Paris was interested at the time, and the collection is huge simply because he found it hard to sell his art to anyone. He seems to have found the conformity required of him and the impositions of his family hard to bear, although he died with the words *'Maman, rien que vous'* on his lips. Perhaps because of this and perhaps, too, because he was unable through his illness to pursue much of the country nobleman's life, riding and hunting, he sought out a city life for himself. He seems to have felt very much at home in the gay metropolitan world of Montmartre, meeting his friends in cafés, drinking far too much, observing – always observing – and absorbing the life that went on around him. Here he was his own man and people liked him for it.

If he is best known for his posters and lithographs, he was also a keen observer of women. None of his portraits is posed in the real sense of the word. It was the spontaneity of a gesture that interested him, and he is as open and honest in his painting as he apparently was in life. Nothing is hidden or ignored, certainly not the ugly or unacceptable; there is a naturalness in his art, and his people are very real. The real revelation of his collection, though, are his horses, unsurpassed, for me, by anyone. As an aristocrat he was no stranger to horses; he had grown up amongst them and as a child had had ample time to watch and study them at close quarters. Look closely at the 'Artilleur sellant son cheval', at the horse, shiny and groomed, standing with scarcely restrained impatience, fairly bursting with strangled movement as the man struggles with the saddle. In seconds this horse will be off and out of the canvas. It was painted when the artist was fifteen. Only two years later he painted the 'Cheval de trait à Celeyran'. This horse strains at the bit, too, but this is not the groomed stud of the earlier picture, this is a tired horse, old and decrepit, every line of its body spelling weariness and the weight of the cart it pulls. Look, too, at the portrait of 'Gazelle, in the same year. Montmartre had not beckoned yet; that was to come in the following year. If ever you thought that Toulouse-Lautrec was merely the world's best graphic artist of all time, then let this collection disabuse you.

Wandering around the museum, which apart from the massive Toulouse-Lautrec collection of paintings and drawings contains much else of interest, you may be distracted by the view, for the collection is housed in the seventeenth-century palace of La Berbie, an episcopal palace originally built in the thirteenth century; *bisbia* meaning 'bishop' in the local dialect. It was Bernard de Castanet's justifiable paranoia that turned the place into a fortress. Over the years, but particularly in the seventeenth century, the huge proportions of these defences were softened by alterations, especially by the decision to turn the military courtyard above the river into gardens.

The **cathedral** is like nothing you have ever seen before;

massive, and so ugly that its eccentricity becomes almost beautiful. A great Lancaster bomber of a place, it looks from a distance like a giant cardboard cut-out fortress; like the toys you used to find in nurseries or the efforts of a film studio running out of cash. It is threatening. The fortified walls hide the roof and the whole building is covered with towers and turrets. The west end simply serves as the base for the 85-metre tower. Propped up against this positive battleship of 29 towers interspersed with thin lancet windows, glued on almost as an afterthought from a different toybox, is the south porch, the Renaissance baldaquin; white stone filigree against the red brick. The effect is dramatic and adds further to the eccentricity. The whole building is bizarre in the extreme. And it was in the Renaissance style too, that the well-to-do clerics of Albi decided, in keeping with the times, that the church should be decorated.

I have already called the building bizarre, but inside this clumsy tank of a church the artists have gone mad. Inside, it is not recognizable as the same church. Nothing can prepare you for the richness of the interior decoration of Albi. Although the decoration largely belongs to the fifteenth century, the body of the church is a fairly pure example of meridional Gothic.

The west wall is taken up with a gigantic fresco, painted on two round towers at the end of the fifteenth century and depicting the **Last Judgment**. It is the work of French painters, but the influence is Flemish. The colours are vivid and brilliant, reds and blue-greens. Friezes of nudes – what the French call *'la foule'* – huddle together, about to be precipitated into hell, some clutching the book of their life to their naked chest. Beneath them men rise from their graves, while the damned devour each other and horrific-looking toads. There is an inscription beneath.

The detail is fantastic and the whole thing has great presence, but unbelievably the entire work has been absolutely massacred by the removal of the central figure, Christ, knocked down to make way for a chapel entrance: only the saints and a clerical hierarchy that includes Pope Innocent III in a mitre remain. It is hard to believe how such a crass decision could have been taken and ironic, too, though perhaps less so when one thinks of its evil founder, that the west wall of this great cathedral should completely manage to obliterate the Christian message and depict merely the malevolent deeds of man and his consequent and awful punishment. For the power of the painting, for me, lies not in its saved clerics and the angels of the upper tiers, nor even in the people rising from the grave, but in those clustered naked bodies of the damned as they tumble into the abyss.

Once the French had moved out the Italians moved in, to start work on the ceiling in Quattrocento style. Against an azure background angels wing their way across the roof and scenes from the Bible are picked out in gold, linked with delicate floriated curlicues. The walls, too, are covered with paintings. But that is not all. The other treasure of Albi is its **choir**, which takes up nearly half the church. Unfortunately you have to pay to go round it, which means fighting your way through postcard-buyers for a ticket and waiting for the verger to open the gates. Because it is shut off like this, you lose the full perspective and a little of its magnificence, but it is fine work by any standards. Apparently Richelieu, passing through Albi one day, refused to believe that the choir was stone and demanded a mallet to tap it. What else could it have been? But it was its fineness that amazed him. The painted stone is carved like lace with intricate patterns and exquisite filigree work. There used to be 96 statues on this rood screen, but since the Revolution, the Virgin, Christ, St John, and a delightful Adam and Eve, deliciously pink and naked against the white stone and each with a large green fig leaf, are all that are left. But on the outside of the choir some of the statues remain, a wealth of prophets and angels.

Allow plenty of time for Ste Cécile, for the detail is complex, even too much to take in. The tendency is to allow yourself to be tempted on to the next treasure without ever having taken in the last. There is another church in Albi and it is Romanesque, with a slightly disfigured door, a cloister, a twelfth-century wooden statue of its namesake St Salvy, and a lovely *pietà*; but just as the Lot has no really good examples of the Gothic, so this Romanesque cannot match much to be found in that *département*. For once I bow to the later period. It would take an extreme purist not to do so. Ste Cécile is a one-off; eccentric, interesting, enigmatic and not to be missed.

Albi is another of those French towns whose tourist board has been busy with arrows directing you round the sights of the city. The soft brick really comes into its own when placed in conjunction with exposed beams. The **pharmacie** in the Rue Timbal, for example, is sixteenth-century, a riot of beams and bricks in criss-cross patterns. The **Hôtel Reynes** is one of the few partly stone buildings in town, with Renaissance windows and galleries. The **Maison du Vieil Albi**, which houses a museum, has a Figeac-style *soleilho*, or *soleilhou* as it is called here, where the merchant owner used to dry his pastel. Then there is the **Hôtel du Bosc**, Toulouse-Lautrec's old home, which still belongs to the painter's descendants and which is now another museum devoted to the artist.

You will probably have to tear yourself away from Albi, but the French countryside is always capable of throwing up somewhere interesting, so follow the D1 to **Castelnau-de-Lévis**, a *bastide* founded under the instructions of Raymond VII to shelter the battle-weary population from the excesses of Simon de Montfort in the Albigensian Crusade. A long straggly pink village with gates and dusty streets terraced above the distant Tarn, it is dominated by the ruins of the once-strong château. It survived until 1821, but nowadays you have to guess at its strength by examining the remains of the massive round towers and the tremendously high watch-tower which leers out over the countryside.

You can drive up to the castle or walk up through the village and seemingly through people's front gardens, waved on by an old lady holding off a hysterical dog. Once at the top our explorations were slightly circumspect as well, owing to the presence of a group of French teenagers who were certainly not there for a history lesson or even to admire the view, and whose style we were obviously cramping. The view from the top of the watch-tower is worth the hard climb, though not for those with a fear of heights; the view from the bottom is good too. This is a grassy ruin with outcrops of chalk, and the grassy banks that now hide the old walls and moats were a blanket of cowslips on the day we were there. Walking along them eastwards, looking out over the Tarn valley dotted with tall poplars, *pins parasols*, red roofs and undulating hills, like a living Cézanne, you suddenly see the towers of Ste Cécile, framed in the landscape.

At nearby Labastide-de-Lévis, treat yourself to some **Gaillac** wine at the Cave Coopérative. The classic wine of Gaillac was traditionally a sweet white, but today the area produces a bit of everything, with the red grown largely on the south bank of the Tarn and the white on the north. Although it produces over a million hectolitres a year, Gaillac is today a shadow of its former ancient self, superseded by different tastes. The nicest wine it produces today is the *perlé*, a light, crisp, dry and slightly *pétillant* white.

Gaillac itself is pleasant enough, another red-brick town, full of fountains, an old abbatial church, and some very pretty gardens, designed by Le Nôtre, above the Tarn, along whose waters Gaillac wine used to be exported. If you wander along the banks you will come across fishermen fishing from the old Quai St Jacques, from where the wine started out on its long journey to Bordeaux and thence to England and Scotland. The gardens, called the Parc de Foucaud, surround a seventeenth-century château of the same name.

The church of St Pierre stands high above the river. It contains a Romanesque choir and a sweet-faced thirteenth-century Virgin, her robes simply flowing around her. It is thought that the gesture of the child on her knees – right hand raised and pointing at His mother's face – was a dig at the Cathars, who denied the generally accepted connection between the Virgin and her son.

He looks a precocious little horror, and that smug smile would be enough to make anyone join the heretics.

Head for home now through a trio of quaint places, **Castelnau de Montmiral**, a perched *bastide* with an arcaded square and entry gate, founded yet again by Raymond VII of Toulouse. **Puycelci** is even prettier, built on the site of a huge, strong castle of which only the ramparts still exist; this is another perched village, from which there is a stupendous view. The small chapel of St Roch was built as a thanksgiving by the people of Puycelci for having been delivered from the plague. Finally, **Bruniquel** – a little mini-Cordes of fewer than 500 people. The château, according to legend, was built by Brunehaut, a Merovingian queen of the sixth century. Bruniquel was a Protestant stronghold. At least two of its gates still stand, including the Clock Gate at the top of an old winding street of stone houses covered in vines and pots of geraniums. The church here has a Romanesque choir and a naïve sculpture on its doorway depicting Adam and Eve being expelled from the Garden of Eden.

Montricoux stands at the entry to the Aveyron gorges. It is an old Templar town whose inhabitants were all imprisoned in 1307. From here you can make for Caussade and Cahors or, if you are returning to Figeac, cut across to **Caylus** on the D958 and D19 north of St Antonin. The Wolf House is another of those imposing Gothic houses similar to the ones at Cordes, with wolf gargoyles snarling from its sides. The fortified church is dominated by a much more modern acquisition: an enormous crucifix by Zadkine, the Cubist. Zadkine was Polish, and so is this work – tortured and moving. Caylus is only about sixteen kilometres from Beauregard on the *causse* of Limogne and very near the abbey of Loc Dieu, where a nineteenth-century building that looks like a hotel encloses the remains of a fifteenth-century Cistercian abbey. Yorkshire travellers will not be over-impressed. Figeac is about 50 kilometres away by the direct road.

From Figeac and the eastern Lot to Conques, the Lot gorges, the Aubrac and the Cantal

There is nothing for it. If you want to get to Conques quickly, you have to go through Decazeville. If you are not driving, shut your eyes or read a book. Decazeville is a blot on the landscape, an industrial mining area of such awful proportions it makes you feel angry and want to turn back. But the minute you turn off the N140 up the D22, Decazeville seems light years away.

You approach Conques up the claustrophobic valley of the Dourdou, a small, gushing river that winds its way round mills and rocks at the bottom of a steep-sided gorge of deciduous trees. The first time I came to Conques was in a thunderstorm, and the road up that tiny valley dripped depressingly. Even in sunshine, little light penetrates and what does is dappled. There is a steep climb up to Conques, a village built on the side of a hill above the Dourdou and the Lot, in the north of that remarkable *département*, the Aveyron, where it borders on the Cantal.

How to gauge **Conques**, though, after places like Cordes and Bruniquel? It is charming, medieval in appearance, with steep cobbled streets. The stone houses are roofed in that wonderful slate fish-scale design so typical of all the Auvergne, giving the place a slightly sombre air. But there is something about Conques that I do not quite warm to. I think it might be the slightly dour Auvergne atmosphere, which will be with us for the rest of this trip. It is a tidy, too tidy, town; neat and prim and pious.

Tourist literature describes Conques as the 'marvel of the Rouergue'. They are not talking of the village, pretty as it is. Conques, with only 400 or so inhabitants, has a Treasure – a real medieval church treasure – thanks to which the monks of Conques were able to build the **church** which survives today, a strong powerful edifice whose three towers lord it over the village in pure Romanesque style.

The story has been told many times, but bears repeating. In the ninth century the Clunian monks who ran the abbey at Conques began to feel fed up. Although the abbey was on the Le Puy-Compostela route and many pilgrims passed through the village demanding board and lodging, Conques was not rich and had no relics, which in the days of the great pilgrimages spelled money.

The abbot Bégon, a bad lot, who had schemed to get his job in the first place, cast his eye enviously around him and hatched a plot. The focus of his plan was Agen, where in the third century a little girl, Faith, had been martyred by the Romans. Beaten, bound to a grate and burned, she died protesting her faith. Her relics were enshrined in the cathedral at Agen and many a miracle was said to have been performed there afterwards. Abbot Bégon chose a monk, a man called Aronisdus, and instructed him to remove his habit, make his way to Agen and apply to join the abbey there as a postulant.

All went according to plan. Aronisdus was a patient man. He needed to be. It was ten years before he was allowed the privilege of guarding the relics. This was what he had been waiting for, and no sooner was he left alone with the bones of the little Ste Foy than he was up and out of Agen, carrying the relics with him, hotly pursued by his fellow monks. Ste Foy, it seems, liked the idea of a home in the Aveyron hills, for a mist descended over Aronisdus and his pursuers, and he got clean away.

What God was to make of this little escapade we shall never know, but Abbot Bégon was well pleased. In no time at all Conques grew rich from the gifts left by pilgrims in the hope that their prayers to Ste Foy would be answered, and Bégon spent the remaining years of his life dissipating that wealth. Ste Foy's 'head' had been left behind in Agen and still more of her bones ended up in Glastonbury, but a reliquary was made to house the bones that made it to Conques and they are still in the original container, an ugly little golden doll, with a bull neck and heavy jaw, the face of a man, studded with the most preposterously large jewels. Indeed, so totally vulgar is it that one struggles to accept its authenticity. It is not every day one sees gold on this scale and certainly not every day that one sees a real medieval treasure. It is housed, along with gifts, in a room off what remains of the cloister, and your ticket is taken by a Chaucerian monk bulging from his cream habit in the way of all true monks; in actual fact he is one of the Premonstratentians who use the abbey today on condition that they allow access to visitors.

The other gifts are equally incredible, though some, like the eleventh-century box in beaten copper decorated with blue enamels, are very beautiful. It is unusual for treasures to survive. Too many trials got in the way – the English, the Protestants, the Revolution. The treasure at Conques survived partly thanks to the village's isolation and partly thanks to the quick-witted mayor at the time of the Revolution. Hearing that the Republicans were on their way from Rodez, he distributed the treasure among the villagers with instructions that they hide it until the danger had passed. When the officials arrived at Conques, they were told that the village had already had its own Revolution; the wealth had been redistributed and woe betide anyone who tried to get it back! And when the danger was over the people of Conques gave the treasure back to their church.

Conques is no stranger to lucky escapes. The church was scheduled for total demolition in 1837 when Prosper Merimée stepped in to save it, though not before the vandals had got at the cloisters. The restoration undertaken is clearly visible today, but it does not detract from the purity of the Romanesque lines. The church presents a balanced, symmetrical and simple front to the world, with its two towers rising on either side of the **west door**.

I am running out of superlatives for these doors, for here is another of the great Romanesque tympanums. It would seem to be quibbling to say that Conques is not my favourite; that in comparison to Moissac or the design of Cahors or even the mysticism of Beaulieu it lacks a certain degree of soul. By any standards this is another masterpiece. Like the others, it is twelfth-century and depicts the Last Judgment: Christ in the middle, His right hand pointing to heaven, His left to hell. To the right of Christ, angels bear scrolls announcing the virtues and there is a series of figures. You will recognize the Virgin and Peter with his keys; they stand alongside the abbey's founder and Charlemagne with his retenue, who had contributed to the first church on this site. Three martyrs are depicted, including St Caprais, Bishop of Agen. One wonders if it was guilt that put St Caprais up there and whether this was a sop to Agen, to whom they had paid compensation for stealing its relics but never once offered to return them. They were not feeling too contrite, however, for there, squatting at the end of the row as if he hoped no one would notice him, is Aronisdus. We can see Ste Foy prostrating herself before God and the dead rising from the grave and, beneath Christ, St Michael and a marvellously evil and cheating Devil weigh out the souls. Hell and damnation are always the best bits of medieval iconography and this is no exception. The monster Leviathan swallows the damned, and there is a whole frieze of grizzly scenes as they are welcomed to hell by Satan amongst toads symbolizing sloth and ripped-out tongues symbolizing slander. There is even a somewhat parochial warning to poachers on the abbey lands thrown in. Poachers will be trussed up on a stake, like game, and, to emphasize the fact, a sympathetic mason has chipped in a rabbit helping to carry the stake away – an early proselytizer for vegetarianism?

Peace reigns in Jerusalem, however, where angels turn away the damned, but we cannot escape the settling of old scores. There are Bishop Etienne of Clermont and his two nephews bound up in a net, captured by a Devil who looks as if he has been drinking too many pints of bitter. They had plotted to loot the treasure. Bégon is there, too, reaping his just reward at last.

Inside, the building is unusually light and also very high for a Romanesque church – about twenty metres. The light is due to the windows in the nave and clerestory, and the height was a deliberate attempt by the builders to add authority. It means that you can see most of the capitals, some of which are historiated. I particularly like the one on the south side of the chancel, depicting the sacrifice of Isaac, the latter holding hands rather trustingly with Abraham and an angel. The gates are said to have been forged from the handcuffs of Christian soldiers captured by the Moors and released thanks to the good offices of Ste Foy.

Conques has several hotels but it is unlikely that you will want to stay the night here if you have just left Figeac, though you might be feeling like lunch. We, however, climbed to the pleasant room we had been offered at the top of one of Conques' tall houses, joking in a half-serious way about what to do if a fire broke out. The owner pointed to his newly installed alarm system and the fire extinguishers. I did not feel all that reassured: we had just climbed several flights of wooden stairs. Why is it that French hotels are so inadequate where fire prevention is concerned? The staircase, apart from being wooden, was also narrow. What good would an alarm be in a case like that? Even if the wood did not burn the building would soon be full of smoke. The hotel was full of exposed beams, in a country where 55 per cent of the population smoke, as against 39 per cent in Britain. It was escape routes that were lacking. All over France, from north to south, British tourists are subjected to the same badly translated and meaningless note on the back of bedroom doors, which advises them if they discover a fire not to panic, not to shout 'Fire', but to run for the chambermaid (in a French family-run hotel?) or take sensible precautions and wait for help. And where on earth would help come from in Conques? Along the gorges of the Dourdou, up the twisty road? From Decazeville? From Rodez? It would be a long wait. As it happened, the hotel did have an escape route on a lower landing, although it was not marked as such. This owner had been trying, at least, but it is an issue that should be examined in more detail.

Dinner was so appalling that we had finished by eight-thirty. The night was warm and young, so we strolled the streets of Conques, up to the top of the hill where the old folk of the village had congregated after supper, and along the tiny streets, where we met the postman's wife and her friends. We complimented them on their village. How beautiful it was, how marvellous their church. Yes, they said, but even the tourists did not bring enough money. There was no work to be had in Conques. Their own

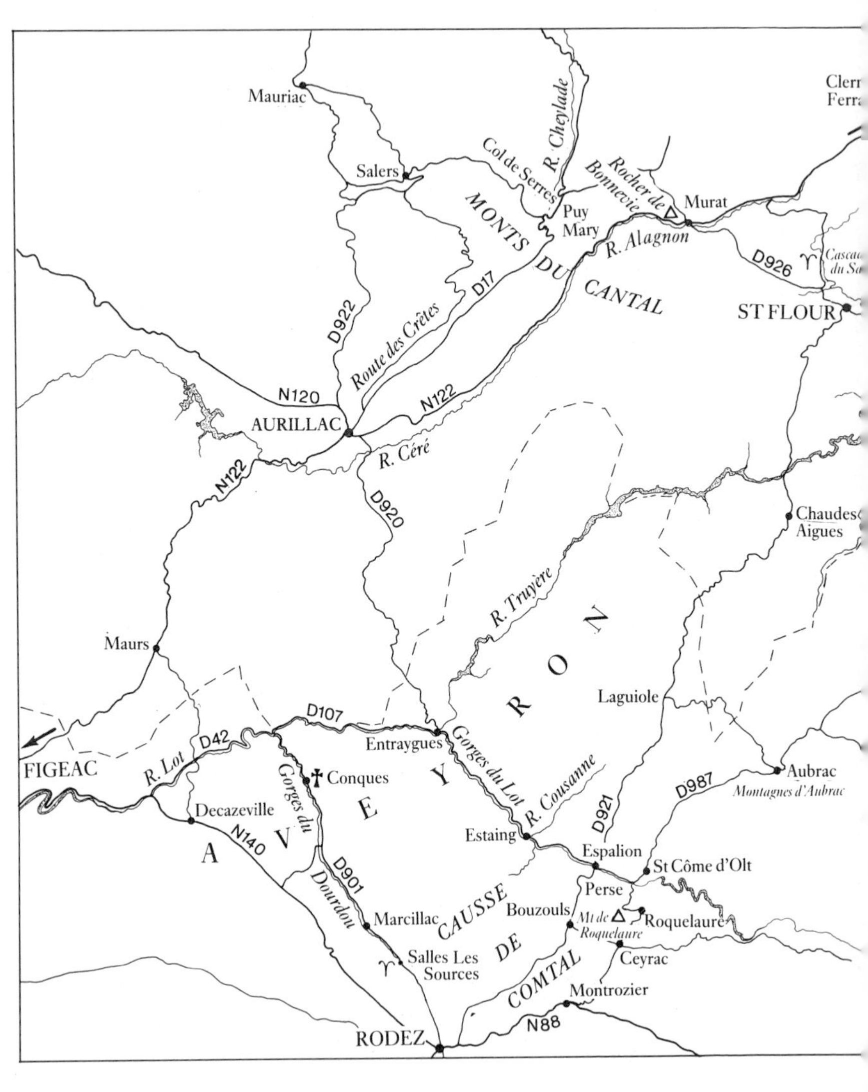
Mauriac
Salers
Col de Serres
R. Cheylade
Rocher de Bonnevie
Murat
Puy Mary
MONTS DU CANTAL
R. Alagnon
D926
ST FLOUR
D922
Route des Crêtes
D17
N120
N122
AURILLAC
R. Céré
D920
Chaudes Aigues
R. Truyère
A V E Y R O N
Maurs
Laguiole
D107
Entraygues
Gorges du Lot
FIGEAC
R. Lot
D42
Gorges du Dourdou
Conques
Aubrac
D987
Montagnes d'Aubrac
R. Cousanne
D921
Decazeville
Estaing
Espalion
N140
D901
St Côme d'Olt
Perse
CAUSSE DE COMTAL
Bouzouls
Mt de Roquelaure
Roquelaure
Marcillac
Ceyrac
Salles Les Sources
Montrozier
N88
RODEZ

young moved away. The young rich, to their astonishment, bought second homes and moved in. It was not how it used to be.

We stood in the warm evening as the skies darkened and the bats came out and the yellow lanterns were switched on, hearing tales of the past. Look at the *'lune rousse'* they said, pointing behind us to the russet crescent in the sky; that means frost. Surely not, we said. The sunset had been pink, and earlier we had picnicked in the heat of the midday sun. It was ten o'clock at night and we stood sleeveless. But the women were firm. We said our goodbyes and walked back through the quiet cobbled streets, the dim light playing round the mass of the church beneath us. It seemed ancient and mysterious, and for the first time I warmed to Conques. Tomorrow would be the first day of May. We took a last look at the moon before going inside, smiling at the folklore. On 2 May it snowed!

You have to descend from Conques to pick up the river road (the D901), turning right when you reach the Lot and following it on its north bank until you get to Entraygues. It is a very scenic road, and the river flows strong and wide. There are pleasant, family-run hotels all along this stretch, which seem to me a far better bet than the tourist prices of Conques.

Entraygues is the first town of the so-called Lot gorges. It sits astride a confluence of the Lot and the Truyère, lost in a valley, with old houses and medieval streets, and an elegant Gothic bridge crossing each river. The castle, built by the counts of Rodez, stands on the semi-island formed by the confluence. There are stepping-stones across the Lot, much used by fishermen, and this, of course, is a fisherman's paradise. Entraygues has built up quite a holiday trade for itself. You can swim and enjoy water sports, and there is a holiday village nearby. It is an attractive town.

It was 1 May, and the markets of the three little towns we passed through were awash with the scent of *muguet*, or lily of the valley, the traditional May Day flower in France. Bunches of green and white stood propped up in buckets. Unable to resist it, we bought some and stuck it in the car ashtray with some water, breathing in the sweet smell. The markets here are very small, local affairs. Only produce grown locally is available. It is useless to look for a tomato if it is not tomato time. But the radishes were good and fresh, and we bought a small slab of butter off the block to go with them.

Between Entraygues and Estaing you will see why I referred to the 'so-called' Lot gorges, for the whole of the upper Lot has been wrecked by hydroelectricity schemes and dams. Some might say that it is nice to see the river in full flood, but I hate the unnatural size of it, the way it flows in straight lines, drowning the trees and bushes. The rapids of the upper Lot used to be famed for their beauty as they flowed through this gorge. There are no rapids now.

Estaing is another harmonious combination of bridge, château and old houses; possibly even nicer than Entraygues. The houses cluster at the feet of the castle built by the Estaing, a family who knew a great deal of fortune thanks to a simple piece of good luck. Dieudonné d'Estaing saved the life of King Philippe Auguste at the battle of Bouvines. From that day life grew better for the Estaing but it all ended with the Revolution, when Charles Hector, an admiral, felt compelled to join the Republicans. His decency and his name got the better of him, however, and in an effort to try to save the king he wrote to Marie Antoinette. This led to his arrest and he was condemned to death. Today the castle is used as a convent, although the nuns will show you round.

Estaing, too, is built on a confluence. The gushing stream of the Cousanne joins the Lot here, meaning that a walk through the town of necessity takes you over a series of footbridges, which adds to its charm. The Estaing family distinguished itself in other ways too, for François d'Estaing, bishop of Rodez, was beatified. His fête day is celebrated in the town on 1 July with much pageant.

Leave this second grey village with its fish-scale tiles and terraced vineyards (the wine all along here is quite palatable VDQS growth) and head for the third. At **Espalion**, with its humpback bridge, you are not far from Rodez, and a hint of red is creeping into the stone, showing up the white of the May blossom which was in full flower. Espalion has a different feel to it altogether, for the land opens out here to enable you to cut across the *causse* to Rodez, and, apart from the houses which overhang the river by the thirteenth-century bridge, it is less quaint than the other two towns. It was a bridge that caused Espalion to exist at all, for the Roman road from Rodez to Javols crossed the Lot here and the town grew up around it.

The château rises above the town on an old volcano and the best view is actually from the Rodez road looking back, when you can see just how separate the hill is from the rest of the town.

From Espalion you can follow the cemetery road to the church of Perse. St Hilarion has a door like a small Conques on the spot where the saint was said to have been decapitated, and from here you can follow the road on to St Côme-d'Olt, a few miles east of Espalion, still on the Lot which here reverts to its old Celtic name of Olt. St Côme is a medieval town with fortified gates and old streets. Some of the houses have Renaissance features but it is notable mostly for its extraordinary church tower, which looks rather like a Mr Whippy ice-cream cornet.

We picnicked above St Côme and the river, in a field with a view over the valley, trying not to crush the orchids which were opening out in the hot sun and in the company of a great green lizard, which ran around the field semi-upright like a mini-dinosaur, diving under bushes or through the grass at the first sign of trouble. We poured some Evian into a cup for the *muguet* and set that out on the rug along with radishes and cheese and the *vin d'Estaing*. Mr Whippy gleamed silver in the light.

We had to drag ourselves up the hill behind us to **Roquelaure**, past the huge rock fall and the car that had come to grief against a tree above the drop, and up to the red castle standing behind the enormous rock which gave it its name. The surrounding hamlet is huddled together for protection; a couple of houses, the castle, the rock and the small church, which was being restored when we visited. It is very plain inside, with only a few heads at the base of a pilaster and a *mise au tombeau.* The real point of Roquelaure is the view, for on either side of the rock it stretches away, across the *causse* to Rodez on one side and up and down the Lot valley on the other. Here, where the valley widens to let in the sun, most of the blossom was over and the trees were in that new spring green they wear early in the year. The temperature was touching the high twenties, yet all around were signs of spring. The idea of Rodez and a large town was not appealing. We leant on the gate taking pictures, watching the cows as they idly chewed their cud, soaking up the view, absorbing the silence.

But we set off anyway across the *causse* of Comtal, bare and dotted with juniper bushes standing to attention. We saw **Rodez** long before we arrived. It climbs up the hill in a superb position, crowned by the cathedral tower. Signs of the twentieth century crowded in on us: garages, supermarkets, quarries; but Rodez is an old town, a Roman town, capital of the Rouergue, populated at the time of the Romans by the Rutènes. Later on the Rouergue was ceded to the counts of Toulouse, but in the fourteenth century marriage took it to the Armagnac and together with that family it fought the English. Rodez has already celebrated its bimillennium. The first bishop of Rodez was St Amans in the fourth century, and the old bishop's palace still stands today, next to the cathedral. The tower is the cathedral's *pièce de résistance*, rising up some 87 metres, solid and formidable, pierced only by a rose window. It was built by François d'Estaing in the early sixteenth century. Inside it is cool and airy in a northern Gothic way. André Sulpice has been busy here too with the choir stalls, and there is an impressive organ.

The old part of town has been largely pedestrianized and it is rich in houses of some architectural merit, many with Renaissance features. The shops are good and there are two good museums: the Beaux Arts, which has some work by Denys Puech, an Aveyron painter who turns up again in the nineteenth-century church at Espalion, and the Musée Fenaille. But somehow I just did not take to Rodez. It glowed warm with its red stone but there was a coolness to it, and the cathedral with its northern features was misplaced under the heat of a southern sun, in spite of the impressive proportions of the tower.

If you are heading for home and the Lot, leave Rodez by the D901 for a look at Salles Les Sources, a pretty village in a rocky cirque at the foot of the Comtal *causse*, where an astonishing spring emerges in a powerful waterfall. Nestling at the bottom of the valley is the deliciously squat Romanesque church of St Paul. Marcillac, a bit further north, is the centre of a wine-growing area, and a small museum in the town is devoted to the subject. Wine has been grown in Marcillac since the third century.

If it is spring, however, or if height and mountains attract you, then there is no need to cross the *causse* to Rodez at all. Instead, turn the other way (north-east) at St Côme and head off into the mountains of the Aubrac. We had to retrace our steps, something we were loath to do exactly, but circling round and round Rodez we could not find the way out that we wanted. Every road except the N88 seemed to be well signposted; even the N88 was well signposted – going the other way. It did not improve either our tempers or our feelings towards Rodez. Finally a guess proved lucky. We turned off on the N88 at Montrozier, a picture as it soaked up the sun above an old bridge and babbling stream, pink against a blue sky.

At Ceyrac we saw the farm women come down the road with armfuls of narcissi, the same as we had left in the Lot, where fields turn white and the scent rises on the air. Outside St Côme again we had to stop the car to allow the men to herd the cows by. They were *genisses*, young cows who had spent their first and only winter cooped up in a barn. Their first taste of freedom made them skittish, and they kicked up their heels, running round and round the car and through people's gardens while the men and the dog chased them fruitlessly with huge sticks and apologies.

Up we climbed, up the D987, up, up into **the Aubrac**. What can one say about the Aubrac? Very little. In the actual village of Aubrac, a sad grey collection of houses with no appeal whatsoever, they used to ring the church bells for two hours every evening to guide the pilgrims in over the wilderness. As you climb you can look back over the Lot valley, rich and green and luscious. Up here it felt different. The air was cooler, the trees were still in bud, the greenness had gone. Mile upon mile of high grassland stretched out around us. It was bleak. Even in the sun it felt bleak.

Why come? Well you could come for the transhumance on the nearest Sunday to 25 May, when the cows, decked in garlands of flowers, move up to their mountain pasture from the valleys. For three days the roads are filled with cattle, and it is the cattle who have right of way. But you need not wait for 25 May. Come for the flowers. It starts with the little mountain crocuses. We saw them as we rounded a corner into snow, thick snow, lying at the side of the road in drifts. They peeped through, delicate purple against the white, and behind the white were the fir trees, framed against the still blue sky. After that come the daffodils: field upon yellow field of the small, pale, wild variety. Wordsworth would have been speechless. As someone brought up in the Lake District, so was I. It was too early for cowslips up here on the open stretches, although we saw them later on in sheltered patches, newly opened and pristine. As we neared Laguiole, the banks were a thick, deep purple with violets. It was a voyage of exclamations as one or other of us saw another stretch of colour, and it was a feature of this part of the journey that was with us throughout the Auvergne, an unforgettable feature. Later on, towards June – for everything happens much later in the Aubrac – the daffodils give way to narcissi.

Laguiole is a ski resort. You can see the *piste* cut through the fir trees. It is a happy sort of place, maybe because everyone feels relieved to find life after the barren stretches. We stopped there largely because Laguiole happens to be the home of one of the up-and-coming chefs of France. Michel Bras's name now takes precedence over the actual name of his hotel, Lou Mazuc, which can be problematical if you do not know his name. It is a pity that with fame has come money, which has allowed him to build a rather appalling entrance on to the old hotel, with all the charm of an airport lounge. Everyone inside looks overly clean and efficient, too. But the food is an experience, drawing on M. Bras's Auvergne roots, and at prices that ought to make London restaurants blush. Book ahead whatever time of year you plan to go, for M. Bras's reputation is spreading and, although one can hardly imagine what brings people to Laguiole, come they do and being France, a good many people come precisely because of his restaurant. If you cannot get in at Lou Mazuc, don't despair. There are several other hotels in town, including the Grand Hôtel Auguy run by a displaced *monsieur* from the Loire whose restaurant is good and manner welcoming.

Laguiole depends on cattle. The town has shops full of skins and in the square is an enormous bronze bull by Guyot to help you get the message. It is not a particularly pretty town, but it has a lot of character. There is a museum of the High Rouergue, but the real thing to see is the market, which takes place every Saturday from May to June and which sets the place buzzing.

Even now you could turn back, but we were hooked by the flowers and pressed on for St Flour, through an orchestra of cowbells that clanked like hand bells along the way. The countryside was less barren here and, although at Laguiole we were at over a thousand metres, there was no real feeling of height after we had left the wastes of the Aubrac. The pasture-land and the cowbells reminded us, but there were no deep-pitched roofs and it felt no higher than parts of the Aveyron which we had just left. On we went through the spa town of Chaudes Aigues, which has the hottest waters (82°C) in Europe, hot enough to heat the central-heating systems of the houses, past the memorial at the side of the road to Jean Baron, aged 21, killed by the Germans on 28 June 1944. The flowers were still with us, joined now by expanses of white wood anemones.

By the time you reach St Flour, you have left the Aubrac and the Aveyron. What a marvellously diverse *département* it is that allows you to picnic beside the pastoral Lot one minute and sit beside snow-drifts the next; that stretches from the Templar village of La Couvertoirade on the wild, southern Larzac *causse* to the deep, wooded hills of Najac. Now you are in the true

Auvergne, **the Cantal** and snow-covered peaks in the distance put in an appearance suddenly. It begins to feel like a mountain land.

St Flour, a dour, grey Auvergnat town, sits on a hill huddled against the winds that sweep down off the surrounding mountains, though you have to approach from the east to appreciate its precipitous position. 'None took you by force except the wind,' the old saying goes – and we were reaching for sweaters now – but it was not as unlovable as I had expected it might be, livened up by a busy market and lots of people. Most of the shops, which had queues of people, seemed to be selling jars of *tripoux* (tripe) and the famous Auvergne sausages. Laguiole had its own cheese, but there is also a cheese of the Cantal called simply after the *département*. Like a soft Cheddar in consistency, it has a deliciously nutty taste. There is *bleu d'Auvergne* too, one of the great blue cheeses. All the Auvergne fare is what one might call hearty. The sausages are served with *aligot* – potatoes puréed with the soft, white, unfermented *tomme de Cantal*, served in great cheesy strands. One menu I saw started with the traditional *pâté à la pomme de terre*; Michelin had described it as 'light' and curiosity led me to try it. It turned out to be creamy potatoes layered between sides of thick pastry. Light it was not. We followed this with a fish course which had sounded like a *coquille* but turned out to be a fish pie, once again laden with potatoes. That was followed by a steak the size of a plate and enough chips for seven, then cheese and dessert. Well, it cost under 70 francs, so maybe one should not complain. The quality of the food was good and it was well cooked. The Auvergne is the centre of what today are called activity holidays. You can ski, cross-country or alpine, you can ride horses, swim, play tennis, walk, or less energetically you can fish. Maybe after a day in the open air you can demolish a meal like that without difficulty, but if you have been sitting in the car all day choose your menu carefully.

The church, based on oratory dedicated to St Flour, the martyred bishop of Lodève, is a bit grim: dark grey basalt, solid and Gothic, no-nonsense and functional-looking from the outside, as if the prime consideration were that it should withstand the elements. It stands on the edge of a large square, next to the attractive episcopal palace housing the Museum of the High Auvergne (containing some local Resistance material and a beautiful eleventh-century St Pierre from Bredons) and is approached through narrow, medieval streets. For all its stern exterior, there is a treasure-trove of things to see inside. Like most of the southern Gothic churches, this has no transept, but it has no other southern features and, although it was built under the orders of the Duke of Berry, no real northern ones either. It has five aisles, which allowed me to avoid the christening of twins going on in one of them.

St Flour does not have a Black Virgin hidden between its two stern towers; it has a Black Christ, a thirteenth-century sculpture in wood called, appropriately enough, 'Le Bon Dieu Noir'. It is a sculpture of a long, thin Christ on the Cross clad in a loincloth. The black face falls to the right and is profoundly moving. All the statuary in St Flour is good. The fifteenth-century *pietà*, more naïve than the thirteenth-century Christ, is reputed to be sculptured from lava. There is a rare sculpture of Ste Trinité, and a fourteenth-century Virgin holding a ruddy-cheeked child – very much an Auvergnat baby. The fifteenth-century frescos are badly damaged.

We left St Flour on the D926 and made for Murat, stopping off to picnic at the château and waterfall of **Le Sailhant**, looking down on the croaking ravens which nested in the cliffs. It was at Le Sailhant that the one-time lady of the house, Anne Henard, hid her Protestant son Charles in the oven to prevent him being captured by the governor of the Auvergne. Later on the castle fell into the hands of the Estaing family. The daffodils had gone, the trees were tightly budded and the clouds raced across the cold sky. The panorama as we approached **Murat** was spectacular. The red cattle of Salers chomped away at the pasture and Murat, in a wide valley, climbed up the Rocher de Bonnevie, crowned by the enormous statue of 'Notre-Dame-de-la-Haute-Auvergne' where once the château stood. On a hill to the left stands the church of Bredons, the only remains of a Benedictine priory.

Murat's heyday was in the third century, but today life centres around cheese, wood and cows. Once again it seemed dour and grey-brown to me, enlivened only by the fact that it was *en fête* and streamers hung across the road, but it had a certain elegance, nonetheless. There is a convenient follow-the-arrow system which takes you up and down the steep streets, past the fifteenth-century *maison consulaire* and the Maison Rodier, past the memorial to the deported of Murat during the last World War and the church with its olive-wood Black Virgin dressed in green on a Baroque altar.

We moved on, wary of the the icy wind and the grey gloom of the towns and thought of golden Cordes, and yesterday's picnic, and the *lune rousse.* The peaks of the Monts du Cantal loomed gelid and keen as we climbed up towards the Puy Mary. The approach reminded me of the Langdales: huge, grassy mountains close-cropped by sheep and the cold. We dropped down into a valley once more just as the sky, which had turned steel grey, broke into a patch of blue again. Tiny calves weighed down by bells jangled along in the fields beside the road, gambolling amongst the daffodils which were back in profusion. Thick, thick growths of delicate yellow zig-zagged across the pasture. But we were used to daffodils now. It was the banks that caught our attention, for they were a riot of colour. Newly opened cowslips, succulent and luscious-looking, poked out amidst lady's smock; orchids and violets painted the grass deep mauve; and best of all were the delicate mountain pansies, mauve too, but mostly yellow. All of them smothered by a tangle of forget-me-nots. For a couple of kilometres we drove beside banks like this, while the light played tricks across the hills, making the shadows swoop across the barren grass.

We saw the sign. Puy Mary closed, it said. But we went on anyway. It was after all May and we assumed that they could not get up here very often to change the signs. At the point where the road divides for the Puy Mary and the Col de Serres, there is a breathtaking view across the Monts du Cantal. You are at 1,364 metres, and above you the hang-gliders launch themselves off a cliff to soar among the peaks before landing down by the Cheylade at the foot of the col. Above you, too, rises the Puy Mary to a height of nearly 1,800 metres, sharp-edged and covered with snow. The road was indeed shut and is apparently rarely open before June. We drove up to the snow level, then came down again and parked beside the ugly café, drinking in the view and wondering what to do. Finally we were forced into a detour, past the extraordinary site of Riom ès Montagnes with its two volcanic cones jutting out from the landscape. Much better, though, if you can cross the Puy Mary to Salers, only about fourteen kilometres away.

That evening in the medieval gloom of Mauriac, with its Black Virgin and classic eleventh-century church, the famous west door carved with stylized creatures from the zodiac, it rained; sheets of icy rain, and thunder clattering round the peaks. When we reached Salers early next morning the clouds parted briefly to reveal the Puy Mary freshly white against the steely sky.

Salers is beautiful; icy cold but perfectly preserved. We were ill clad for this kind of weather and set off around the town at a brisk pace, forced to turn our backs to the arctic wind on occasion as it whipped through our pullovers. The streets and houses are the same brown-grey basalt you see all over this part of Cantal, stuck together with strips of white mortar. It is cobbled and turreted, fortified in the fifteenth century against the exploits of roaming bands of Englishmen left over from the Hundred Years War; and almost as much, one cannot help feeling, against that wind, which whips off the surrounding *puys* and blasts across the town.

There are two gates still standing, and visitors are well advised to park outside and walk in under either Le Martille, with its squat arched tower, or Le Beffroi. Salers is not a large town, but there are plenty of nooks and crannies and curious wynds that make you feel as if you are really exploring something. It is a medieval delight of old buildings and shops, including the old apothecary shop sporting a disgusting pickled snake winding round the inside of a jar.

The main square, Place Tyssandier d'Escous (named after the local agriculturalist who was responsible for the revival of the distinctive, red cattle of Salers), is surrounded by some lovely houses, some of them quite bizarre shapes, and the Renaissance building called the *Bailliage*, a rather cold Renaissance, this, apart from the first-floor window – which flowers in splendid isolation. Although Salers was indeed a *bailliage*, with a royally appointed administrator, this building was not the home of the bailie at all; but this hint of Scotland set me wondering whether 'Escous' might not be a corruption of 'Ecosse' (Scotland). There was, I decided, a definitely Scottish air to Salers, with its tough, sober beauty.

The Street of the Templars is probably the oldest street in town, and their house dates from the twelfth century. The porch is an esoteric wonder of lions, medallions and an all-seeing face. The château was razed in 1666 by royal decree, but there are still ramparts and walls, a commanding view over the mountains and the fish-scale slate roofs that grace nearly every building.

The oldest part of the church, which has a curious tower, is the Romanesque porch, decorated with grotesque faces and symbolic animals. The rest is fifteenth-century. Even on a Sunday fake organ music fills the air, a habit that is spreading all over France in churches that are open, and one I am not too enthusiastic about. There is an Entombment, a work of Flemish influence in coloured stone, placed near the back on the south side. The face of Christ in death is one of despair and pain, emphasized somehow by the rich dress of the people around Him, whose faces are rather obscured by their costumes. As at Monestiés, St John looks too young by far, and Salome holds Mary in an absent-minded sort of way, engrossed by the scene in front of her. The long hair of the Magdalene streams out from under her veil.

Amazingly enough, the church is also the proud possessor of no fewer than five Aubusson tapestries depicting various biblical scenes. The 'Adoration of the Shepherds' on the left of the choir is attributed to Ribera, and the picture in the Notre-Dame-de-Grace chapel shows the victory of the Salers people over the Huguenots in 1586, a victory commemorated to this day by a procession to nearby Notre-Dame-de-Lorette every 1 February.

But it was too cold and we fled to the warmth of the Hôtel des Remparts, a good place to stay the night if you need to, to wrap our hands round cups of hot coffee. It was time to go west, descend into some warmth. The D35 winds circuitously almost right up to Salers; as it turns west it becomes the famous Route des Crêtes with outstanding views in all directions. We headed down it for Aurillac and home.

From St Céré to the Corrèze: Beaulieu, Tours de Merle, Collonges, Turenne

This is a gentle voyage round the southern reaches of the Corrèze, a quiet, leafy *département* of some charm. The route does not stretch too far north as it seems senseless, on a holiday in the Lot, to make an excursion which takes you half-way back to England. Brive-la-Gaillarde is a pleasant market town that visitors might be able to explore on arrival, if they take the motor-rail. Much of the east of the *département* borders on the Puy-de-Dôme in the Cantal. There is a Resistance Museum at Neuvic, for the Corrèze, even less populous than the Lot (.07 people per square kilometre), was a Resistance centre. We shall stick firmly to the southernmost corner.

Take the D940 out of St Céré and head north for the last of the great and remarkable Romanesque tympanums at **Beaulieu-sur-Dordogne**. If you are fed up with tympanums then leave out Beaulieu entirely, but the loss will be yours, for Beaulieu ranks alongside Moissac, Conques and Cahors. It owes much to Moissac, with its central, supportive and decorative pier, the delicate ribbon-work, the galloons and the rosettes of the lintel. But where Moissac is powerful, Beaulieu is mystical and quite simply beautiful.

It has been suggested that the theme of this doorway is not so much the Last Judgment as the Second Coming of Christ, the theme of Matthew 25:31: 'When the Son of man shall come in His glory and all the holy angels with Him, then shall He sit on the throne of glory . . .'

It seems to me that this is right, for this door is lighter in tone by far than Moissac. Christ is not pointing to heaven or hell, as at Conques. His arms are wide extended in a welcoming gesture. This mandarin-featured God is glad to see anyone. Great importance has been placed on the Cross as the means by which all this joy has been brought about. It occupies a position slightly to the right of Christ's head, gazed at by the many assembled and emphasized by angels carrying instruments of the Passion: you can see two of them emerging from the clouds carrying the crown of thorns. There is nothing judgmental here.

The double lintel offers a striking frieze of beasts and monsters, and the central column, composed of four prophets, is one of those graceful piers with scalloped edges. The sculptures in the porch are badly damaged, but you can still make out a few Vices and Daniel in the lion's den, among other characters.

Inside, the church, which was the abbatial church of a twelfth-century Cluniac order, is built in Limousin-Romanesque style, whose main features tend to be barrel-vaulting in the aisles buttressing the vaulting of the nave, and an emphasis on the tower, which at Beaulieu is octagonal and quite high. Apsidal chapels open off the central apse, around which there is an ambulatory, common in pilgrim churches, a feature which allowed the crowd to circulate freely. Apart from the capitals, though, the interior is dark and simple as though its simplicity were a deliberate foil for the joys outside.

There is a small treasure in the church of which the main item is a twelfth-century Virgin in silver gilt. A last look at the door

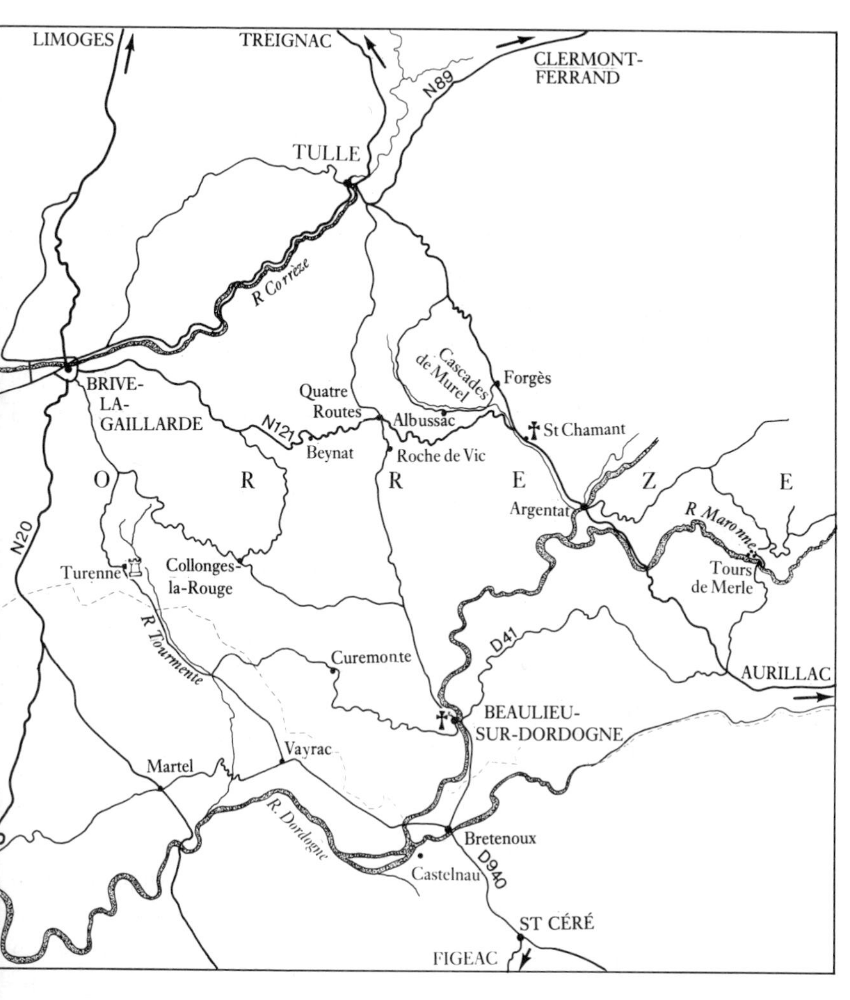

LIMOGES
TREIGNAC
CLERMONT-
FERRAND
N89
TULLE
R Corrèze
Cascades
de Murel
Forgès
Quatre
Routes
Albussac
St Chamant
BRIVE-
LA-
GAILLARDE
N121
Beynat
Roche de Vic
O
R
R
E
Z
E
Argentat
R Maronne
N20
Turenne
Collonges-
la-Rouge
Tours
de Merle
R Tourmente
D41
Curemonte
AURILLAC
BEAULIEU-
SUR-DORDOGNE
Vayrac
Martel
R. Dordogne
Bretenoux
D940
Castelnau
ST CÉRÉ
FIGEAC

before you leave shows you very clearly the curiosity of this church: a Limousin structure with a Languedoc iconography.

Do not leave Beaulieu without seeing the Penitents Chapel in its romantic setting on the river bank, and then follow the D41, which allows you to cut across to the **Tours de Merle**, an extraordinary grouping of ruined towers in an area of the Limousin called Xaintrie, in the foothills of the Auvergne. You can park the car in the lay-by on the D13 and then walk down the little path to the towers and the wild river Maronne, every step smelling strongly of the yellow broom that climbs the hillside.

Even ruined, the towers are impressive, jutting out of the thick undergrowth on top of their hill with the angry waters of the river at their feet. This is a real lair, a real medieval hideaway, and it requires no great flights of imagination to see what life must have been like in this valley during medieval winters. *Madame* at the postcard house, looking herself rather like a bit part in a medieval movie, was very willing to talk. There was rarely a spring here, she said. They usually went from winter straight to summer, and she waved her hand away to the left in the direction of the Monts du Cantal, making further explanation unnecessary.

From the dusty depths of a pile of old newspapers she produced a small and quaint book on the towers – barely twentieth-century in layout and type, never mind literary style – which emphasized the 'audacious' suspension bridge, the 'rustic freshness' of the spot and its 'calm chestnuts', and ended on a note of patriotism, about how the ruins inspired in people those very French attributes of fervour, bravery and love of beauty. She took the money and searched for change, which I checked, half expecting to see golden *écus* in my palm.

The towers of Merle are the remains of a castle built in the eleventh century by the fierce and clannish lords of Merle. In time their sons, too, put up buildings, until no fewer than seven towers sprouted out of the chestnut woods on the hillside. The downfall of the *repaire* was the advent of artillery, which rendered the hitherto impregnable fortress vulnerable to attack from neighbouring hilltops and thus severely threatened for the first time in its history. It was abandoned. A sad list of important dates in the antique guide book ends with the year 1640, but even that entry is a mite too effete for a Merle lord, one feels. Falconry School, it reads.

There is a legend, of course, for such a place would have to have a legend, just as it also has a secret passageway that links the church of St Cirgues-la-Loutre to the château of the lords of Vayrac, co-*seigneurs* of Merle. The legend concerns Bertrand, called *le merle* because he whistled like a blackbird to summon his troops. He and his men established themselves on the banks of the rocky Maronne in a wild valley, and it was to Merle that they brought Eléonore, beautiful daughter of a neighbouring lord, whom they had kidnapped and forced into marriage with Bertrand. One evening as Eléonore cradled her child, a woman appeared. 'I am Aïda', she said, 'I come from the North and my tribe has taken the road to the sun. I ask for shelter as my son is ill.' Eléonore, well brought up, offered the woman the customary hospitality of the times and welcomed her in. Bertrand, however, was more suspicious and, eyeing her golden necklace and the bear's claw which hung round her neck, inquired who she was. Aïda replied that she was queen of the Bohemians and, adding a prophecy that their son would be a great leader, she gave Eléonore the bear's claw.

Ten years later, when Eléonore was offering hospitality to yet another stranger who had arrived at the gates, he identified in the drawing that Aïda had carved on to the table at the house clues that would lead to a secret treasure hidden in a nearby cave. This was the Merle Treasure, which allowed for the building of the remarkable fortress. The baby, Hugues, did grow up to be a powerful lord and was never separated from his bear's claw, but he was killed in battle and took the secret of the treasure to his grave.

High season brings tourists and *son et lumières* to the Tours de Merle; the latter make a spectacular show, by all accounts.

I cannot quite decide whether I like the idea or not. There is something about the 'rustic wildness' of the Tours de Merle which should, maybe, be left untamed.

Argentat, west and slightly north of the Tours de Merle, is best seen from the bridge, where the houses down by the river with their cobbled front gardens and pruned plane trees add a great deal of charm to an otherwise pedestrian place which was once an important port on the navigable Dordogne. The *gabares* that we met on the Lot, sailing barges that plied up and down the river, were well known on the Dordogne too, very often named after the town itself – *argentats*. North-east of Argentat, French engineering takes pride of place and signs direct you to vast stretches of ruined river. As with the Lot, where once there were rapids, now there are landscaped concrete slabs holding back billions of litres of water. If you find this interesting there are many dams that you can go and look at. I find it utterly distressing. By any standards, the Dordogne must rank as one of the great rivers of France, yet the upper reaches of it are lost to us.

For natural waters take the Tulle road out of Argentat (tympanum addicts stopping at St Chamant). At Forgès, take the D113 to Albussac and then the D113E to the Cascades de Murel, where you walk through deep, green woods to find the waterfall. Both Quatre Routes, and Beynat have possible lunching places: Le Tourtel at Beynat, and the Auberge Limousine and the Roche de Vic at Quatre Routes. The name Roche de Vic refers to a former oppidum nearby, at the summit of the *puy*. Today, there is an orientation table there.

From Beynat it is an easy drive on the D130 and D14 to the rose-pink rip-off of **Collonges-la-Rouge**. That is probably grossly unfair. Before the Société des Amis de Collonges-la-Rouge took over this holiday village of the nobility of Turenne, it was falling into a sad state of neglect and disrepair. Today the sandstone buildings with their grey roofs, draped with the sort of luscious wistaria that spells great age, are pristine and clean, and every bend produces a new and delightful angle. But Collonges is dead. Shutters on most of the houses are tightly closed (although admittedly there is a tendency in this part of the world to live in darkened houses). For all that it is beautiful. Parts of the walls still stand, as does the Porte Plate, which has lost its tower. There are arches leading into secluded flower-filled courtyards. There are exquisite manor houses with *lauze* roofs and Renaissance doors, exposed beams and lovely chimneys. The Castel de Maussacamis has an entrance gate with a roofed porch, while the Vassignac manor house is a wonderfully eccentric arrangement of towers and roofs. Holiday houses and abandoned homes are sadly common sights in the south-west and one grows accustomed to them. The point about Collonges is that it is not only dead; it is a museum. There is nothing real about it; no washing hanging from the windows, no lived-in feel to it.

Coachloads of tourists – Germans on the day I was last there – drive up and park in the car park outside the village – and whoever heard of a French town or village without cars? The sight of a coach is like a slap on the wrists at your lack of originality – everyone else knows about the place and has been here before you; if they are from your own country it just makes it worse. Any sense of discovery is, of course, an illusion, but one that it is pleasing to labour under. Centuries ago hordes of English roamed round here – in great armies.

Collonges, in any case, is not built for crowds. In the height of summer you have literally to squeeze in and out of the medieval doors, unable to see anything of the exhibition inside. You queue to see everything, and always, when it gets to your turn, the lights go out. Collonges is full of those maddening contraptions so beloved by the French, the *minutiers*. Here at Collonges, money is required to switch the lights back on again. Once in the church or museum, you are obliged to see it at the pace of everyone else, for to linger over anything is to hold up the people behind you.

The church is fortified in Limousin style. Inside there is more piped organ music, and outside is the last of the Toulouse tympanums: a tiny Ascension, pink on red. Christ, His right hand raised in benediction, ascends into heaven surrounded by angels. Ranged beneath him are the Apostles and the Virgin. It is small stuff compared to Beaulieu, but much better than you will get elsewhere.

The nicest part of Collonges is by the Ancienne Chapelle des Pénitents, where you cannot help but rejoice to notice that the door looks a bit old and they have forgotten to paint it. It is a leafy part of town; the simple red building framed by the green of the planes and the chestnuts and the blue sky.

But if you are aching to get back to the real world, head across-country, westwards and slightly north, to the home of the masters of Collonges. In many parts of this book you have read of the powerful **Turenne**, and you should not leave the Corrèze without a visit to the spectacular seat of this influential family. I do not know how much of the real world you will see in Turenne. It is not a museum, though it is certainly closed for much of the year, and many of its quaint old houses are holiday homes. By and large I prefer this alternative to exploitation. You see Turenne long before you get there, as it sits on top of a perfectly formed green breast, the ruins of the castle and its keep, the Tour de César, towering against the sky. It is a dramatic sight, symbolic of the power of the family it represents. Answerable to no one, the Turenne minted their own money and ruled over an area far to the south of them, creating their own ordered world where they were masters and few dared gainsay them. Turenne's little state ended in the eighteenth century when one of the viscounts, heavily in debt, sold up to the king.

It is a twisty road up to the château, but don't lose your nerve. Once at the top you can climb up to Caesar's tower, called after the Roman oppidum which used to exist at the top of this hill, and visit the guardroom in the Tour d'Horloge. The view from the top is terrific. The green, pastoral landscape of the Limousin swims around you, rising to the foothills of the Auvergne in the east. On a clear day you can easily see the Monts du Cantal and look down the Lot border to little Curemonte with its two châteaux, in the throes of being done up by the villagers, and to Castelnau, arch-enemy of Turenne, and then away over the Gramat *causse*.

Somewhere near Turenne I know of a small hotel where you wake in the night to nightingales and dine cheaply on ceps, *escargots* and farmyard duck. Have fun finding it! Me, I need my 'fix'. I shall head back to familiar places where the air is warmer, the land more arid and the stone more golden. Back to the Lot and the welcome of Mas de Cauze, to sit on the terrace in the last of the sun with a glass of Cahors and some of Mme Rossignol's *chèvre*, perhaps, watching lazily as Guy tends the tobacco and the vesper bells of St Projet toll out. The sun sinks across the timeless valley.

Traveller, go gently:

Les brebis sont au bercail et l'homme simple va dormir
entre sa flute et son chien noir.

APPENDICES

Syndicats d'Initiative

The Comité Départemental de Tourisme du Lot, 46000 Cahors, tel: (010) (65) 35 07 09 will be able to help you out with every aspect of your holiday but the local Syndicats d'Initiative will also be able to help. Here is a list. Prefix telephone numbers with the international code for France (010) and the Lot area code (65).

46320	Assier	–
46130	Bretenoux	Tel: 35 59 53
46330	Cabrerets	Tel: 31 27 12
46000	Cahors	Tel: 35 09 56
46160	Cajarc	Tel: 40 65 20
46100	Capdenac-le-Haut	Tel: 34 17 23*
46110	Carennac	Tel: 38 48 36*
46170	Castelnau-Montratier	Tel: 21 94 21*
46150	Catus	Tel: 22 70 31
46250	Cazals	Tel: 22 82 84*
46600	Cressensac	–
46700	Duravel	Tel: 36 50 01*
46100	Figeac	Tel: 34 06 25
46300	Gourdon	Tel: 41 06 40
46500	Gramat/Padirac/Alvignac	Tel: 38 73 60 or 38 75 22
46120	Lacapelle-Marival	Tel: 40 81 11 or 40 83 39
46210	Latronquière	Tel: 40 26 62*
46110	Les Quatre Routes	Tel: 32 12 40*
46320	Livernon	Tel: 40 57 33*
46140	Luzech	Tel: 30 72 32*
46160	Marcilhac-sur-Célé	–
46600	Martel	Tel: 37 30 03*
46800	Montcuq	Tel: 31 80 05*

46200	Payrac	Tel: 37 65 15
46220	Prayssac	Tel: 30 61 44*
46700	Puy-l'Evêque	Tel: 30 81 45*
46500	Rocamadour	Tel: 33 62 80 or 33 62 59
46400	St Céré	Tel: 38 11 85
46330	St Cirq-Lapopie	
46340	Salviac	Tel: 41 51 38*
46200	Souillac	Tel: 33 00 82*
46190	Sousceyrac	Tel: 33 00 82*
46110	Vayrac	Tel: 32 52 50

*Town hall

Accommodation

For camping, caravanning, hotel, gîte or horse-drawn caravan reservations:
Loisirs-Acceuil dans le Lot
Chambre d'Agriculture, avenue Jean-Jaurès, 46000 Cahors.

Camping and caravanning

Camping à la Ferme (camp sites on working farms) are listed in the *French Farm and Village Holiday Guide,* published annually and available from all good bookshops, some libraries and the French Government Tourist Office at 178 Piccadilly, London W1, tel: 01-499 6911.

Canoeing

There are various clubs, including:
Club Canoë-Kayac MJC
Impasse da la Charité – BP42, 46000 Cahors, tel: 35 06 43

Car Hire: Cahors

Avis:	Station Shell, Place de la Gare	Tel: 30 13 10
Europcar:	avenue Jean-Jaurès	Tel: 30 19 20
Hertz:	134 avenue Jean-Jaurès	Tel: 35 34 69

Also:
Train/Auto SNCF, 179 Piccadilly,
London W1. Tel: 01-409 1224

Caves with paintings open to the public

Cougnac, near Gourdon	Tel: 41 06 11
L'hospitalet, Rocamadour	Tel: 33 63 15
Pech-Merle, Cabrerets	Tel: 31 23 33

Caves and gouffres with formations open to the public

Bellevue, near Marcilhac-sur-Célé	Tel: 40 63 92
Lacave	Tel: 37 87 03
Presque, near Autoire	Tel: 38 07 44
Roland, near Montcuq	Tel: 31 88 50

Châteaux open to the public

Assier	Tel: 40 57 31
Castelnau-Bretenoux	Tel: 38 52 04
Cenevières	Tel: 31 27 33
Larroque-Toirac	–
Montal	Tel: 38 13 72
Rocamadour	Tel: 33 63 29
Roussillon	Tel: 36 87 05

Cycling

Train/Vélo: SNCF, 179 Piccadilly, London W1. Tel: 01-409 1224

Festivals and fêtes

There are various festivals held every year in Gourdon, Souillac (jazz), Cahors (blues), St Céré, Montcuq and elsewhere. Every village, however small, has its own fête day. Details from the local Syndicats d'Initiative.

Fishing

Contact the Fédération Départementale de Pêche
40 Boulevard Gambetta, Cahors, tel: 35 50 22.

Gîtes

Many available gîtes are listed, along with photographs, in the *French Farm and Village Holiday Guide.* This is published annually and is available from all good bookshops, some libraries and from the French Government Tourist Office at 178 Piccadilly, London W1, tel: 01-499 6911.

Chambre d'hôte (bed and breakfast) rooms are listed in the same guide.

The national French body handling gîtes is:
Fédération Nationale des Gîtes Bureaux de France
34 rue Godot-de-Mauroy, 75009 Paris.

The local Lot body is:
Association des Gîtes du Quercy
Chambre d'Agriculture, 430 avenue Jean-Jaurès
46000 Cahors, tel: 36 67 01; and ferry companies.

Museums

Cahors, rue Emile-Zola	Tel: 35 10 80
Pech-Merle, Cabrerets (prehistory)	Tel: 31 23 33
Figeac, The Champollion, Place Vival	Tel: 34 06 25
Labastide-Murat, Murat Museum	Tel: 31 12 45
Martel, The Raymondie	Tel: 37 30 03
Rocamadour, Treasure	Tel: 33 63 29
Rocamadour, Cires Roland le Preux	Tel: 33 63 08
St Cirq-Lapopie, Rignault	–
Sauliac-sur-Célé, Open-Air Museum of Quercy	–

Riding

Contact: Association de Tourisme Equestre du Lot, BP 103 46002, Cahors, tel: 35 07 09.

Swimming

Swimming pools at:
Bretenoux-Biars
Cahors
Cajarc
Castelnau-Montratier
Figeac
Gourdon
Labastide-Murat
Lacapelle-Marival
Lalbenque
Leyme
Limogne
Luzech
Montcuq
Payrac
Prayssac
Puy-l'Evêque
Salviac
Souillac
Souscreyrac
St Céré
Vayrac
Vers

In the Lot at:
Albas
Anglars-Juillac
Arcambal
Caillac
Cajarc (water sports)
Castelfranc
Crégols
Cuzac
Douelle
Duravel
Grézels
Larroque-des-Arcs
Luzech (water sports)
Mercuès
Parnac
Pradines
Prayssac
Puy-l'Evêque (water sports)
St Vincent-Rive-d'Olt
Tour-deFaure
Vire-sur-Lot

In the Dordogne at:

Bétaille
Bretenoux
Creysse
Floirac
Gintrac
Girac
Gluges
Martel
Pinsac
Prudhomat
Puybrun
Souillac
St Denis-Martel
Varac

In the Célé at:

Boussac
Brengues
Cabrerets
Corn
Espagnac
Sauliac

In lakes at:

Alvignac
Aynac
Cajarc
Catus
Cazals
Comiac
Laval de Céré

Walking

The following Sentiers de Grande Randonnée go through the Lot. (details from Syndicats d'Initiative):
GR6 (Alps-Ocean) Souillac to Figeac by Rocamadour
GR46 Brive la Gaillarde (Corrèze) to Vers
GR65 Le Puy-Compostela (Montredon to Montlauzun)
GR36 Channel-Pyrenees (Bonaguil) (Lot-et-Garonne) to Cordes (Tarn), Lot Valley, Laramière
GR652 Gourdon-Bonaguil (Lot-et-Garonne)

There are also circular, arrowed routes for motorists – *Sentiers de Promenade* – around many centres.

SELECT BIBLIOGRAPHY

ENGLISH

Books

Baigent, M. Leigh, R. and Lincoln, H. *The Holy Blood and the Holy Grail.* (Cape, London, 1982)
Barber, Richard *The Companion Guide to South-West France.* (Collins, London, 1977)
Ford, Hugh *Nancy Cunard: Brave Poet, Indomitable Rebel.* (Chiltern Book Co.)
Grigson, Geoffrey *The Painted Caves.* (Phoenix House, London, 1957)
Grant, Loan *A Lot to Remember.* (Out of print)
Hare, Augustus *South-Western France.* (George Allen, London, 1890)
Hartley, A. (ed) *The Penguin Book of French Verse: 4, The Twentieth Century.* (Penguin, London, 1966)
Hitching, Francis *Earth Magic.* (Cassell, London, 1976)
Johnson, Hugh *The World Atlas of Wine.* (Mitchell Beazley, London, 1971)
Kendall, Alan *Medieval Pilgrims.* (Wayland, London, 1972)
Ladurie, Emmanuel Le Roy *Montaillou.* (Penguin, London, 1980 and Scolar Press, 1978)
Lands, Neil *Beyond the Dordogne.* (Spurbooks, Bucks, 1978)
Lindsay, Jack *The Troubadours and Their World.* (Muller, 1976)
Michelin Green Guide *Dordogne: Périgord-Limousin.* (1976)
Penton, Anne *Customs and Cookery in the Périgord and Quercy.* (David and Charles, Newton Abbot, 1973)
Savage, George *The Languedoc.* (Barrie and Jenkins, London, 1975)

Sieveking, Ann and Gale *The Caves of France and Northern Spain.* (Vista, 1962)
White, Freda *Three Rivers of France.* (Faber and Faber, London, 1962)
Woods, Katherine *The Other Château Country.* (John Lane, The Bodley Head, London, 1931)
Gregory of Tours: *The History of the Franks.* (transl. Thorpe, Lewis) (Penguin, London, 1974)

Pamphlets

Hamilton, Bernard 'The Albigensian Crusade'. (Historical Association, 1974)

Newspapers

Hope-Wallace, Philip 'Into a State of Grace'. (*The Guardian*, 9 June 1969)
Schwarz, Walter 'Souvenir of a belle epoque'. (*The Guardian,* 27 August 1984)

FRENCH

Books and Pamphlets

Benoit, Pierre *Le Déjeuner de Sousceyrac.* (Albert Michel)
Bulit, R. *Gourdon en Quercy.* (Claude Soulié, Gourdon, 1971)
Chaussade, Jean and Raymond Picard, *Ombres et Espérances en Quercy 1940-1945.* (Privat, Toulouse, 1980)
Clottes, Jean *'Inventaire des Megaliths de la France – Le Lot',* Supplément à Galia Préhistoire édité par le Centre National de la Recherche Scientifique. 1977, 552pp.
Fourgous, Jean *A Travers le Lot.* (Imprimerie Tardy Quercy, Cahors, 1980)
Houlet, Jacques *Châteaux du Lot.* (Nouvelles Editions Latines)
Juillet, Jacques *Saint-Céré.* (Editions S.A.E.P., Colmar-Ingersheim, 1974)
Noel, Aimé *Figeac d'hier et d'aujourd'hui.* (Imprimerie Moderne USHA, Aurillac, 1984)

Saint-Marty, L. *Histoire Populaire du Quercy: des origines à 1800.* (Ré-édition Quercy Recherche, Cahors, 1980)

Torre, Michel de la *'L'art et la nature des ses communes'.* Nos. 12, 15, 19, 46, 47, 81, 82 (Nathan, Paris)

Guide de la Vallée du Lot. (Association pour L'Aménagement de la Vallée du Lot, 12300 Decazeville)

Guide de L'Aveyron. (Collection Connaissance du Pays d'Oc, 34006 Montpellier, 1982)

Le Guide des Chateaux de France: 46: Lot, Max Pons. (Hermé, Paris, 1981)

Guide du Lot. (Collection Connaissance du Pays d'Oc, 34006 Montpellier, 1980)

Le Lot: Pays de Quercy. (Editions J Delmas et Cie, CAEL, Paris, 1985)

Michelin: Guide Vert: Auvergne (Bourbonnais); Causses (Cévennes-Bas Languedoc); Côte de l'Atlantique; Pyrénées

Magazines

Quercy Recherche. (Boite Postale 127 46005 Cahors): numerous editions.

Vieilles Maisons Françaises: Patrimoine historique: Lot (No 103 Juillet 1984, 93, rue de l'Université, 75007, Paris)

INDEX